MEN AND MASCULINITY

D1387779

MEN AND MASCULINITY

From power to love

Roy K. McCloughry

Hodder & Stoughton
LONDON SYDNEY AUCKLAND

British Library Cataloguing in Publication Data
A catalogue record for this book
is available from the British Library

ISBN 0-340-53153-3

Copyright © Kingdom Trust 1992

First published in Great Britain 1992

All rights reserved. No part of this publication may be
reproduced or transmitted in any form or by any means,
electronic or mechanical, including photocopying,
recording, or any information storage or retrieval system,
without either prior permission in writing from the
publisher or a licence permitting restricted copying.
In the United Kingdom such licences are issued by the
Copyright Licensing Agency, 90 Tottenham Court Road,
London W1P 9HE. The right of Roy K. McCloughry to be
identified as the author of this work has been asserted
by him in accordance with the Copyright, Designs
and Patents Act 1988.

Published by Hodder and Stoughton,
a division of Hodder and Stoughton Ltd,
Mill Road, Dunton Green, Sevenoaks, Kent TN13 2YA
Editorial Office: 47 Bedford Square, London WC1B 3DP

Photoset by Hewer Text Composition Services, Edinburgh
Printed in Great Britain by Clays Ltd, St Ives plc.

For Helen

For she is wise, if I can judge of her,
And fair she is, if that mine eyes be true,
And true she is, as she hath prov'd herself;
And therefore, like herself, wise, fair and true,
Shall she be placed in my constant soul.

The Merchant of Venice, II, vi

CONTENTS

PREFACE

It is so often the case that debates which take place in the media or in pubs are only taken up by the Church after a lapse of many years. Yet if we are to engage in a critical dialogue with our culture as Christians it is important that we anticipate such debates in order to participate in them when they occur. This book is an attempt to bring a Christian perspective into a debate which is already well under way and yet which has not really been taken up by the Christian Church. It is my hope that it will be an encouragement to men and women who find themselves struggling with issues surrounding the men and masculinity debate.

I am writing as a Christian who has a conservative view of scripture but, as I point out in the book, it is no longer the case that those who have a high view of the authority of scripture are necessarily conservative in their views on subjects such as gender. This book has its roots in my own attempts to grapple with scripture and in the many hours of debate with friends and colleagues on gender issues. It is also rooted in my own search for help in this area, which will continue long after this book has been forgotten. As with so many books, it was written because I could not find any book on this vital subject which covered the areas in which I was interested. Consequently the book is interspersed with reflections from my own pilgrimage.

This book is not meant to be the last word on the subject. It will, I'm sure, be one of many books on this subject written from a Christian viewpoint for the task of making the masculinity world-view explicit and then developing a Christian critique of it is an enormous one. However, I hope that this book will hasten the need for debate in this area. I hope also that both men and women will find it a book which is encouraging as well as challenging. So many of the debates on gender which men have participated in have been silent about the world-view held by men, and I hope that I have opened the door a little on the world of masculinity for us to be able to evaluate it together.

It is important that this book contains accounts of both theory and practice, and my experience of the men's group, outlined all too briefly in chapter seven, was more important to me personally than perhaps is indicated there. It has also been crucial to my own pilgrimage to be able to discuss the majority of these issues with my wife, Helen, with whom I have learnt so much about partnership, mutuality and equality. This book is dedicated to her.

This book has been part of a pilgrimage more than any other I have written. This is not only due to the effects of the research but also to many conversations with men and women who gave their time to help me. At the outset of this book I had decided to keep a list of everybody whom I had to thank but when the list grew past the 200 mark I felt sure that I must have forgotten somebody and backed out. All kinds of people have been interviewed, or allowed conversations to be recorded, or have been willing to chat about their own lives.

Nevertheless, this book would not have seen the light of day without the help of a small group of friends and colleagues. Rowena White and Sally Livsey, my researchers, not only dug up all kinds of material but sat and talked with me about it until I understood it! Alan MacDonald read the manuscript in an earlier draft and kept me going with his encouragement. Martin Offord, Michele Taylor, Glynn Harrison, David Lyon and Steve Stickley all made helpful comments on parts of the book. Rod Beadles read a near-finished draft and made valuable face-saving comments throughout. I am indebted to my friend David Cook who read the manuscript closely and made extremely helpful suggestions. Helen Bookless and Elizabeth McKelvey, who were in turn my personal assistants during this project, not only typed draft after draft but commented on the manuscript and saved me from many errors.

During 1989 I was privileged to be the chair of an educational charity known as Men, Women and God, whose work is concerned with raising the profile of gender issues in Great Britain. This is my small contribution to them in honour of their work, in lieu of my chairmanship that year. Long may their work continue. As ever, I am most grateful to the trustees of the Kingdom Trust, who employ me – Peter Ellis, Richard Farnell, Hilary Holden, Wendy Sayers and Martyn Eden – for the extraordinary support they have given to this project and to all who have supported the Trust over the last three years. The Trust exists to bring the Christian faith to bear on issues which ordinary Christians face in the modern world, and I am especially grateful to all those people and churches who view my work as mission to the modern world and who are prepared to support it with their donations and prayers.

At the end of each chapter there are several questions. They are designed for use by groups but I hope that they will be of help to all who read the book. Those who start small men's groups, who are not sure how to start the ball rolling, may find them a useful focus for discussion, although I would hope that most groups will quickly leave them behind as they develop a life of their own. Some of them are intended to provide a focus for an entire evening's discussion. There is also a mix between questions which are intended to clarify or illustrate things that have been said in the book and personal questions which depend on people being willing to tell their own story. Although the bias of the questions is towards men and their experience, I hope women readers will also find them helpful.

The book has already been read by several women in

manuscript who have commented that many women will find it helpful. I hope that they are right. Many of the issues which I have raised in the book may also be true of women, but it has not been part of my intention to draw attention to this. I do hope that women who read the book will debate the issues raised in it with men. Where the subjects raised are part of the experience of both men and women, we will all profit immensely from each other's insights.

Space and style have dictated some limits for the book. It contains theological reflection on social issues but is not a theological treatise. I hope to develop a more detailed theological treatment of the issues in another context. Likewise, those looking for detailed social analysis will find it emerging in symposia and articles over the next few years. Despite this interest in masculinity my professional interest remains economic and social ethics, and I will be returning to this theme in another book to be published shortly.

My calling to relate the Christian faith to the modern world is a fascinating and challenging one. The modern world is still a place to celebrate as well as critique and I hope that this book will convince some of the importance of engaging in mission and dialogue with that world. My considerable debt to many of its leading thinkers is evident throughout this book. I would like to acknowledge my indebtedness to the writing and insights of Joseph Pleck, David Gilmore, Robert Bly, Victor Seidler, Shere Hite, Deborah Tannen and Arlie Hochschild.

Although this book is primarily intended for Christians, many close friends of mine who are not Christians have stated their intention to read it. I await their comments with special interest. It has been my goal in this book to focus on Jesus Christ as the one who should be the hero and mentor for men. My hope for them is that this book should reawaken a desire in them to become disciples of Jesus Christ. My friendship can offer them nothing more precious than that.

Roy McCloughry
West Bridgford, February 1992

1

THE INVISIBILITY OF MEN

I was playing football in the playground when I slipped on the greasy tarmac and cut my knee badly. As I bent over holding my leg, tears threatened to come into my eyes. A schoolmaster walking at speed down a nearby path on his way to a lesson called out to me, 'Be a man, McCloughry, be a man.' Trying to staunch the flow of blood with only limited success, I remember thinking that a clean hanky would have been more use than his half-baked advice. The episode was only one of several which made me ask how a man was meant to behave. What did it mean to 'be a man', 'act like a man'? Surely one day I would be a man just by waiting for long enough. It seemed there was more to being a man than meets the eye. There were all kinds of expectations and ideas built into that phrase 'be a man'. It didn't seem to mean the same as 'be yourself'. It was more like trying to be like somebody or something else. Certainly, standing on the playground with blood pouring from my knee and tears coming to my eyes, 'being myself' was not an option. I began to learn that 'being a man' was about strength, skill, reason, autonomy, control, achievement, success. With these lessons well learnt a 'real' man could 'go far'. Anything else was 'left to the girls' because it wasn't worth having.

In those days the only place I would find the word 'gender' was in a Latin grammar. But now issues which focus on gender are among the most important which face us today.

Since everybody in the world is either male or female our experience of ourselves and of the world around us cannot be separated from the fact that we are men and women. It is all very well for us to talk blithely about 'humanity' but we experience our humanness as men or women. This raises the question as to whether men and women experience the world around them and the people they are in the same way or whether that experience is very different. Do men and women perceive God in the same way? Issues of gender affect our personal relationships including our marriages, they also affect how we bring up children. Many people see their role in society as determined by their gender and see the rise of feminism as a threat to social order as they have known it. Some women view the Church as an institution dominated by men which excludes women from participating fully in it. Gender also affects how we conduct mission to men and women. Do men need to be approached differently with the Christian Gospel, and if not why are our churches so empty of men?

Gender is an issue in which we are all implicated and which we cannot avoid. Some social issues such as nuclear war or the third world could be seen as options for those who are interested in such things but all of us have already got opinions on gender issues and express them in the way we treat people throughout the day, and in the way we approach our personal relationships. How vital it is to face up to our prejudices, fears and experience of what it means to be a man or a woman. This is an area in which we can learn from other people and where we need to be open to their experience of gender. Christians need to be especially careful to make sure that what they believe about gender arises out of their Christian world-view.

Many men think of gender as an issue which interests women. They see themselves as getting on with the business of life. Other men think of gender as a cover women put up when they want to moan about men. Whatever the reason, gender has had a bad press among men. Just a mention of the word causes their eyes to glaze over, yet recently there has been a spate of interest in the issue of men and masculinity. This seems to puzzle many men who don't seem to think of themselves as a subject worthy of study.

My personal assistant recently went with her husband for a medical check-up. The doctor addressed her husband, who was also a doctor, rather than her. When he did address her he patronised her and called her 'dear'. Trying to make conversation he asked her what she was doing and it came out that she was working for someone who was writing a book on men and masculinity. 'Oh,' said the doctor, 'is that really necessary?' 'Yes!' she said, through gritted teeth.

Over the last couple of years I have met many such responses. A man asks me what I am doing, I tell him I am writing a book about men. After a pause he looks puzzled and then asks, 'Why?' If I had said that I was working on a book on the dietary habits of the American Indians, the same man would have responded immediately, 'How interesting.' Incomprehension is the order of the day. Of course other men do respond differently. They get excited and say, 'What a vital subject, I'd like to read that.' What a difference between the two responses!

Perhaps the best reason for men developing an interest in gender issues is self-awareness. Until recently there was not a great deal to help them. I walked into a well-known book shop three years ago and asked the woman behind the counter where they kept their books on men. This appeared to stump her for a while, but she then recovered and said, 'Women's studies . . . there, or humour'! I stood in front of the hundreds of books in the women's studies section which seemed to be about every conceivable aspect of the lives of women, but found nothing about men.

Since then I have stood in front of women's studies sections in nearly every major city in Britain. I have always been the only man to do so, and only recently have I begun to find one or two books about men. There is a wealth of books and articles on the subject if you know where to look, but the fact that they are not sold in the high street must mean that men do not want to buy them. Women, it seems, not only reflect a great deal on their lives as women, but are prepared to pay out hard cash to help them do so.

Among Christians things are no different. There are good books on 'women's issues', focusing on theology or the Bible and feminism. Yet again there is practically nothing on men. Anybody wanting to hear good lectures on feminism and theology from diverse perspectives, can find them without too much trouble but try finding something for men and the world of ideas turns into a dry desert. We do not even have a comparable word for 'feminist'. What would it be anyway? 'Masculist' sounds more like something you wouldn't tell your family doctor about than somebody with an interest in men and masculinity. Why this lack of interest and incomprehension?

The Invisibility of Men

One vital part of the answer to these puzzles is provided by Michael Kimmel who is now a writer in men's studies in America. While he was doing his PhD at Berkeley he sat in on classes on feminist theory. He was the only man in the room. At one seminar he witnessed an exchange between a white woman and a black woman. The white woman said that all women share the same oppression; whatever their colour or class, all are equally oppressed. The black woman did not agree; she asked the white woman, 'What do you see in the morning when you look at the bathroom mirror? You see a woman. I see a black woman. For you race is invisible because that is where you are privileged.' Michael Kimmel's reaction to this was to say, 'When I look in the mirror, I see a human being – a white, middle-class male. Gender is invisible to me because that is where *I* am privileged. I am the norm. I believe most men do not know they have a gender.'[1]

Colleges and universities do sometimes have courses on 'men's studies' and these have been set up to enquire into masculinity as something which needs to be explained rather than something that can be assumed. Many academics have been suspicious of this development. One asked, 'Aren't all courses that don't have the word "women" in them about men?' That is precisely the point. The position of men in our society means that they have been able to shape it around themselves. The experience of men has been read as 'human' experience rather than the experience of men as men. It seems ridiculous, but this is a relatively new area of study.

Michael Kimmel's experience is the starting point for this book, and understanding it is vital to understanding the book. Those men who have had similar experiences to him are now learning to see their masculinity as something which needs to be explained and even wrestled with, but often when I talk to men I get the feeling that the vast majority of them presume that their masculinity is an expression of common humanity. There is an old saying that 'a fish discovers water last' and many men have taken their masculinity for granted so long that they cannot get to grips with it. This book has been written to enable men to evaluate things which they have been living with all their lives but have never had to face before. There are some men reading this book for whom this thought is so new that they ought to put the book down and talk to their partners, friends or parents about this issue before reading on.

The way the history books are written gives little space for the exploits and achievements of ordinary women. Science, technology and models of managerial behaviour largely represent the behaviour and thinking of men. One of the main points made by feminists has been that the idea that the experience and perspective of men can also represent that of women is unjust. Their claim is that although they may have disagreed with what men were doing they could not express this difference since they had no power in society and were therefore not heard by men. The main evidence for this is the English language itself where women are meant to listen to men using 'he' or 'him' to refer to 'she' or 'her'. But try turning the language round and notice how the heads come up in surprise!

The way in which men's views have also purported to represent the views of women has led to women becoming *socially invisible* as a gender. Differences between men and women seem to have been restricted to sexual differences but the idea that women may have different views on politics or a different approach to family life or even business life has not been considered until recently. One of the ideas behind the women's movement has been that women should draw attention to the fact that the differences between men and women cannot be restricted to sexuality but are pervasive throughout public and private life. This point of view did not just affect women. Men came to see their point of view as the norm and did not have to grapple with the fact that it arose out of their point of view as a gender. This lack of reflection by men led to masculinity itself making men *personally invisible*. Many men are not aware of the effect the masculine world-view has on them because they do not view themselves as men but as persons. It is ironic that this insight which in other contexts expresses a high ideal, namely that we are people and not objects, has in this context been a barrier to our discovering our true humanity which can only be experienced as a man or as a woman.

Over the last twenty years women have developed a way of speaking about themselves, which draws attention to the fact that they have a distinctive world-view as women. The women's studies sections of high street book shops do not just contain books about sexuality and sexual differences. There are books about literature, industry, art, as well as books about family life and human relationships. Over the same period men have not developed a distinctive approach with which to talk about themselves, their world-view and their assumptions about life. One of the indications that this is true is demonstrated when men are asked what it means to be a man. In my experience of asking such a question of other men I have found that many men are at a loss to know what to say. It is an issue that they have not reflected on. Because of this lack of reflection such men frequently resort to stereotypes which are readily available to them as convenient ways of talking about themselves, but which do not describe who they are as men.

So there is an inequality between men and women in that while women are acutely aware of themselves as women, men are invisible to themselves as men. This invisibility does not only generate negatives such as prejudice and discrimination. It also prevents men from celebrating what it means to be a man. If they have never explored themselves, and if their language and self-image depends on well-worn stereotypes then they are unable to celebrate their humanity.

'Introspection'

What happens when men do attempt to look at themselves and become self-aware? One of the major problems is that such self-analysis is viewed as *introspection*. It is true that introspection, rightly understood, is not about being quiet or shy but is about being focused on the self. It is also true that people who are obsessed by themselves cannot mature or grow spiritually since they think that the whole world revolves around them.

Nevertheless, we are also to understand ourselves. Just as some people are obsessed with themselves, others are completely ignorant of themselves and have no insight at all. Some men seem completely unable to talk about themselves. The fact is that when men accuse others of introspection or navel-gazing they are often adopting yet another avoidance tactic of dealing with the issue of who they are. Such lack of insight can make people infuriating to live with since they find it difficult to take responsibility for their own behaviour. When such men are Christians this is an even greater puzzle, since the Christian life is a pilgrimage from the self towards God. We start out focused on the self and as we journey we become more aware of the self in order that we might lose our hold on it and grasp instead those things of which God wants our lives to be full.

Self-awareness is an essential part of that self-control which is one of the hallmarks of a mature Christian character. It is an essential part of a journey towards being able to love others and also to act justly. But if some men are unwilling even to undertake this journey then they condemn themselves to being stunted spiritually. Contemporary masculinity is functional and not spiritual, it has more to say about 'doing' than 'being'. Men cannot embrace spirituality without learning to become critically aware of their masculinity. One of the reasons for this is that spirituality and masculinity occupy similar territory in men's lives. Both generate ideas of authority, identity and security and men cannot be sure that they are being liberated by true spirituality unless they can critically evaluate the source from which it is being generated. One of the things I have been interested in over the last twenty years has been the way in which men who are deeply spiritual have often had to come to terms with their own sense of what it means to be a man as part of their pilgrimage.

Compartmentalism

Many men change their behaviour according to the context, either because they see themselves fulfilling different roles or because they have divided their life into watertight compartments which are sealed off from one another. I remember meeting a man who was very relaxed, loving and cheerful in an informal setting, but who became extremely formal and overbearing when at his place of work. He increasingly experienced a tension between the two which he found difficult to resolve. It was as if he became a different person when he was at work, or that a different side of his personality came out at that point. The reason I ended up speaking to him after a conference which I was addressing was that he wanted to be the same person whatever the context, he felt that he was taking the culture of his workplace as a given and was fitting himself into it but was adding to the problem for other people who were having to do the same. He was so used to playing roles that his home life now felt as if he was also playing the role of husband and father. He needed to discover his true identity which he believed to be the relaxed, friendly, companionable person he was at home.

Another man I talked to who was a banker completely separated his work life from his home life, his wife did not even know the names of the people he worked with nor had she ever been to his place of work. The problem in his life came when he was facing a professional crisis which affected him to such an extent that his marriage almost broke up. He had no desire to talk about the crisis at work with his wife, since he had always made a virtue of keeping it separate. When the story did come out he found that behind his lack of communication at home was the additional burden of his having internalised the pressures he was facing at work. In the end he had to experience a very painful personal breakdown in order to be able to admit that he needed help and that he was dependent on other people.

These are both quite stark and dramatic instances of a general tendency among men to place various parts of their lives in separate compartments. We all change slightly in different contexts, because the expectations around us are different, and at our place of work we are known for skills that we do not practise when at home, but the tendency to fragment our experience is not just restricted to the work/home dichotomy.

Men *are* affected by what happens in the rest of their lives and in so often seeking to suppress it they may lack understanding of why they are behaving as they do. Those who have never faced up to insecurities which are based in their relationship to their parents as a child because they were never affirmed or loved, may occasionally wonder why they constantly seek affirmation in their work or are driven by the need for promotion when such promotion may be inappropriate or even a negative influence on the rest of their lives.

The end result of such compartmentalism is that men can suffer from living in parallel worlds. In their work life they are surrounded by values such as competitiveness and self-interest. In the commercial world aggressive behaviour may be applauded since it wins contracts and puts competitors down. Power relationships are important and having authority over people is seen as a measure of prestige and status. But when a man comes home tired from the office and from the self-interested commercial world, he steps into a world where such things are anathema. At home he is meant to be the loving husband and father who is caring and who nurtures those around him with his love. Aggression, self-interest and power are not acceptable in the context of family life or of friendships with other people. Women who work in such worlds find that they too are affected by problems of compartmentalism and this may be because the culture of work has been based on a masculine world-view which they are asked to adopt in order to be successful. We shall go into this in depth when we come to look at the issue of work more closely.

The transition between work and home can be very difficult, and those who cannot make the transition may prefer to remain faithful to the values they work with outside the home, remaining formal, aloof and distant within the home. Such men may confine their activities within the home to practical tasks such as mowing the lawn or painting the shed, and may even read stories to the children or play football with them, but they find it difficult to be the loving, vulnerable and 'human' person that their family wishes they would be. Often the wives of such men will go along with this, being willing to trade emotional support for a secure home which is bought by the efforts of their husband at work. Inwardly they do not derive satisfaction from this arrangement, and husband and wife can quickly grow apart as the wife begins to resent the lack of friendship and emotional support and may develop a life of her own in order to find them.

However, there are many men who find their *raison d'être* in their life within the home or in their leisure activities and for whom the world of work is a regrettable necessity. Some men would prefer to play with the children or play golf to developing computer programmes or doing people's accounts. Such men may be viewed within the world of work as not having the cutting edge or the commitment which is necessary in order to be thought of as successful and worthy of promotion. In business where the rewards are extremely high it is not enough just to 'put in the hours', one has to become a company person in both image and soul.

When asked why they behave in this way men may respond that it is much simpler to keep things separate than allow them to become muddled up with one another. In other words they see the issue as one of complexity, yet they find themselves beholden to other people in different areas of life who are making demands on them to which they are responding differently. One of the components of a typical mid-life crisis is that men have been beholden to other people for so long that they do not know who they are themselves. The idea of separating parts of their lives and keeping them distinct, far from being about complexity and simplicity, ends up being about identity and security.

Isolation

Succumbing to these tendencies within conventional masculinity can be very isolating for men. We shall see in future chapters that even if men do not view other men as competitors, their friendships with them can be instrumental. In other words, friendship can be a means to an end (knowing the right people) and therefore subordinated to the values of one's working life. More often, however, the instrumental nature of friendship is found in the fact that men often relate to one another through some joint activity. In recent research about how children relate to one another, it was found that when two small girls were placed in a room together and their behaviour recorded by a hidden camera, they quickly began to ask questions of one another and established a rapport based on knowing something about the other person's life. When two boys were placed in the same situation, they quickly went to the toys placed in the room, which the girls had ignored, and began to play with the toys. Sometimes they played in isolation from one another and at other times they related to one another through the fantasy games they had made up. But at no time did they question one another about background or seem inquisitive about the other person's life.

This research is not meant to conclude that boys never question one another or are not interested in each other, nor that girls never play in isolation from one another. But it highlighted tendencies which can be seen in adult life for women to use conversation to express intimacy whereas men do not do this directly. When men get together with friends their friendship may be expressed through the medium of a game of golf or attending a football match or another activity which they both enjoy, but it is extremely rare for men to sit together and talk about each other as an expression of friendship. When they talk, it is often about issues in the public world, or about things at work.

The meaning of male and female friendships is very different. Men prefer activities to conversation, and men's conversations are usually less intimate than women's conversations. Men may say they want intimacy but often mean companionship. They prefer loyal commitment to intimate disclosure. If a friend has turned up to play squash every week for the last twenty years this may be taken to mean that he is a close friend and may be preferred as a sign of friendship to his opening up about the intimate details of his life. Such friends infer from the fact that they share things in common that what they are experiencing is intimacy. This also applies to men sharing the same objective interests in their conversations; one man's response when asked about his best friend, 'We are pretty open with each other I guess. Mostly we talk about sex, horses, guns, and the army.'[2] This objectivity may be a strength from the standpoint of the tasks men tackle when at work, but if men do desire intimacy then it will not serve them well in the area of relationships.

Perhaps the word 'friendship' is a key word in the debate about masculinity. Many men admit that they do not have close friends but do not know how to go about forming such friendships. One writer who wanted to look at the subject of male friendship constantly found that he was misunderstood to be talking about homosexuality.[3] It appears that the legendary love of David for Jonathan may now only exist in sermons, partly because men have no time to give themselves in such relationships because they see themselves as 'too busy', and partly because they just do not know how to go about forming such friendships since they do not know who they are and do not have the language to either enquire about or understand their friend. Perhaps men are reduced to having acquaintances and colleagues who can be shut up in a compartment. One widow remarked that though her husband's funeral was large with three hundred people attending, most of them men, 'It was strange that he had no friends . . .'.

One study of friendships between men makes the following comment:

> . . . there are times when a man becomes aware that something is lacking. Inferred intimacy seems to work well until a disturbing problem demands more from the relationship than unquestioned acceptance. At that point, many men find themselves without the kind of friend on whom they can rely.[4]

It is that last comment which strikes home. Many men are searching for a friend because life has become difficult for them. They are suffering from stress, divorce, unemployment or are questioning whether they have got it right with their lives driven by money, sex and power. But when things go wrong men find that the person they have played squash with every Friday night for the last twenty years does not want to talk about it. Many men are looking for a friend and they feel lonely and isolated. That may be the starting point for a great deal of personal reflection. Certainly those men who fear becoming more aware of themselves, who compartmentalise their lives and feel isolated, need to make a number of changes in their lives if they are to celebrate life more.

Changing Assumptions

The hope of women that they will be one day treated in all respects as equals and not written off as 'feminists', or merely appreciated by men for their beauty or their sexual attraction, lies ironically in men discovering themselves as men. Until then the views of women will in many areas be seen by men as mere deviations from the norm. This is not mere social analysis but the daily experience of millions of women. As social and sexual historians have documented, women find that men interrupt them when they are talking, do not listen or hear what they say, tell women they are wrong or that they shouldn't feel the way they do, accuse them of being 'illogical', expect them to be supportive of their views in public even when they disagree. Men believe that their view of the world is 'natural', 'normal' and 'right', they therefore cannot come to grips with their bias, prejudice and shortcomings.

Those women who have been on a pilgrimage to find an identity for themselves as women, hope to find at the end of their journey that they can be integrated into life with men. This is a vain hope until men have been on their own pilgrimage which may turn out to be very different from that of women. But until then it remains true that men who are compartmentalised and isolated cannot love with *all* their mind or with *all* their heart and therefore cannot love their neighbour as themselves.

Any analysis of the changing role of men in the modern world cannot be theoretical but must grapple with the experiences of men. How easy it would be for men to listen to a lecture or read a book in order to change. But we learn most from what we experience together. Over the last decade there has been an attempt to found a men's movement in Britain and America. But many of the groups appeared to assume too much before they ever met. Those who joined men's groups and wrote books on masculinity usually did so because they had been deeply influenced by feminism and shared its assumptions, but to a great extent both the women's movement and the men's movement were built on socialist foundations. This provided the language as well as the vision for their journey and although they talked a great deal about being inclusive and about laying down power, they excluded a great many people by adopting left-wing views which many people could not share. From the standpoint of those who do not subscribe to left- or right-wing politics but who consciously pick their way through such minefields looking for a Christian third way, it is important to be discerning about what they have to offer.

We share with those groups the belief that the old masks of power and dominance which men have traditionally worn should now be decisively rejected, yet stripped of our masks we feel faceless, as if we cannot be ourselves without adopting some role or hiding behind the stereotypes of conventional masculinity. This book looks at the possibility of coming to terms with the masks that men wear and encourages us to take them off and accept what is underneath.

The story of many of the men's groups in Britain is about the void that many felt was facing them as men when the old certainties had gone. Andrew Tolson wrote about the experience of a men's group in Birmingham in the seventies as follows:

We wanted to rediscover the experience of becoming a man – taking seriously our shortcomings, and learning from the analysis. But we soon discovered that no one really knew, or could express, why he had joined the men's group in the first place. As men, we had no language to formulate our uncertainties; no way of showing to others our responsiveness or concern.[5]

If we all wear masks created and sanctioned by the images of modern society, then we will only be more alone. If one of us wears a mask while the other takes it off, then the vulnerability for that person may be too great to bear, for all their fragility is open to gaze while the other's defences are intact. But if as men together we can first identify the masks and then encourage each other to take them off, we can then discover in our new vulnerability acceptance, love and grace. At present such words make many men feel uncomfortable or raise a laugh.

Perhaps this is because masculinity is often defined in terms of not being feminine or 'like a woman', and this desire of men to get as far away as possible from being thought of like a woman means that masculinity and femininity are thought of as polar opposites. We even talk of 'the opposite sex'. But this polarisation is based on fear which is fuelled by insecurity. The Christian perspective is quite different. It solves the problem of insecurity first and then shows that men and women share a sameness which makes the lists of characteristics considered masculine or feminine accessible as an expression of humanity open to us all.

Until such an insight becomes commonplace then men will shift their gender identity as women change in order to still be thought of as masculine. The other strategy which men will adopt is excluding women from occupations and behaviour considered to be part of the core identity of what it means to be masculine. Many books which have been written recently about the subject of masculinity contain the idea that masculinity is in a state of crisis[6] because the old role models have dropped away leaving uncertainty in their wake. While women were submissive men could delude themselves that the macho man was acceptable, but as John Lennon points out we have to find some other way of living as men:

> Isn't it time we destroyed the macho ethic? . . . Where has it gotten us all these thousands of years? Are we still going to have to be clubbing each other to death? Do I have to arm wrestle you to have a relationship with you as another male? Do I have to seduce her – just because she's a female? Can we not have a relationship on some other level? . . . I don't want to go through life pretending to be James Dean or Marlon Brando.[7]

Women are showing themselves to be good in areas men have previously considered their own and there is now little exclusive territory for men to call their own. This is another reason why men should be interested in gender issues. The world is changing and men must change with it. Masculine conventions are not serving them well.

A Map for the Journey

This book is for people who want to wrestle with these issues. The next chapter sets out some of the tools that are needed in order to tackle the job. It then moves on to a discussion of feminism and how men respond to it. Having located one of the central problems as attitudes to power we then move on to look at power from a Christian perspective. Alternatives to conventional masculinities are slowly emerging and the 'new man' and the 'wild man' are two of the most important, for reasons I bring out in the chapters on them.

The book then moves to the story of the men's group which I have been a member of for several years. Many of the insights of this book were forged in that group rather than through reading books and the story is about the kinds of models for which men who are committed Christians are looking. That leads on naturally to a consideration of the person of Jesus Christ because he was a man too. Can men still follow him or has he nothing to offer us in this debate? Another essential issue is the revelation of God as father. How do we deal with the problems that come from this and how does the fatherhood of God relate to the problems which men are experiencing as fathers today.

The book then moves on to considering two areas: relationships and work. There are three chapters on sexuality, intimacy and communication and two chapters covering work and men's response to 'women's work' both inside and outside the home. The book concludes with a call for us to celebrate our humanity by recovering our self-awareness as men.

The first task is to make sense of some of the tools we shall need on the journey. What is the difference between maleness and masculinity, for instance? We've got to get these straight before we can move on.

QUESTIONS

1. What do you think the phrase 'be a man' means?
2. 'I do not think most men know that they have a gender.' Do you think this statement is true?
3. Do men you know talk about themselves?
4. How would you characterise the strengths and weaknesses of the ways in which men view friendship with other men? (It may help to list them on a board.)
5. Why do you think some people have a tendency to keep different areas of their life in separate compartments?
6. Do you think that masculinity is defined as 'not being feminine' or 'not acting like a woman'? If so, how do you see men responding as women change their roles?

NOTES

1. This story and quote was taken from the *Guardian*, 29 September 1988.
2. L. R. Davidson and L. Duberman, 'Friendship: Communication and Interactional Patterns in Same-Sex Dyads', *Sex Roles*, 8, (1982), pp. 809–22.
3. Stuart Miller, *Men and Friendship* (London: Gateway, 1983).
4. Drury Sherrod, 'The Bonds of Men: Problems and Possibilities in Close Male Relationships', *The Making of Masculinities: The New Men's Studies*, ed. Harry Brod (London: Allen and Unwin, 1987), pp. 213–39. This quote from p. 222.
5. Andrew Tolson, *The Limits of Masculinity* (London: Routledge, 1988), p. 11.
6. See for instance Leanne Payne, *Crisis in Masculinity* (Eastbourne: Kingsway, 1988) or some of the essays in *The Making of Masculinities*, ed. Harry Brod (London: Allen and Unwin, 1987) particularly the essay by Michael S. Kimmel 'The contemporary "crisis" of masculinity in historical perspective', pp. 121–54. See also Elaine Showalter, *Sexual Anarchy* (London: Bloomsbury, 1991), p. 9.
7. John Lennon quoted by Kimmel, op. cit., p. 121.

2

MEN, MALENESS
AND MASCULINITY

One of the key distinctions I want to make in this chapter is
the difference between maleness and masculinity. The focus
of this book is on masculinity rather than maleness which I
see as being about the 'givens' which cannot be altered by
cultural change. Maleness is about the fact that men have
testosterone in their systems and their genitalia are of a
certain sort. Masculinity is about the values, expectations
and interpretations which men have attached to the idea of
being a man. These ideas can be challenged and changed and
it is therefore possible if men see masculinity differently for
men to behave differently.

It is important to distinguish between 'sex' and 'gender'
as the difference between the two is the distinction between
maleness and masculinity. The sex of a person is traditionally
related to issues focused on biology and physiology but
gender is about the cultural understanding of what it means
to be a man. What message do men use their bodies to convey
to the outside world and what do they understand it means to
be a man in terms of their own self-consciousness?

The difference between maleness and masculinity needs to
be illustrated. Imagine two posters hanging on a wall. One is
a picture of Sylvester Stallone in his film role of Rambo, his
muscles are rippling, he carries a gun. In the other poster a
man with a naked and muscled torso is cradling a baby in his

arms. Both are men and both are male, the muscle ratio on the body denotes maleness in both cases, but the masculinity of each is very different. In the Rambo picture the muscles reinforce the message, 'Look out, I'm a threat.' In the other the message is, 'You're safe with me'. One is a picture of violence, the other a picture of meekness – the gentleness of the strong.

If male aggression is attributable solely to biological causes then there is not much that men can do about it. They cannot be held to blame for something they cannot control. But if such behaviour is socially constructed; if it is learned behaviour, then anything is possible. These two models stand at the two poles of explanation. At its worst the former succumbs to determinism or 'nothing buttery' – the idea that people are 'nothing but' their biology. The latter model is one of social relativism where everything is manipulable. But we know that there are many things about gender which appear to be given and are not manipulable.

Between these two poles are statements such as this one from Arthur Brittan in his recent book *Masculinity and Power*: 'The socialisation case assumes that a man's and a woman's body respectively provide *different* foundations on which the social and cultural world builds its gender system. Biological differences are the starting point for the construction of an edifice of gender differences.'[1]

A Christian view of creation states that it is essential to see people as more than their biology. The creation story in Genesis is about God making people in his own image, and the man and the woman are not reducible to biology for God breathes into them. From day one they are living, thinking, loving, imaginative and creative people. Christianity therefore resists reducing people either to their biology or to social conditioning, preferring to emphasise the wholeness that comes from the creation story.

This book examines how men use the ideas behind masculinity to make sense of their lives. In particular I am concerned to ask whether the images of masculinity have been hijacked by ideas which do not allow men to experience or explore the 'created wholeness' that their humanity represents. Should masculinity be likened to a pair of glasses which enables men to focus clearly on the world and on themselves, or should it be likened to a pair of blinkers which only enable men to see what is directly in front of their eyes but blind them to everything else? The added complication to this is that masculinity is largely invisible to many men as I have illustrated in chapter one. It is my hope that by bringing out the series of cultural norms and stereotypes by which men currently make sense of their lives, and showing some of them to be distorted, men will feel liberated to look for new ways of being a man. I hope that all kinds of men will be stimulated to look again at the life of Christ as the model for their lives.

Stereotypes and Norms

Many of the images surrounding masculinity are stereotypes of what it means to be a man. A dictionary will tell you that a stereotype is 'an over-simplified mental image of a person'. It can apply to a whole race or class, or it can be narrow as applied to 'women's libbers' or other easily identifiable groups. Instead of dealing with the diversity of different kinds of people we tend to create stereotypes out of the characteristics of the group which are most easily observable. For instance rugby players may be stereotyped as being big, liking bawdy songs and drinking excessive amounts of beer. Bankers could be stereotyped as being neat, obsessional and having no personality. Production-line workers could be stereotyped as liking pornographic pin-ups, smoking in their tea-break and going to Majorca for their holidays. We can see that stereotypes can be grossly unfair, but because we cannot meet every banker, rugby player or production-line worker and assess them individually, we tend to create a picture in our mind of what they are like as a group. The same is true for men and is especially true of the idea of being a 'real man'. It may help to write down, at this point, your own stereotype of men or real men to compare with the rest of this book.

In the whole area of gender, stereotypes have become extremely important. There have been many attempts to describe the ways in which men and women are different and in what ways they are the same. In one study[2] university students were asked to choose adjectives from a list of 300 as being typically associated with either men or women. They were able to do this with over ninety per cent of them and there was a wide measure of agreement between the male and female students. Adjectives such as affectionate, gentle and appreciative were associated with women, whereas men were seen as enterprising, ambitious, courageous or confident.

Sex Roles

Traditionally, the way to look at gender has been through the use of sex roles. The behaviour of men and women was seen as being dictated by our biological make-up and since this could not be changed the way in which men and women typically behaved was seen to be a good guide to how they should behave. Many of us grew up with this kind of approach. We were given very clearly defined images of the kind of behaviour expected of men and the kind of behaviour expected of women. The problem was that individual people wanted to behave quite differently because they were not 'average people'. To take a simplistic example, when I was a young man men wore trousers and women wore dresses. As jeans came in men and women both began to wear trousers but it never became acceptable for men to wear dresses. It was not 'done'. All kinds of sanctions were attached to behaving in a way which was different from the norms.

This approach to gender had real weaknesses. Firstly, it did not take history seriously. Men have viewed themselves very differently in different periods. Secondly, it did not take culture seriously. Men behave differently in different cultures. Thirdly, it did not take power seriously. Enshrined within the role models we were given was the dominance of men over women in our society. Fourthly, it did not take people seriously. The boxes marked male and female came first and then people were measured up to them. It ended up being reductionist. Instead of finding explanations of human behaviour which allow people the freedom to be different even within their gender, it imposed straitjackets on us. Masculinity became associated with power and the public realm, femininity with subordination and the private realm. These roles were seen as 'natural', 'moral' and even 'godly'.

How we view sex roles depends on two considerations.[3] Firstly, those characteristics which are 'typical' of women or men (sex role *stereotypes*) and secondly, the behaviour considered 'desirable' for women or men (sex role *norms*). The characteristics and behaviour which go to make up sex roles are drawn from aspects of personality, i.e. men may be characterised as aggressive, achievement-orientated or inarticulate, and have specific social roles such as breadwinner, husband or father. So sex role *stereotypes* are widely shared beliefs about what the sexes actually *are* whereas sex role *norms* are widely shared beliefs about what they *should be*.

How do people see themselves compared to the 'typical' man or woman? A person who sees themselves as strongly masculine, as measured by the association of their personal attributes with typical sex roles, is also likely to strongly identify psychologically with that sex role. Sex roles are the means by which we make sense of our own behaviour as men and women. But we understand what these roles are by a mixture of stereotypes and norms which we learn throughout our lives. If 'real boys' are meant to like playing sport then those boys who like playing sport will feel secure, but those who hate it may well feel that their gender identity is insecure until they can find something else strongly associated with being a 'real boy' which they identify with. Such boys will suffer from 'sex role strain'[4] which comes from not living up to or fulfilling sex role stereotypes and norms.

Among researches on gender it has become common to distinguish between traditional male roles and modern male roles. Traditional roles have been described by anthropologists working in primitive societies and by studies of ethnic communities and working-class neighbourhoods. But modern male roles have come out of middle-class communities and studies of men working in contemporary organisations and bureaucracies. Traditionally masculinity is seen as valid if it depends on physical strength and aggression. Such men are not meant to be emotionally sensitive or expressive and are not meant to be vulnerable or weak in any way. However, anger is tolerated, a traditional paradox within male roles. The modern man is seen as masculine more through economic achievement and the power he exerts at work. His intelligence may be an important factor and he may be seen as masculine if he is able to be sensitive and expressive in romantic relationships with women. However, control over the emotions is crucial to modern masculinity and emotional expression must be confined to relationships with women. Anger is discouraged as control is so important.

Traditional men prefer the company of men, perhaps in the pub or club, and see other men as providing validation for their masculinity. Women are necessary for sex and bearing children but these relationships are not intimate or romantic. Women should defer to male authority. There is a double standard which views sexual freedom as okay for men but not for women. The modern man prefers the company of women. It is women rather than men that validate the modern man's masculinity. Men's relationships with women are intimate and romantic, and heterosexual relationships are the only necessary provider of emotional support. Women are companions rather than subordinate to men. But men's relationships to other men are weaker and less emotionally important. These insights are derived from Joseph Pleck's path-breaking study entitled *The Myth of Masculinity* and constitute his summary of the conclusions of many researchers in the field. He cites one study by Komarovsky which reports about college students that:

> men now disclose more to female than male friends. It is now men's relationships with other men – rather than with women – that seem to be only arrangements of convenience. Male-male relationships often appear now to derive primarily from workplace contacts and to be expressed primarily through drinking and watching sports on television.[5]

The distinction between traditional and modern parallels a distinction between middle-class and working-class cultures. It is important to realise that the argument is not that we are all now modern men but that as culture has evolved the modern image of masculinity has increasingly become the one which men measure themselves against. However there are still strong elements of the traditional man present in contemporary society and some men will revert to traditional values when they feel insecure about modern values.

Ideal Men?

The ideals and norms which govern male behaviour are on a continuum. At the top of the ladder are those ideals which represent all those characteristics which people believe an 'ideal' man should have. At this level there is a great deal of similarity between masculine and feminine ideals. Gentleness, patience, kindness all figure as virtues of the ideal man. Many of the characteristics would be considered feminine. At the lower levels there are the more typical and more readily identifiable masculine stereotypes. These are essentially competitive or sports orientated.

The fact is that the more idealised the norm is, the less people feel that it is attainable even if they could possibly be like that. People may reserve admiration for such an ideal but compare themselves more with the minimum achievable than with the maximum ideal, which is out of reach. Interestingly, the kind of person that Jesus Christ is portrayed as closely resembles the highest ideals of masculinity but many people would regard him as 'out of reach'. So when we portray Jesus as an ideal person we may end up admiring him from afar but feeling that it is hopeless trying to emulate him because of the gulf between him and us.

It is interesting that male norms include many sex-neutral and feminine characteristics, for example, intelligence, sensitivity to the needs of others, warmth, and romanticism. The ideal male and the ideal female share many traits in common yet many men are aware of norms which emphasise the difference between men and women. One study looked at four factors which make up the sex role norm: 1) No Cissy Stuff: the stigma of anything even vaguely feminine; 2) The Big Wheel: success, status, and the need to be looked up to; 3) The Sturdy Oak: a manly air of toughness, confidence, and self-reliance; 4) Give 'em Hell: the aura of aggression, violence, and daring.[6] It is important to score highly in at least one of these factors in order to be considered a 'real man'.

Women and men have different views of each other's sex role. The proliferation of Mills and Boon style romances feeds off the view held by women that men should be expressive, intimate and romantic. But although the modern man is meant to be more emotionally expressive many men, as we shall see in later chapters, have real problems with articulating their emotions and see a conflict between being vulnerable emotionally and holding on to ideas of control and objectivity which are at the heart of masculinity. It has been interesting to observe men I know being romantic with a woman until marriage but then quickly settling back into behaviour more associated with conventional masculinity than emotional vulnerability. So it is easy for the sex roles which we try to live up to to be a great source of strain for us as the person we are fails to live up to the expectations of our gender generated by the society we live in.

A man may be made redundant through no fault of his

own, who has until now been completely dependent for his personal identity on the idea that he is the breadwinner for the family. The social changes around him completely dislocate his sense of personal self-worth and social status. He may respond to this by becoming depressed but may also become aggressive, over-compensating in one area for his perceived lack of masculinity in another. Whatever the cause, many men are aware of the fact that they do not measure up to what is required of them by contemporary views of masculinity and this is a problem for them since they may find it difficult to express what they are going through.

The 'Deep Structure' of Masculinity

One of the phenomena which needs to be explained is the persistence of similar roles for men across cultures. Despite the current fashion for explaining masculinity as socially constructed there does seem to be a remarkable continuity in the ways men perceive what it means to be 'manly' or what has to be done to achieve 'manhood'. One of the most important of these perceptions is the notion that masculinity or manhood is different from growing up from a boy to a man. Achieving manhood does not just happen due to the process of the child becoming an adult, but it is something that must be 'achieved' often against the odds. In many cultures boys have to go through a rigorous period of testing in order to 'prove' that they are 'men'. There is no guarantee that they will succeed but failure brings with it heavy social penalties. This idea is found among peoples of very different background: hunters and fishermen, warriors and peaceable folk, peasants and urban workers. There are a lot of words used of men which ungender them such as 'effeminate', 'unmanly', or 'emasculated'. When I was a schoolboy, those who were 'different', or who were quiet and not very good at sports were called 'eunuchs' and were taunted publicly by other boys. Such words are used frequently of men and with great force.

Women do have a biological threshold which signals the

onset of 'womanhood' and that is the beginning of men-struation. Boys have no such dividing line. Girls can identify with their mothers and can learn from them and model themselves on them, but boys can only learn about being a man by breaking the links with their mothers and modelling themselves on their fathers. Where the father is absent or engaged in pursuits which are difficult for boys to emulate or admire boys are presented with a real problem of security, they need to become men and are not sure how it is done. This can lead to anxiety which in turn can lead to anti-social behaviour such as violence or excessive drinking as boys try to 'prove themselves' by emulating the most extreme examples of 'macho' behaviour.

In his book *Manhood in the Making: Cultural Concepts of Masculinity*[7] anthropologist David Gilmore compares some of the ways diverse cultures have found to prove manhood. On Truk Island in the South Pacific, the men are fishermen and are obsessed with their masculinity. They maintain their 'manliness' by going to sea in tiny dug-out canoes to spearfish in shark infested waters. Those men who will not go are laughed at by both men and women who call them effeminate and childlike. 'When on land, Trukese youths fight in weekend brawls, drink to excess, and seek sexual conquests to attain a manly image. Should a man fail in any of these efforts, another will taunt him: "Are you a man? Come, I will take your life now."'[8]

On the Greek Island of Kalymnos the men are sponge-fishers and dive into deep water without any equipment, taking the risk of being crippled by the 'bends'. Again they prove their manhood by showing they have contempt for death. To take precautions is to be called 'effeminate'. In East Africa boys from the Masai, Rendille and Jie cattle-herding peoples are taken from their mothers and subjected to circumcision. If a boy makes any sound, blinks or cries out under the pain of the knife 'he is shamed for life as unworthy of manhood, and his entire lineage is shamed as a nursery of weaklings.'[9]

In nearby Ethiopia among the Amhara masculinity is called *wand-nat* which is characterised by aggressiveness, stamina, and 'courageous action' which means never backing down when threatened. To show *wand-nat* young men participate in whipping contests called *buhe*. All able-bodied adolescents must take part but the ritual is bloody, 'faces are lacerated, ears torn open, and red and bleeding welts appear.' Any sign of weakness is greeted with taunts and mockery. As if this were not enough, adolescent Amhara boys are wont to prove their virility by scarring their arms with red-hot embers. In these rough ways the boys actualise the exacting Amhara 'ideals of masculinity'. On his wedding night a man's potency must be demonstrated by waving a 'bloody sheet of marital consummation before the assembled kinsmen.'[10]

Gilmore gives countless other examples of similar phenomena from different cultures. He cites British boarding schools as places where 'trial by ordeal' was commonplace, and tests of manhood, which included violence and cruelty, were seen as essential. Boys were taken away from mother and home to become men. This produced all kinds of problems for such boys who wanted mother but dare not show it and who developed the 'stiff upper lip' instead of the trembling lips of the crying infant.[11]

In American culture the idea of becoming a man is explored by many authors including Ernest Hemingway, Norman Mailer and William Faulkner; the stories of the wild west where John Wayne exemplified the 'real man', gangster movies and now the Rambo cult with its bringing together of violence with the 'obvious masculinity' characterised by the muscled torsos of actors such as Sylvester Stallone and Arnold Schwarzeneggar.

The people of Tahiti in French Polynesia and the Semai of Malaysia have very different attitudes to masculinity. In Tahiti for example, the emphasis is on casual behaviour. Women seem to be as powerful as men and are permitted to do almost everything that men do. Some beat their husbands, others take part in male sports, even wrestling with male opponents. The artist Paul Gauguin said of them that 'there is something virile in the women and something feminine in the men.'[12] There are no jobs reserved for one sex rather than another. Men have no fear of acting in ways which western people might consider effeminate. They do not hunt or indulge in strenuous activity since food is plentiful and easily found. Men who work too hard are criticised by other men. They are passive and are expected to ignore insults. There is no concept of male honour. In fact masculinity is a matter of no concern for Tahitian men.

Where life is easy there seems to be little need for concepts of manhood that place emphasis on stress, risk, bravery and violence. The men feel little inherent need to 'act like men'. The Semai people are similar in their passivity. Gilmore sees in this an indication that feminist writers may be correct in talking of the idea of masculinity as cultural rather than biological and universal.

In order to survive all societies must be good at both production and reproduction. In most societies men are responsible for the former, women for the latter. Manhood can be seen as the point where the boy becomes a producer rather than a consumer and by doing so adds something of his own to his community. In concluding David Gilmore draws a rather surprising conclusion:

> I was prepared to discover the old saw that conventional femininity is nurturing and passive and that masculinity is self-serving, egotistical and uncaring. But I did not find this. One of my findings here is that manhood ideologies always include a criterion of selfless generosity, even to the point of sacrifice. Again and again we find that 'real' men are those who give more than they can take; they serve others. Real men are generous even to a fault. . . . Non-men are often those stigmatised as stingy and unproductive. Manhood therefore is a nurturing concept.[13]

Of course this nurturing is indirect. Men do not have breasts as women do with which they can feed infants. It is more obscure and difficult to see but 'men nurture their society by shedding their blood, their sweat, and their semen, by bringing home food for both child and mother, by producing children, and by dying if necessary in far away places to provide a safe haven for their people.'[14]

Although this is an interesting conclusion it is also dangerous. In the modern world many men believe that being the breadwinner is enough. If a man has a family of course he must provide for it, but to see this as the end of his nurturing reduces men to an instrumental role in their children's upbringing. Men can nurture and love their children, friends and wives directly. They do not need to hide behind the masking nature of provision, valuable and necessary though it is. The virtue of Gilmore's insight into masculinity is that it sees nurturing as central to manhood rather than being something unique to women which men must try and graft onto traditional concepts of masculinity.

There is one other point which must be stressed and which arises out of this work. These anthropological studies show that masculinity is something which is external to men. It is a social construction of something which has to be achieved by boys in order to prove themselves as men or something which has to be put on, like a suit of clothes, in order for men to be seen as masculine. It is the external nature of masculinity, as presented in images, expectations and conventional wisdom that is one of the reasons behind the constant comparisons men make between their inner self and their knowledge of what masculinity consists of within their own culture. It is this externality that has also led to masculinity being portrayed in many recent books as the wearing of masks.

Fulfilling Expectations

Men who do not fit in to the expectations being generated around them can find themselves talked about, vilified and ignored by the communities they live in. They may grow anxious and worried and deteriorate psychologically and physically because of this. One researcher comments that violating sex roles has the most negative consequences amongst those who believe that conformity to sex roles is important.

Men who see themselves as inadequate in some ways may over-compensate in others in order to prove to society that they are indeed as masculine as the next man. American sociologist Diana Russell argues that rape is not so much a deviant act as an act of over-conformity to a perceived masculine stereotype. 'An extreme acting-out of qualities that are regarded as super-masculine in this and many other societies: aggression, force, power, strength, toughness, dominance, competitiveness.'[15] The behaviour of a boy who plays with dolls is seen as more inappropriate than that of a girl who plays football. Yet it is also the case that if men fulfil masculine stereotypes this can lead to serious effects in their own lives. They take greater risks exposing themselves to danger and stress, die younger and suffer stress as breadwinners. They succumb to stereotypical behaviour which encourages smoking and heavy drinking, and often shrug off adequate medical attention. If they repress their emotions these will undoubtedly surface again causing emotional scarring, and they can be lonely, viewing other men as competitive and forgoing friendship which they desperately need.

It appears that men cannot win where the dominant stereo-type requires of men that they act in ways which are scarcely human and that are far removed from the behaviour of the people God created them to be. Many men feel that more is expected of them than they can possibly live up to. They lose themselves in their work, constantly feeling inadequate as husbands and fathers. They are called upon to be tough and self-interested in the workplace but within the home they are to be loving, intimate and altruistic. This dualism in their lives is a source of stress as the organisation of the labour market together with masculine stereotypes means they cannot possibly succeed at both, since they are set up as polar opposites. Many men succumb to over-identification with their work, hoping that they will receive enough respect within the family for their role as breadwinner to enable them to get by as fathers. While research shows that many men behave similarly to women in their response to newborn babies and would like to take part in childcare, they rarely allow themselves to become vulnerable enough to make such desires known, thereby perpetuating the stereotype for another generation to live up to.

Men are caught in a 'catch-22' situation. If they consciously seek to fulfil masculine stereotypes they may submerge their own personality and cause themselves harm in the process, yet the call to abdicate from such stereotypes is a call to distinctiveness which few men can bear. The sense of inadequacy and isolation felt by men who do not 'measure up' as men, can lead them either to become violent, to immerse themselves in their work, or to succumb to psychiatric illness and stress.

Men need to become critically aware of masculinity and begin a pilgrimage from masculinity to humanity. To do this we must ask questions about why being feminine entails becoming weak, or why being emotional is equated with 'loss of control'. It will mean looking at the over-identification of masculinity with employment and the consequences within the family of the absent and the distant father. It will mean rejecting exploitative sex in favour of vulnerability and intimacy, and ridding ourselves of the fear of homosexuality in favour of strong and loving relationships with other men.

It is particularly important to be aware that it is artificial to tie masculinity to maleness and femininity to femaleness as we shall soon see: one of the responses men have made to the analysis of the women's movement is to 'get in touch' with the feminine within them in order to become whole. But what is true for men must also be true for women, who must be free to draw on virtues and strengths considered masculine by a society which conforms too rigidly to gender stereotypes. It may well be true that when talking about masculinity men 'resonate' with it more deeply than women. Nevertheless it remains true in the person of Christ that he conveys to us in one personality the whole range of virtues and strengths which our society has split up into two lists according to sexual characteristics.

Having outlined some of the issues surrounding the idea of masculinity it is important to recognise that the reason we are interested at all is because the women's movement has raised so many questions over the conventional behaviour of men. Over the last twenty-five years publishing houses that specialise in women's studies have brought out hundreds of books but they have been met by silence from men. Are some men right to dismiss feminism as the rantings of neurotic women or are women putting their fingers so accurately on the real issues that men feel threatened by this and dismiss it only because they feel defensive?

QUESTIONS

1. Make up your own illustrations for the difference between maleness and masculinity.
2. In what way does the creation view of people differ from the biological or social models?
3. What are the stereotypes of men you are most aware of?
4. Do you feel under pressure to conform to certain sex roles? Where is that pressure coming from? (i.e. parents, friends, society?)
5. Do you think that the Second World War had much impact on men's interpretations of masculinity?
6. Do you agree that masculinity is something which has to be 'achieved' or 'put on'? If this is true, what do you think the impact of this is on men a) who feel they achieve it with no effort, or b) who feel that they cannot achieve it?
7. What kinds of pictures of 'ideal' men can you find in our society? What would your picture of an ideal man look like? Try drawing one!

8.   Do you think the picture of masculinity as 'wearing a mask' is apt? Do you ever find yourself doing this?

NOTES

1.   Arthur Brittan, *Masculinity and Power* (Oxford: Blackwell, 1989).
2.   J. E. Williams and S. M. Benett, 'The Definition of Sex Stereotypes via the Adjective Checklist', *Sex Roles*, 1 (1975), p. 327–341.
3.   Joseph H. Pleck, *The Myth of Masculinity* (Cambridge, Mass.: Massachusetts Institute of Technology Press, 1981), p. 10.
4.   Pleck, op. cit.
5.   Pleck, op. cit., p. 141. The insights leading up to this quote depend heavily on pp. 140–1.
6.   R. Brannon and D. David, 'The Male Sex Role: Our culture's blueprint for manhood, and what it's done for us lately', (eds.) D. David and R. Brannon *The Forty-Nine Per Cent Majority: The Male Sex Role* (Reading, Mass.: Addison-Wesley, 1976), quoted in Pleck op. cit., p. 139.
7.   David Gilmore, *Manhood in the Making: Cultural Concepts of Masculinity* (London: Yale University Press, 1990).
8.   Gilmore, op. cit., p. 12. The conversation in quotes is from Mac Marshall, *Weekend Warriors* (Palo Alto, Calif.: Mayfield, 1979), p. 92.
9.   Gilmore, op. cit., p. 19.
10.   Gilmore, op. cit., pp. 13–14.
11.   On this see John Chandos, *Boys Together: English Public Schools, 1800–1864* (New Haven Conn.: Yale University Press, 1984).
12.   Paul Gauguin, *Noa Noa* (New York: Noonday Press, 1957), p. 47.
13.   Gilmore, op. cit., p. 229.
14.   Gilmore, op. cit., p. 230.
15.   Diana Russell, 'Rape and the Masculine Mystique', paper presented to the American Sociological Association (New York, 1973), quoted in Pleck, op. cit., p. 146.

3

RESPONDING TO FEMINISM

Men regard feminism with universal apprehension. Those convinced of their own superiority may respond by dismissing feminism as being the whining of neurotic women. These comments are not usually for public consumption unless the company is like-minded. Although these men may be characterised as chauvinists there is more than a hint of fear in the air as they dismiss feminism out of hand. They feel that women have come to take something from them rather than to give them something. Their suspicion is that the issue is not partnership or equality but replacing male power by female power. They do not understand women and do not want to, and they take the silence of their partners as willing obedience and contentment with their lot rather than seeing it as resignation, despair or even fear of the consequences of speaking out.

The vast majority of men are not like that. They see themselves as hard-working, polite, and distantly friendly with women. They may even feel that women have a point, but they either think that it is somebody else's problem or that it is a social issue which is irrelevant to their daily life. For them, introducing the issue of gender into their lives is like people constantly harping on about the poverty in the third world. The issue is all right in its place but one mustn't get too obsessed with it.

These are the men whom feminists need to convince. The

problem is that they do not have the same world-view as the majority of feminists. For them the only possibility of change is some kind of conversion experience centred on gender issues. One of the luxuries patriarchy offers men is complacency. It has always been more difficult to overcome especially when the men involved are so 'nice' to women.

There is a third kind of response to feminism which comes from a minority of men who have been brought up alongside women who have become feminists. These men have tried to listen and have been ideologically convinced that their partners and woman friends have a point. They have taken on board the challenge that feminism throws down to men to change the way they see the world. Some of them have set up men's groups in order to respond to feminism and some of these have successfully brought out new issues for men, enabling them to grapple critically with the images and masks so prevalent in contemporary masculinity. Yet they are hounded by guilt. They are sensitive to the accusations of women that they as men are responsible for what has happened to women. They see themselves as the oppressors of whom women are the victims.

Some of the men who have joined such groups have commented on the breastbeating that went on and the sense of guilt which dominated the proceedings, stopping the men from finding their own way forward and always bringing them back to a debate with an ideology that seemed to condemn them rather than liberate them.[1]

A fourth type of response focuses on finding a way forward for men which can learn from feminism and what women are saying to men whether they are feminists or not. This view is different from the others in that it is not hostile to feminism as is the first response, nor does it ignore it as does the second. It does not surrender to feminism, as does the third response, but it seeks to develop a way forward for men which is pro-active and not reactive, but within which there is a critical awareness of both the strengths and the weaknesses of feminism. Such a position seeks to provide men with a positive vision of what it means to be a man while being willing to accept that men have behaved in an oppressive way in the past. It is this fourth way which provides the ethos for this book.

Before we can look at this way forward it is important to look at the main tenets of feminism, realising that what was in the initial stages a women's movement centred on the cause of liberation and equality with men, has become an ideology which is extremely demanding and which is split into various camps and disciplines. Any good bookshop with a women's studies section will show how many hundreds of books have been published by women on issues related to feminism in the last twenty years. How are men to evaluate this torrent of analysis and make some response to it? What is it that men are grappling with in order to go forward?

The Personal is Political

The women's movement was dominated from the outset by an important insight which was that 'the personal is political'. Kate Millett's book *Sexual Politics*,[2] which was published in America in 1970 and a year later in Britain, was responsible for articulating this insight. Whatever men did to women they did as representatives of their gender, class and subculture. Their actions, far from being unique, were typical of a whole class of actions, carried out daily by men on women. So the unique became typical, the private became public, the personal became political.

Far from being an act of personal aggression, rape became symbolic of male aggression. It was not only violence and abuse of one person by another but a statement of worthlessness by one gender about the other. Kate Millett's concept was extremely powerful. It gave women the means to talk about 'men' in general rather than focusing on their experience of one man, but it also did the opposite. It enabled a woman to see 'men' in her man; to see his anger, sexuality and weakness as 'typical' of all men. Out of this emerged a series of male stereotypes. The problem with this was that women were creating a 'way of seeing' men which was essentially reductionist. Of course some men had reduced women to a common denominator for years, but now men were the objects of stereotyping rather than the perpetrators. The diversity of men's personalities became mere variations on the same theme.

Perhaps feminists did for men what men could not do for themselves. For in seeming to reduce them to a common stereotype they provided a picture with which men could now compare themselves. For the first time men as a gender could see themselves as others saw them. Feminism made masculinity visible. The claim of men that their actions were entirely personal and not representative of contemporary masculinity was increasingly seen as a lack of self-awareness. If men wished to free themselves from it they had to develop insight. Before the women's movement forced this reflection of their own image on them, they could avoid this painful liberation of themselves.

The raising of self-consciousness was different for men than it had been for women. Women had to make the transition from the personal to the political but men had to make the transition from the political to the personal. They had to see that the world of institutions, power and authority was a world of people. These people were not to be treated as instruments, diverse means to effective ends. They were not merely important, they were in some sense sacred. If men did behave as if they related in some way to the same stereotype then liberation for them included recovering a sense of personal identity by freeing themselves from that kind of stereotype. Admitting its existence was the first step.[3]

Some women had undoubtedly come to the women's movement through experiences of deep and very personal suffering. They came not only to find liberation but also solace and understanding. I know of several women who joined a women's group after experiencing the breakdown of a relationship. For them it was more true that the personal *became* political; they came with a personal story to a women's group and were given an understanding of it in terms of social processes and gender injustices. Rather than advocate personal reconciliation which would have meant that life continued much as before, the women's movement counselled women to nurture their anger against men. It was seen as righteous anger. It was this anger that provided the momentum for the women's movement. They had a common enemy in men. As Rabbi Julia Neuberger has pointed out in her writings on the women's movement this sometimes led to problems, 'Feminism, in its heady 60s and 70s days, was so angry that it failed to establish realities. Everything was men's fault. Nothing was women's fault.'[4] Nevertheless, this sense of common cause gave women everywhere a degree of unity which was to fragment as their cause prevailed. It is true of any minority cause which battles as an underground movement in the name of freedom that its unity begins to disappear as the enemy is overcome and the plurality of the different groups which had been hidden behind the common front asserts itself.[5] Now women disagree as to whether even the initial skirmish is over. Feminism, like Marxism before it, has become divided into a wide spectrum of interests from lesbian separatism to biblical feminism.

One of the main motivating forces for the women's movement was anger. But there was disagreement about the origins and the consequences of that anger. Feminism interpreted it as a righteous expression of injustice rather than as an expression of personal hurt. Such women were portrayed as a political movement which was seeking to bring about change, rather than as women who wanted to 'get at' their partners. Men tended to respond to this in two ways. Their corporate response was to see the women's movement as a threat to the establishment, but because they could not see the world from women's perspective this was not seen as an improvement but as a destruction of all that society stood for. Some men regarded women's anger as a personal insult.

In both cases the anger itself placed men on the defensive and made them unwilling to even attempt to see the world from the perspective of feminism.

Why was the anger important? Many men would have preferred a situation in which they could have sat down with women round a table and discussed the situation quietly and, as they would put it, 'rationally'. But women knew from experience that this would mean that they would be dismissed. The anger of the women's movement was seen to be the only means by which women could shake men out of their complacency and force them to listen. Anger was the herald that went before the many powerful arguments of the women's movement. It signified that change must come and the first change had to be that men had to listen. If men felt hurt or wrongly accused then this was not as important as the fact that justice must be seen to be done. After all, women had been hurt and oppressed for many more years than men.

Patriarchy[6]

One of the essential insights of feminists was that society is dominated by and represented by men. The language of public discourse uses male references to speak for women. The laws of inheritance until recently favoured men. Professional advancement was and still is difficult for women whose place was supposed to be in the home. The Church preached that women were to be subservient to their men, and women promised to obey in the marriage ceremony. Such a society made women voiceless in the public realm. Status and worth seemed to be increasingly dependent on employment and women's work within the home had no monetary value,[7] and often felt like a second option. Some women who had been brought up to look to motherhood as the crowning glory of their femininity found the reality arduous, isolating and taken for granted.

Patriarchy means that those things that men do are considered to be important and the language that refers to men is taken to include women. Margaret Mead, the anthropologist, comments:

> In every known human society, the male's need for achievement can be recognised. Men may cook or weave or dress dolls or hunt humming birds, but if such activities are appropriate occupations of men then the whole society, men and women alike, votes them as important. When the same occupations are performed by women, they are regarded as less important.[8]

In our society this has not only happened through rigid gender stereotypes but a lot of women who are praised for being mothers and staying at home feel that they are not receiving the support and value that our society gives to such things. We remain a society that regards men's activities as the main source of value. Why has it been so difficult for women to enter certain occupations? Margaret Mead continues:

> In a great number of human societies men's sureness of their sex role is tied up with their right, or ability, to practise some activity that women are not allowed to practise. Their maleness, in fact, has to be underwritten by preventing women from entering some field or performing some feat. Here may be found the relationship between maleness and pride; that is, a need for prestige that will outstrip the prestige which is accorded to any woman.[9]

Whereas in a previous generation women had learned to be the producers during a war which made men scarce on the ground, when the soldiers returned women had to give up their jobs and react to men for whom war had made macho masculinity a strong option. Homemaking was the response of an extreme feminisation of women, and the women's movement may never have got off the ground were it not for this over-reaction after the Second World War.

Patriarchy was viewed by the women's movement as an unjust system which gives power to men at the expense of injustice for women. Feminism was much bigger than the complaint of individual women against the actions of their men. Feminists saw that this injustice was inherent in the structures of our society. It was present in the way that the law treated women and it was also true in the world of economics. But the dividing line was not now between managers and workers but between men and women, where men were the oppressors and women were the oppressed.

It was for this reason that feminism was so often wedded to socialism, as is much of the response by men to the problems of gender injustice. The belief was that if only one could change political and economic structures and bring in a socialist new age then egalitarianism would bring the freedom that men and women wanted. This analysis, rooted in Marxism, has always been a target for Christian criticism because while it calls itself radical, it is extremely optimistic about the degree of change that can be accomplished by politics. However, feminism was part of a movement to the 'new politics' which felt that its goals could not be achieved through the structures of the parliamentary model. It became part of a world of pressure groups which were used not only on the gender issue but also by other groups working in the areas of peace, race, and ecology. The hallmark of the new politics was that it was participatory in style rather than being representative.

Power and Change

The first insight that the personal is political made the oppression of women into a universal cause. The second insight was that patriarchy was so pervasive that the system of privilege upheld by men was regarded as normal. The third insight follows from the other two, which is that 'men change but only to hold on to power, not to relinquish it'.[10] Feminists suspected that men would be willing to change the law, and introduce equal opportunities regulations, as long as they did not have to change personally. The wedding of feminism with socialism had led feminists to believe that by changing the structure of society people would change as a result. But even after the establishment began to give way, in part, the enormity of the problem could be seen in that both the personal and the political needed to change for justice to be done. The issue was not just power-sharing, leading to justice, it was also how to move from power to love in the personal sphere.

The response of men has to be both corporate and personal because the issue is about justice and love together. If some men respond to feminism by loving their partners as equals this is part of the answer but is not enough. The women's movement is not only up against the issue of personal sin, it is also up against the issue of structural evil. If all the men in our society became loving 'new men' that would not mean that our society would cease to be patriarchal. Similarly we can change the structures of our society but that does not mean that men cease to treat women badly. Some power is needed which can confront the personal and the structural dimensions of life. Biblical feminists have seen Christianity as that power.

The question which women faced was whether men could change at all. Many women, especially those influenced most by feminist thought, felt pessimistic. This was put in three different ways. The first viewpoint was that men *cannot* change. The basis for this was in the biological model of men which we have already examined. Men are who they are because of their genetic make-up. Their competitiveness and aggression are due to biology and not choice.[11] Some women, among them Christians – espccially those who were conservative in outlook – said that men were not meant to change but were made to go out to work and be the providers while women were equipped by virtue of their biology to remain at home and look after the children. This view tried to make a virtue out of the fact that many men were bad at nurturing others but good at providing for them. This was the view of men as traditional breadwinners.

The second view was that men *choose* not to change. It is not that they cannot change, as in the first view, but that they decide not to. In other words, some women felt that although men know that they should co-operate with women they will refuse to do so. Men might buy in to a new way of talking about women and may appear to be changing but will not let go of the reins of power. They will regard the intrusion of women into their world as a phase that they are going through and will put their heads down and wait for it to blow over, hoping that women will return to their traditional occupations within the home.

The third viewpoint was expressed by those feminists who saw feminism as arrival rather than as journey, and who did not seek integration with men. They saw men as *irrelevant* to change. In their view the future of women lay in their life as sisters together and not in the integrated world of men and women. This self-sufficiency of feminism was most radically expressed by those lesbian separatists who saw the need for sperm to propagate the species but saw no need for a relationship with a man.

More generally there were three ways in which this self-sufficiency operated. The first was the biological self-sufficiency to which we have already alluded. Secondly there was an ideological self-sufficiency in which women could create a parallel world in which they redefined history from women's perspective and created new attitudes to science, sociology and other intellectual disciplines. Thirdly there was relational self-sufficiency in which women found in one another the friendship, support and group identity which was missing from their relationships with men.

The Process of Liberation

The question that now faced women was that if men were not going to change, personally, where would women who felt this injustice get their support from? Many women had discovered a sense of solidarity with other women through the women's movement. Some saw their support continuing to come from women while others saw feminism as a preparation to renewing their relationships with men on the basis of equality.

We have already discussed two different attitudes to the women's movement: those who see it as arrival and those who see it as a journey on to something else. For the first group the process had only two stages: from exploitation to separatism. Those who saw it as a journey were necessarily part of a three stage pilgrimage: from alienation through recognition to integration. For some women, however, the third stage was resignation.

Whereas the *separatist* model ends up being about the adequacy of relationships between women, men having been discarded as a bad lot, the *integrationist* model is ultimately about all kinds of relationships, including those between men and women. Each of the three stages is vital to the success of the venture.

Alienation Although the exploitation of women was a key theme of the women's movement, it was in many cases secondary to alienation. This was threefold. Firstly, women felt that they had no chance to explore themselves within the confines of roles allowed them by a patriarchal society. Secondly, women felt that a sexist society forced them to view other women as potential rivals rather than sisters. Thirdly, they were unable to relate to men properly while that relationship was characterised by power and not by equality.

Recognition Women needed to come together to discuss, share, be angry and find strength and understanding. They found they could not do that in the presence of men. Early in the history of the women's movement sympathetic partners were barred from meetings which were to be women only. Sympathy, it was decided, could not overcome the short-comings of being a man. Women began to recognise in one another their own stories, hopes, fears and hurts. As women broke through the constraint of discrimination in area after area other women began to see that the world could and was changing in their favour. They found recognition and strength in sisterhood. This fellowship of women together was the second stage.

Integration The third stage is only emerging at the moment. 'New women' needed 'new men' if integration was also to be successful. If women were to relate to men and not to give up on them they too needed to wrestle with themselves. Yet men had no agenda of their own, they were wrestling with what women said about them rather than formulating what they wanted to say about themselves. Integration hung in the balance. Women had been changed by their struggle. They were new people for a brave new world, but were there sufficient new men to allow them the space, flexibility and support to take their place in it? It seemed that utopianism was at a premium once again.

An Alternative The alternative seemed to be a realistic (if not a weary) resignation. Women had changed but men had not. Since women had discovered sisterhood in their fight against a common enemy maybe the existence of the common enemy was of use after all. If the enemy was to continue maybe the only good thing to come of this would be that sisterhood would persist. Perhaps that was where women should stay. They should not reject men, just realise that the value of life lay in being women together under the yoke. This was resignation rather than integration; but it was not separatism. Or at least if it was, it was a separatism of the heart rather than of the body.

Biblical Feminism

In many ways such a mapping of feminism is simplistic in the extreme for it leaves out many ideas which have been important to the women's movement. The position of Christian men and women on the issues raised by feminism has been diverse. Some Christians have seen traditional norms as receiving the blessing of scripture and a great many books have been written by conservative Christians to support this case.

But some men and women sought to look at scripture 'with new eyes' rather than to unthinkingly give its authority to interpretations which may have owed more to culture than previous generations had realised. This exercise lay at the heart of an approach to feminism which was inspired by the Bible. The fruit of this was focused particularly in books such as Elaine Storkey's *What's Right with Feminism?*, published in 1985 as part of a publishing venture inspired by Tim Dean, then editor of *Third Way* magazine. This magazine had as its *raison d'être* the provision of a biblical perspective on politics, social ethics and cultural affairs, and was influential especially within the evangelical movement. At the same time an educational charity known as Men, Women and God became established in the UK to bring an awareness of gender issues into the Church. In the US the Commission for Biblical Equality occupied a similar position with theologians such as Katherine Clark Kroeger and Berkley and Alvira Mickelsen performing the same function within the conservative tradition. Books started to appear on both sides of the Atlantic by both men and women theologians who were raising the questions which the feminists were grappling with, but in a Christian framework.

It is important to note that such a movement was by no means a blanket endorsement of feminism. Theologian, Mary Evans, based at London Bible College, had already published her own penetrating analysis of women in the Bible which was an important contribution to biblical scholarship.[12] Elaine Storkey's own book divided feminism into liberal, Marxist and radical camps, seeing them all as having their roots in the thinking of the Enlightenment period which was antagonistic to Christianity.[13] The elevation of reason over faith and the equation of the natural with the free were seen as important weaknesses of feminism, when subjected to critical scrutiny. The denial of human fallenness and particularly the idealisation of women came in for especial criticism. However, although the philosophy and stance of the feminist movement came in for heavy criticism, the injustices they had identified, the persistence of patriarchy and the issue of power were something which biblically inspired feminists felt they could support. The parallel with the abolition of the slave trade was quite compelling. In this area the Bible had been used to advocate slavery for many years but when the abolitionists came to look at it with new eyes they found in it the insights that would eventually bring slavery down. It is one of the texts which was key to their insights which is also key to the insights at the heart of biblical feminism, 'There is neither Jew nor Greek, slave nor free, male nor female, for you are all one in Christ Jesus.'[14]

Subsequent work by other conservative theologians added to the feeling within the evangelical movement that one could no longer assume that a person who was conservative in their view of the authority of scripture would also be a conservative on gender issues. The old theological map was no longer a guide in this area. In other areas such as sociology, economics and politics the same reinterpretation was under way by people who had a high view of scripture but were willing to come to radical conclusions.

As a result of this Christian women who may have felt that they had to choose between a biblically based Christianity and what they had learned from feminism were encouraged to see that they could have a rigorous approach to scripture and take on board many of the issues which were at the heart of the women's movement, especially the issue of equality. In the next chapter some of these issues emerge as we consider the issues surrounding power. Over the years there began to be a change in the way non-Church organisations approached the issue of leadership and who was given a platform from which to speak. Change within a male-dominated Church was slower but even here people began to see that some subjects, which had been considered 'biblical' but which endorsed male power, had more to do with cultural assumptions than with the authority of scripture.

The Beauty Myth

Both inside and outside the Church, the debate continues as to whether feminism has begun to achieve its objectives. Certainly the world has changed in the last twenty years with many more women in the professions than before and a rising number of women in the workforce as a whole. American thinker and scholar, Naomi Wolf, suggests that having taken strides forward many women still feel dissatisfied with themselves because of the pervasiveness of the 'beauty myth' as chronicled in her book of that name.[15] She feels that the progress of women in society has been put on hold and that women are confused, divided and dispirited with younger women doing little to take the women's movement further. Why has this happened?

> We are in the midst of a violent backlash against feminism that uses images of female beauty as a political weapon against women's advancement: the beauty myth. It is the modern version of a social reflex that has been in force since the Industrial Revolution. As women released themselves from the feminine mystique of domesticity, the beauty myth took over its lost ground, expanding as it waned to carry on its work of social control.[16]

Thirty-three thousand American women told researchers that they would rather lose ten to fifteen pounds in weight than achieve any other goal. Women spend millions of pounds each year trying to achieve some image of beauty. With the weight of fashion models twenty-three per cent below that of ordinary women they are chasing images which are difficult to achieve and cause many women to feel a sense of failure and inadequacy when they look in the mirror, rather than a sense of freedom or self-acceptance. Why mention this at the end of a chapter on feminism?

Firstly, to show that the struggles women are experiencing are multifaceted and constantly changing. It seems as if women cannot win. Feminism is not a phenomenon of the sixties which we can now evaluate as history. Each new generation of women struggles with its own issues. Men cannot 'make up their minds once and for all time' about women's issues, if they care about women. The issues are constantly changing.

Secondly, in a book which has a great deal to say about masculine stereotypes, competitiveness between men and hierarchical organisation, it is salutary to remind ourselves that these things are at the heart of the beauty industry for both consumers and producers. It is easy to portray men as competitive and women as co-operative but when it comes to notions of beauty women can be extremely competitive with one another. They also constantly compare themselves with stereotypes portrayed in women's magazines and elsewhere in the media often succumbing to narcissism as a result. Many beauty products are made at the expense of animal cruelty or environmental damage, as Naomi Wolf points out. She calls for a redefinition of beauty which is 'non-competitive, non-hierarchical and non-violent,'[17] and which allows a woman to express herself in any way which feels comfortable to her rather than having to follow the dictums of the beauty industry.

There is another reason for raising this issue. Most of this book assumes that if equality between men and women is to persist then men must lay power down for equality and partnership to result. This is seen as a desirable thing. But there is another path to equality which is not desirable and that is that men could become objects in the same way as women have been for so many years. In recent years statistics show that anorexia nervosa, the illness which results from a person believing that they are overweight and starving themselves, is increasing among men. Traditionally anorexia has been seen as a condition found among women who are sensitive to their own body image. But now men are being marketed the ideas of 'the beauty myth' which have caused so many problems for women. *Playgirl* magazine which features male nudes for women has been on the newsstands for several years. Beauty products for men are a multi-million pound industry already. In the last few years glamorous male strippers such as the Chippendales have played to packed audiences of enthusiastic women as well as appearing on prime-time TV. Posters of eroticised male torsos sell at a brisk pace to both men and women from high-street stores. A popular tabloid newspaper in the UK which regularly features topless models now finds space for similar photos of men. The eroticisation of the male body is well under way. It is defended as good business, fun, aesthetic, entertaining, and the ultimate defence of all business life which is that it allows business people to say 'we are only meeting the demand from our customers.'

Some women may smile at this and see a sense of rough justice in it all. Now men will learn what women went through. It serves them right. Play them at their own game. Commenting on the reaction to the exhibition of photographs of male genitalia by artist Robin Shaw, journalist Katie Campbell wrote that:

For centuries male artists had been depicting female models, but when women assumed the role of interpreter, turning men into a passive muse, suddenly the male critics became hysterical. Suddenly they experienced what women have felt all along: the vulnerability – and often the humiliation – that attends such intimate exposure.[18]

The exposure of the male body may seem to convey a message when draped in the guise of fine art, but what of the more tawdry exposure of the male body? Is this the kind of equality that we wish for one another? Is the right response to the treatment of women as sexual objects to make men sexual objects as well? Or should we be fighting for dignity for each other as an expression of the partnership between men and women in our society? Partnership is the word – for men cannot protest at the commercial exploitation of their bodies without doing the same for the exploitation of women's bodies, otherwise hypocrisy hangs heavy in the air. There are many false philosophies in our world which promise liberation but deliver bondage. False notions of beauty, material wealth, freedom through attaining power, and even utopian visions of equality, are all illusory. In some cases men and women face the same temptations but where the problems to be overcome are very different men and women need to fight for justice and freedom together.

Yet many men still cannot decide whether feminism is a veiled personal attack on them as individuals or whether it is an attack on the edifice of masculinity. If it is the former then feminism will win few friends among men who will retreat further back into conventional masculine defences. But if it is an attack on masculinity as being responsible for the persistence of patriarchy, then men can respond for they are entrapped by the same idolatry. If women had focused on the common bondage which patriarchy places both men and women under, there might have been a wider affirmation of feminism by men who wanted to lose their chains. On the other hand, if men never had felt the sharp sting of incisive accusation the degree of change that has come about in the last twenty years might never have arrived at all.

QUESTIONS

1. 'Men regard feminism with universal apprehension.' Is this a fair statement?
2. This chapter outlines four responses to feminism made by men. With which do you identify the most?
3. In what ways do we still live in a patriarchal society?
4. Do you think men should change? If so, should such

change be carried out for their own benefit or the benefit of others?

5. Do you think feminism represents the views of women generally?

6. In your view, what changes have come about in society because of feminism? Are these welcome changes?

7. Some women feel hostile to men. Do you think they have good reason to feel this way?

NOTES

1. See the discussion about men's groups in '"Personally Speaking": Experiencing a Men's Group', *The Achilles Heel Reader: Men, Sexual Politics and Socialism*, ed. Victor Seidler (London: Routledge, 1991), pp. 45–61. This account portrays the struggle men have to meet in groups. It also shows the way in which some men have been so dominated by political language, movements and agendas that they find it difficult to talk personally without mistrust and suspicion. It is important that such men's groups are not seen sentimentally as some kind of 'answer' to the questions men are currently facing. There is nothing necessarily magical about a group of men meeting together just because it is quite unusual for men to do so. Some groups seem to intensify the tensions between men and split up as a result.

2. Kate Millett, *Sexual Politics* (London: Virago, 1977).

3. In her book, *Slow Motion: Changing Masculinities, Changing Men* (London: Virago, 1990), Lynne Segal takes as her starting point the idea that there is a plurality of masculinities adhered to by men. She says that 'it is the *differences* between men which are central to the struggle for change.' (p. x) You cannot assume that the elderly and young, gay and straight, black and white, macho men and new men, anti-sexist and chauvinistic, aristocratic or working class, all share the same views as to what it means to be a man. Men are not uniform or monochrome in their aspirations. Masculinity has fragmented as a result

56 MEN AND MASCULINITY

of pluralism. Feminism has not always come to terms with this and has often appeared to be more at home with a single stereotype of men than with admitting the diversity of their experience.

4. Julia Neuberger, *Whatever's Happening to Women? – Promises, Practices and Pay Offs* (London: Kyle Cathie, 1991), p. 137.

5. In his book on the family entitled, *The Subversive Family: An Alternative History of Love and Marriage* (London: Jonathan Cape, 1982), Ferdinand Mount says: '. . . as the evening up develops, as women's civic rights slowly begin to become undisputed facts, utopian feminism is itself under pressure. For it has always relied on the plain shocking facts of civic oppression to support its apocalyptic arguments. It was the arranged marriage, the denial of the vote, the inequality of legal rights, the brutish masculinity of Church and State that fed the yearning for a marriageless, de-sexed utopia.' (p. 246)

6. In his treatise entitled, *Authority* (London: Secker and Warburg, 1980), American social philosopher Richard Sennett distinguishes between patriarchy, patrimony and paternalism. Under patriarchy the man is dominant as the head of family and society is seen as an extension of family life. Property passes down male bloodlines. Old Testament Israel is a good example of patriarchy. Under patrimony, as in modern Japan, this model has extended outside family life to other spheres such as the social organisation of industrial life. The difference between these two is that under patrimony relationships which are not familial are recognised. Under paternalism, men are still dominant but their dominance is symbolic. In this case the family analogy may not apply at all since 'what a child learns about its father's protectiveness is not what a young adult will learn about a boss.' (p. 54.) Despite these distinctions, the women's movement has followed Kate Millett in talking of a society dominated by men as 'patriarchal' and I have followed this use of the language.

7. On the issue of the economic value of women's work in various contexts cf. Marilyn Waring, *If Women Counted: A New Feminist Economics* (London: Macmillan, 1989).

8. Margaret Mead, *Male and Female* (Harmondsworth: Pelican Penguin, 1962), pp. 157–8.

9. Mead, op. cit.

10. Rowena Chapman, 'The Great Pretender: Variations on the New Man Theme', *Male Order: Unwrapping Masculinity*, eds. Rowena Chapman and Jonathan Rutherford (London: Lawrence and Wishart, 1988), p. 235.

11. I am not asserting that male aggression is due only to social conditioning. Male aggression obviously owes a great deal to biological influences. The difference between men and women in the committing of crimes of violence or indeed any crime, is extremely marked. Ninety per cent of murderers are male and over a third of all married women suffer violence and/or the threat of violence from their husbands. [Source: Rosalind Miles, *The Rites of Man: Love, Sex and Death in the Making of the Male* (London: Grafton, 1991), p. 232.] When it comes to sexual offences men are between thirty to forty times more likely to be convicted than women. [Source: Liam Hudson and Bernadine Jacot, *The Way Men Think: Intellect, Intimacy and the Erotic Imagination* (New York and London: Yale University Press, 1991), p. 119.]

12. Mary Evans, *Woman and the Bible* (Exeter: Paternoster, 1983).

13. Elaine Storkey, *What's Right with Feminism?* (London: SPCK/Third Way, 1985), p. 133.

14. Galatians 3:28.

15. Naomi Wolf, *The Beauty Myth* (London: Vintage, 1991).

16. Wolf, op. cit., p. 10.

17. Wolf, op. cit., p. 286.

18. Katie Campbell, 'Foreign Bodies', the *Guardian*, 14 August 1990.

4

THE POWER PROBLEM

If feminists are right in pinpointing the problem of power
as the key issue between men and women, how should we
respond to this as men? Some people have told me that the
reason they are not interested in Christianity and even feel
hostile to it is that they believe it is Christianity which has
endorsed male superiority and has kept patriarchy alive for
so long. They are unimpressed by Christian talk of a loving
God when the relationship between the sexes seems to be a
power relationship rather than a loving partnership. Is not
the Christian God also a God of justice?

This is an important issue as we live in a world obsessed
with power. We can protest that we are exempt and do
not abuse what little power we have, but the only credible
evidence of that is whether we share power;[1] just as a credible
defence against materialism requires generous giving. Many
men have become so used to a world in which they hold
power that they are not aware of any other perspective.
The first step in overcoming prejudice or discrimination is to
recognise its existence. The same is true of all discrimination.
Black and Asian friends tell us that they are suffering from
racism, 'disabled' friends tell us of the discrimination against
them, but we have no 'ears to hear' them. We are reluctant
to put ourselves into their shoes. There are enough problems
in the world without making more for ourselves.

We should be quick to hear such a protest. If Christians

are committed to love and justice then the complaint should be enough. The burden of proof lies with those who say it doesn't exist or it isn't true. Masculine power is invisible to many men and therefore, instead of saying that women are wrong, we should ask ourselves how we can widen our perspective. We cannot deal with the problem until our eyes are opened and we can recognise it. Reading books can help, listening to women and discussing the issues with them can also open eyes and unstop ears. We are blind to the familiar and we are reticent to change anything which gives us power. Indeed it is important to recognise that power itself is not a bad thing, but it is always qualified by what it is used *for*. The question I ask in this chapter is whether the power which men have over women in our society can be justified at all and, specifically, whether it can be justified by Christianity, or whether it is in fact subverted by Christianity.

So though men may recognise the existence of male power over women they may see this as something which is good and right. Christian men may even see this as having a divine sanction. This makes the problem even worse. In order to change their views such men have to swing through the whole spectrum from seeing male power as God-ordained to seeing it as a barrier to God's purpose in the world. For many men such a shift in perspective will change their world-view and alter their behaviour more than any other change in their lives.

Yet I believe that such a shift is an essential part of the pilgrimage Christian men must make if they are to emulate Jesus Christ. He is the key. It is all too possible to construct complex theologies which rationalise male power, but the personal goal of every Christian is to become more like Jesus Christ – to be his disciple. Even those who are not Christians admire Christ and respect him.

Quite often the fact that Christianity is seen as part of the problem rather than part of the solution is expressed as a dislike for the writings of the Apostle Paul, or for the traditional teachings of Judaism as patriarchal. Many people feel that 'Jesus was a nice chap but it's a shame about Paul'. Claire Rayner, a well-known writer and 'agony aunt' summed up the popular impression of Paul's views on women very well:

> He didn't like women very much . . . only certain kinds of women; dull, sexless women. He wasn't very keen on women who had energy and a mind of their own. If they were submissive and obedient and good girls then he thought they were all right, but any woman who stood up for herself, he wasn't really keen on was he?[2]

Psychiatrist Dr Anthony Clare, hosting the radio programme on which she said this, commented that, 'She sums up in a characteristically pungent way the mindset of the Church as anti-flesh, anti-sex, anti-women.'[3] He is right: many people who are searching for some way out of the mess we have created in our relationships will look anywhere but to Christianity for the answers. Christianity has been written off as oppressive and patriarchal, giving divine sanction for men to claim rights over women. I do not believe that this view in any way represents the views of the Apostle Paul, quite the opposite. I see him as someone who welcomed freedom for women from traditional Jewish patriarchy but was concerned that such sudden freedom should not be misunderstood by those who were critical of the early Church.

Freedom and Diversity

The problem lies mainly with the interpretation of several passages in the New Testament written by the Apostle Paul and therefore I am going to look briefly at the Pauline texts. They seem to contain the idea that men have 'authority over' women. For instance, Ephesians 5:22–3 says, 'Wives, submit to your husbands as to the Lord. For the husband is the head of the wife as Christ is the head of the church. . . .' This hinges mainly on the interpretation given to the Greek word *kephale*. We have traditionally translated this 'head' and this has come down to us in the phrase 'the man is the head of the household'. Others translate this 'source'. A whole doctrine has been based on these passages known as 'headship'.[4]

Many married couples, including some who will read this book, believe in the idea of headship but use it in a way which has nothing to do with 'male power' or with the man having 'authority over' the woman. They see it as a call for men and women to be loving, Christlike and respectful. Their marriage is chacterised by mutual submission. In practice their life together is one of partnership and mutuality. They struggle together with difficult decisions and seek wisdom outside the marriage if they cannot resolve an issue. The man would not dream of being coercive, standing on rights or claiming authority just because he is a man. Such strong loving relationships can be found in churches today. The criticisms I make here of the use of the term headship are not meant to apply to such people.

But there are other relationships where loving partnership is not an apt description. Some men believe that this teaching gives them 'an edge' over women. In this situation it is the fact they are men and not women which gives them added 'authority'. In what follows in this chapter I want to address such men. I am concerned about movements both inside and outside the Church which wish to give men more power and 'authority over' women. Some men seem to divorce the idea of being a husband from the call to be Christlike and can be coercive, imposing their view of the world on others. I have met a great many women who are submissive to such husbands because they have been brought up to be so but whose lack of protest is being exploited by men who are insensitive and sometimes even cruel, yet who claim to be acting as Christians. Such women are often angry at the imposition and lack of respect which marriage has brought them.

In still other situations men refuse to contribute either spiritually or in being a husband and father. Such men need to be challenged and encouraged to make more of a contribution to marriage and family life. Sometimes this can be because they fear that being 'stronger' will lead to their becoming authoritarian. They need to be urged to use their gifts and insights and to become more Christlike in lifting burdens from their partners which are due to their not 'pulling their weight'. Criticising ideas of 'male power' does not mean that men should avoid the responsibilities involved in partnership.

In preparing this book the Kingdom Trust conducted a number of interviews with married couples who were Christians. Many of them had strong marriages which were admired by others. We focused on the idea of headship and on their understanding of it. The most important finding from that research was that they felt free to give very diverse interpretations of what it meant. Those who believed in 'it' could not agree about what 'it' was. Some said it was about the man taking the final decision when both disagreed; others opted for the man taking the initiative in the marriage over spiritual matters; still others talked of the husband being the protector of the wife; while others said that the husband should discipline the children. In a few cases the interpretation placed on the word headship matched those things which the wife (when interviewed on her own) felt were deficient in her husband. In other words they viewed headship as a normative but empty box into which they could place something which was important to them.

Theologians are confused as well. It is easy to meet theologians who believe that the passages on headship are clear and unambiguous, the problem is that they disagree. I remember attending a debate between eminent theologians in Great Britain. I listened all day to the various arguments but at the end of the debate they agreed to differ. Those who viewed the passages hierarchically and those who viewed them as expressing equality and mutuality then went home leaving me wondering what the rest of us were meant to think if we didn't have a PhD in theology! It is against this background that I offer some thoughts on the passages.

Equality and Mutuality

The main passages in which the word *kephale* appears are 1 Corinthians 11:3–16 and Ephesians 5:22–3. 1 Timothy 2:11–15 is also an important passage but does not contain the word *kephale*. The same word is used of Christ as the head of the Church in Colossians 1:18 and Ephesians 1:22. Christians are divided about the meaning of the passages in which this word appears. Some people appeal to these passages as something we need to recover if we are to 'get back' to the stability and order of more traditional days. Whether such days ever existed is a debatable point. Gillian Warren expresses this belief in a divine order which is normative when she says:

> . . . the order God has given us is Christ-husband-wife-children-pets. That's the way it works best. . . . If we will dare to enter into God's original design for marriage, each taking our full part, we shall discover a new fulfilment, delight and peace in our relationship. The satisfaction we all seek will be found in following Father's instructions. His design is for our greatest happiness.[5]

It is undoubtedly the case that families, indeed relationships of all kinds, are breaking down.[6] Is the idea of a created order for the family with the man at its head the answer?

A marriage which is characterised by one partner who is the head of the family and the ultimate decision maker will also tend to be characterised by stability. I remember one man proudly telling me that he and his wife had never had a row. The reason was apparent when you looked at his wife. She wouldn't have dared to question him. In their case there was a trade-off between her freedom and the stability of the marriage. Other women say that it is more 'peaceful'

if they 'submit' to their husbands. But the Bible knows
nothing of peace without justice. Imagine slaves rowing a
galley in Roman times. They may have come to terms with
their lot, they may feel happy in their hearts, they may be
aware that God is with them, but from a biblical point of
view they do not enjoy *shalom*. Their situation is not just
and their contentment does not make it so.

The creation story shows us God's original intentions for a
world in which sin and evil did not yet exist. In this world the
man and the woman are created in the image of God to have
dominion over the world that God had created. A blessing,
the command to be fruitful and increase in number, to fill
the earth, to subdue and to rule are given to both the man
and the woman. In Genesis 1 man and woman are related
to God and are placed by him in the garden as the pinnacle
of creation. Genesis 2 tells the story from the perspective
of the relationships in the garden. It is here (verse 18) that
God says, 'It is not good for the man to be alone. I will
make a helper suitable for him.' Those people who think
that the pattern of male-female relationships is a 'creation
ordinance' and therefore normative for all cultures and all
times, often go back to Adam naming Eve as his helper. He
had done the same to the animals, doesn't this imply that
he had authority over her as well? Ethicist David Atkinson
resolves this dilemma helpfully when he says:

> . . . the question of female subordination to male domi-
> nation is raised *descriptively* in Genesis 3 as a *consequence*
> of sin, not normatively in Genesis 2. The notion of Eve as
> 'helper' does not require the sense of subordination, for
> the word is used many times of the help that comes from
> God (cf. Psalms 33:20). Not until Genesis 3:20 does Adam
> use the standard naming formula for his wife; in 2:23 the
> 'naming' is more delight than domination.[7]

Even before the fall it was not good for the man to be on
his own. Autonomy is not the will of God. The picture in

Genesis 2 is of partnership, mutuality and equality in an innocent freedom in which the man and the woman relate to one another, celebrating their sameness (verse 23) and also their difference. In Genesis 2:18, 20 the word 'suitable' (*kenegdo*) denotes equality and adequacy.[8]

It was only with the introduction of sin and evil into the world that mutuality was disrupted and a loving relationship became a power struggle. Dominion gave way to domination. The woman became locked into this relationship because her desire was still for her husband. There is a great gulf between God's original intentions for man and woman and this outcome of sin and evil. I cannot see how we can talk of a man's authority over a woman being 'natural' since there is nothing natural about a distorted relationship which came about through disobedience. If we persist in sanctifying the pervasiveness of male power in our world we turn the outcome of the fall into the norm, enshrining that which is evil with sacred power. Genesis 3:16 is a prediction of the effects of the fall rather than a prescription of God's ideal order.[9]

It may be protested that the Old Testament is patriarchal, and this is true, but God's process of redemption takes place within history, and the record of the Old Testament shows the struggle to redeem mankind taking place slowly, and only coming to fulfilment in Christ. There is a gulf between the accurate *description* of religion as patriarchal and the *intention* of biblical religion to bring equality, freedom and complementarity between the sexes.[10]

Is there a creation pattern in the Bible with the man having authority over the woman? I cannot see it and believe that where theologians interpret the passage as hierarchical they struggle to do so. John Stott comments:

> . . . men and women were equal beneficiaries both of the divine image and of the earthly rule. There is no suggestion in the text that either sex is more like God than the other, or that either sex is more responsible

for the earth than the other. No. Their resemblance to God and their stewardship of his earth (which must not be confused, although they are closely related) were from the beginning shared equally, since both sexes were equally created by God and like God.[11]

The passage in the New Testament which is cited more than any other about headship is Ephesians 5:22–33. This passage comes after the calling to 'live a life worthy of the calling you have received' (4:1); 'Be imitators of God' (5:1); and 'Submit to one another out of reverence for Christ' (5:21). The book of Ephesians as a whole is about God's new community and the new ways in which people are to behave 'in Christ'.

Whereas after the introduction of sin into the world men 'rule over' women, here the emphasis is completely different. Husbands are to love their wives 'as Christ loved the church', that is sacrificially, by putting her interests first. In Genesis 3:16 women 'desire' their husbands in a 'selfishly grasping way'.[12] Here the wife is to 'submit to' her husband. The words mean only to respect and do not mean obey.

In other words Christian relationships of all sorts are to be characterised by mutuality based on respect, love and service (cf. 5:21). Each partner is to honour the other. The word 'head' in this context does not mean that the man can claim power over the woman. That would be to revert to the unjust pattern of the fall. Elsewhere in scripture the word 'head' is linked to Christ's example. If we want to look at what it means, we look at him. This is the key to the debate on gender. Behaviour by Christian men which does not emulate Christ is not Christian behaviour, however many arguments are used to reinforce it. Where the Bible is used to reinforce male power it is one of the greatest single barriers to Christian witness in the modern world.

In the process of redemption God is reversing the effects of the fall and this must bring a challenge to those who have the strongest views of male 'authority over' women. They must ask themselves whether this is the only area in which the direction of the fall is allowed to stand. God's intentions have not changed. Redemption means buying back something which is already yours but which has been under the temporary control of someone else. If I pawn a watch at a pawn shop it still belongs to me even though someone else has temporary ownership of it. Throughout history God is buying back what is already his and because of this we would expect there to be a direct relationship between God's original vision and the vision restored through redemption. If there is no hierarchy in Eden, and there is not, will God introduce it in redemption? The answer must be 'No'. Equality, freedom and mutuality remain the goal and the characteristics of all relationships in the kingdom of God.

From Roles to Relationships

A lot of the discussion on the biblical text and its meaning focuses on the roles of men and women. We have already seen that gender roles are composed of norms and stereotypes and that these can provide stress for those people who feel that they do not fit them. In the post-war years there has been considerable relaxation over the question of roles. When I talk to someone of my mother's generation they seem to have lived in a world more characterised by conformity to given roles. There was less freedom to express oneself as an individual outside the social interpretation of how men and women should behave. When listening to the struggles of younger men and women over their relationships, people from an older generation frequently comment that such conversations just did not happen in their day.

More recently the emphasis has changed from given roles to the quality of relationships between men and women. Co-education, youth culture and career opportunities for women have opened up a new world of options for younger people. One of the good things about this is that younger people feel more free to be themselves than previous generations. But this freedom can in turn lead to problems. There can exist some confusion about personal identity and, in an age which is focused on personal fulfilment, there can be a nostalgia for a previous generation in which 'men were men and women were women'. This is not to say that older gender roles have completely disappeared. They have been maintained in those families and traditions which are most socially conservative and which have resisted social change, seeing it as undermining healthy and important patterns of family life.

We have already seen that God's original vision for men and women was one of partnership together. They were partners in the divine image, in the task of managing the world and family life, and also partners in humanity sharing 'sameness' as well as expressing 'difference'. These things were disrupted by the introduction of sin and evil. It is not only the case that mutuality is disrupted by power leading to the appearance of domination of men over women but it is also the case that division is introduced and this leads to the appearance of roles for the first time. In Genesis 3:16 and Genesis 3:17–20 God explains to the man and the woman the consequences of their disobedience. Here for the first time we find that the consequences of the fall for the woman are that she is addressed only in the area of relationships and family life. But the consequences for the man are seen to be in the area of work and the environment. The task which was shared has now been divided into different realms and roles have appeared. It is important to realise, as it is with the introduction of power, that the pervasiveness of such roles may not be due to any created order intended by God, since there is no indication of this before Genesis 3. It appears that this division is a result of the introduction of sin and evil into the world. How important it is to make this distinction.

Some of us have made separate and different roles for men and women sacred but the Bible does not make them sacred. What the Bible does place before us is the idea of 'calling', and it is important that Christians are committed to every individual, being able to follow their 'calling' rather than being squeezed into roles that are defined so narrowly that a person is not able to discover or fulfil their 'calling'.

Where a man and woman get married it is important that both freely agree about the style of their marriage. It may be that both prefer a relationship in which the man takes the 'lead' in some way which they give definition to. There is a great difference between such marriages being seen as one of a choice of styles and being the norm for all marriages. Yet no marriage can claim to express the character of Christ if a woman or a man is coerced in any way. It is important to remember that the word 'authority' is never used in the New Testament to describe the role of the husband, nor is the word 'obedience' used of the wife.[13]

Jesus explicitly rejects secular definitions of authority when he draws a distinction between the attitude of the world and the attitude of his disciples, saying that in the world people lord it over one another but that he who would be greatest of all must be least of all and servant of all (Mark 10:42–4). On another occasion (Mark 9:33–7; Luke 9:46–8) Jesus is asked by the disciples who will be the greatest. His answer was to stand a child beside him and say, 'Whoever welcomes this little child in my name welcomes me; and whoever welcomes me welcomes the one who sent me. For he who is least among you all – he is the greatest.' Typically Jesus refuses to answer the question that they have asked. His point depends on the fact that people with great power and authority in his day saw themselves as elevated above the world of children who they ignored and did not treat with any respect. Jesus defines authority in terms of servanthood and love. The person who welcomes an insignificant dirty child is the person who is most Christ-like and being Christ-like is the only definition of authority that a Christian man can attain.

Seeing men as having authority over women also creates stress for men. All too often there is a confusion between *role* and *style*. Listening to sermons and talks on headship, men can easily be persuaded that they have to behave in an authoritative manner. This usually means that they have to behave in a way which they perceive as more masculine. They become more aggressive, insist on their rights, and generally make themselves a nuisance. Many men are not at ease in the garb of patriarchy and only want to get back to being loving, friendly and gracious. It is no wonder that men often feel inadequate because they cannot live up to the demands made on them by the stereotypes of authoritarian masculinity. *The crucial difference which the Bible makes, but which contemporary models of masculinity reverse, is that between taking authority over women and having the respect of women.*

One of the things that the feminist movement has been trying to get over to men is that many women do not trust men any more. The violence, pornography, promiscuity and patriarchy which has come through a male-dominated society has left many women reeling. It is rather typical of the misunderstandings between men and women that at a time when women are not prepared to make themselves vulnerable to men because of their experience of them, men themselves are responding by standing on some supposed authority.

The crucial question which faces the Church is whether the Church is distinctive in its Christian witness by endorsing male headship. I quite understand that people see the break-up of society and want to opt for a model that brings stability. But in a world where men still have power and where women are protesting about the abuse of that power in violence, rape, injustice and exclusion, is it not more distinctive and Christ-like for the Church to recover its belief in the equality of men and women and honour women in a way which is prophetic in a patriarchal society. So many people say that moving from the world to the Church makes no difference because it is just another institution dominated by men.

If change is to come men must first learn to listen to women, secondly to admit that much of what they say is true, thirdly to make changes in their lives in order to renew their partnership with women. The problem with this yet again is that it necessitates men making themselves vulnerable to women at a time when women appear to men to have the upper hand. The strange thing about this is that men see this as taking away their masculinity rather than seeing that only a man who is secure in himself can make himself vulnerable in this way.

The choice is not between being macho and being a doormat. Men fear that if they make themselves vulnerable or 'give their lives away' they will be trampled on and will fade away. What I am saying is that having power over a woman is not what makes a man. Men find their model and their security in God who the Bible declares to be a Rock. By this it means that God is a place of certainty and security which doesn't change even when our lives are shaky. Men's identity is not defined by reference to women, it can only be defined in relationship with God. From the standpoint of this kind of rock-like security, the most macho poseurs look the most insecure underneath it all. What a relief to give up the performance, chuck away the masks and restricting roles and be yourself!

Where trust has gone and *relationship* is deficient there is no point in asserting *role*. In loving strong marriages where people are equal and enjoy rapport and friendship they do not talk about headship, it is irrelevant. Yet where a marriage fails it adds insult to injury to try and appeal to 'authority'. When a happily married couple come to a point where they disagree about something, the wife doesn't ritually give up her position to defer to her husband over something where he may be morally wrong.

Husbands are not in the right more than wives. To say they are more logical and therefore better at decision-making is to reduce truth to logic *and* to capitulate to the distortion, propagated since the Enlightenment, that men are rational and women are not. When I lecture in social ethics I do not teach my students the ethics of decision-making by saying that where people disagree a man must make the final decision because it is more likely to be right! The idea of tying headship to decision-making insults women's moral insights and places men under undue strain. If persistent disagreement arises in a marriage both partners should seek outside counsel if they are humble enough to admit that, since they both can't be right, either of them could be wrong. For the man to impose his point of view at such a sensitive time seems to me to be incredible. It is no wonder that couples who believe this usually say that 'it has never come to that'!

Many men who say they believe in headship, say that they do so because they believe it is the biblical language and therefore they have to struggle with it. They long to be able to say convincingly that they are totally equal with their partners. The majority of men that I talk to about this, and who still believe in the concept of headship, are mystified as to what it actually means in real life. In concluding this chapter I want to put a finger on the key question which men must ask themselves in order to clear up the implications of this debate. The question is, 'Do you believe men and women are equal or do you believe that men are superior?' This question clears a lot of the wood away so that we can see clearly. If men and women are not equal then they are unequal and one is superior to the other. This book is stating that there is no more fundamental equality in life than equality before God.

For some men headship is a bank of fog between equality and superiority. In it there are people trying to find their way towards equality but who still feel they should use language which is biblical. There are also men who use the term as an acceptable word for superiority and they are moving in the opposite direction. The first group will greet this book with relief, the second with anger.

Many men in this second camp will want to say something like 'Men are different' or 'Men are authoritative in some areas'. The question is, in what respects is the Church honouring women? Can it give a clear message about that to the world? Many men reading this book who believe in headship do not believe in the superiority of men. For them there is comfort. For everything that they have so far put in the category of headship can be placed on more certain ground theologically. Some say it means that husbands should love their wives; fair enough, the Bible states that and it is essential in marriage. As we noticed earlier in this chapter, others hang different concepts on the peg of headship believing that it is about initiative, protection, decision-making, etc. Some of these ideas are purely cultural or particular to certain marriages, whereas others are important facets of all marriages but are not roles restricted to men alone. Where there are important insights for us all they can all be contained under other headings of love, justice, mercy, friendship, loyalty or other such words.

The Effect on Men

We now come to one of the most crucial insights in the book which is the connection between male power and the masks which men wear so often. *Men cannot retain the idea of power over women and also avoid the fragmentation which leads to the inner life of men being split away from the outer image. The two are intimately connected.*

It is because equality before God is central to God's intentions and because dominance is a result of the fall that men come into problems themselves where they believe this is a valid norm. In order to have power over women such men must believe that there are grounds for doing this. We have seen that men elevate reason as a part of the core identity of masculinity. So in order to continue dominating women rather than joining the protest at the injustice, such men believe that not only are they different but that they are also superior in some way. Such a belief is reflected in sophisticated research on the biological superiority of the male sex, theological treatises on the superiority of men, as well as the bar-room vulgarity that women are 'only good for one thing'.[14]

Yet men know intuitively that they do wrong, can be capable of evil and are vulnerable just as women are. These are indications to men that they share a common humanity with women. Men also know that not only are women sometimes more capable than men in areas traditionally considered masculine (decision-making, etc.), but that men seem to have particular problems in areas such as violence. Psychologically, spiritually and socially men have the evidence that they are fallen human beings just as women are. If men persist in believing that they are superior to women then they can do so only at the expense of a pretence which comes into their lives. This pretence is at the heart of the ideas of masculinity. It is a split between what a man knows to be true inside himself and the image he portrays to the outside world, as well as the ideology he propagates.

If men will cling to power over women, even if they use biblical terms to describe it, they can openly do so only at the expense of wearing a mask which hides their vulnerability. Until a man is willing to lay down power, with its connotations of superiority, he cannot be whole. There are men reading this book with mounting anger who at the end of it will refuse to give up the idea of male power because they have lived with it for so long – their marriage assumes it and their Church teaches it; but if they want to be whole then they must admit that they share a common sin and a common humanity with women and face the future together. Men cannot retain power over women and also have integrity. To live they must split off the inner life from the outer image. If they convince themselves of this pretence then their own sense of vulnerability will become submerged in order for them to be able to live out their belief in superiority.

There is another vital side to this insight which is the link between truth, grace and freedom. But I want to leave that until the section on the men's group in chapter seven.

To state that men are superior to women can lead to men believing that they have rights[15] over women and this can lead in turn to subjugation rather than to the mutual submission that Paul underwrites. In extreme situations this can lead to violence and abuse. Some men will not listen to their wives, do not share with their wives, and fall back on 'authority' to get them through situations which should have been characterised by their vulnerability.

In America in 1989, according to the *US Department of Justice Report to the Nation*, ninety per cent of all crimes committed against married partners or former married partners were committed by men.[16] In 1983 *Time* magazine dedicated a series of articles to domestic violence commenting that:

> Nearly six million wives will be abused by their husbands in any one year. Some 2,000 to 4,000 women are beaten to death annually. The nation's police spend one-third of their time responding to domestic violence calls. Battery is the single major cause of injury to women, more significant than accidents, rapes or muggings.[17]

In her book on masculinity Rosalind Miles quotes a survey carried out by the Polytechnic of North London for the Hammersmith and Fulham Council. This found that of the women in the borough, forty-eight per cent had been attacked or threatened by their partners in their own homes; thirty per cent had been assaulted at least once; thirteen per cent had been threatened with death; thirteen per cent had been raped; and ten per cent had been attacked with a weapon.[18]

Yet physical violence is only the tip of the iceberg as far as the effects of male power are concerned. Peter Rutter is a psychiatrist in private practice in San Francisco and has written a book called *Sex in the Forbidden Zone* which analyses the 'epidemic of sexual relationships between men in authority and the women they are meant to help'.[19] Doctors, psychotherapists, lawyers, clergymen and teachers are shown to be susceptible to abusing the trust which women place in them. Rutter comments that 'ninety-six per cent of sexual exploitation by professionals occurs between a man in power and a woman in his care.'[20] Needless to say the book rocked the professional world when it came out in 1990.

One of the most tragic books I have read recently is *Battered into Submission* by James and Phyllis Alsdurf. They document the incidence of wife abuse within Christian homes. The book contains a typical but agonising testimony:

> After marriage my husband treated me as a non-person with no value other than through him. He cited scripture passages in support of his treatment of me. Any time I objected to his behaviour or to his decisions, he told me that I was to submit to him just as totally as if he were Jesus Christ. He firmly believed that if I were obedient and submissive, God himself would take care of me, therefore he was free to behave as irresponsibly as he liked without fear of hurting me or our child. He felt that God wouldn't allow us to be hurt unless it was God's will.

We must not allow ourselves to be deluded about the kind of lives some people are living. Behind the facades people put up, even in our churches, real agony is going on. She continues:

> My husband took no responsibility for his actions at all, I spent many agonising hours in prayer and fasting seeking to drive out every vestige of sin from my life. I believed that when I finally learned what God was trying to teach me, my husband would respond with love. But the more I submitted to him, the more arrogantly he displayed his flagrantly abusive behaviour. I sought counsel from pastors and friends. Many didn't believe me. It's not hard to understand why. How could such an upstanding member of the church and community be capable of such a miscarriage of God's justice.[21]

Her story continues in their book but this extract shows us

that the combination of a dogmatic approach to Christian doctrine and a belief in masculine superiority can be a recipe for grief where men believe they have rights over women. Is it not time for the Church to call men to emulate the person of Jesus Christ rather than dealing in such danger? Let the Church reverse the priorities of masculinity. *Real* men lay down their lives for other people. *Real* men move from power to love.

Over the last decade men have been offered several models of manhood in response to the discussions of men and masculinity started by the women's movement. Among these have been two from which we can learn a great deal. Both use the conclusion of the women's movement as their premise. The first is the idea of the *'new man'* and the second is the more recent idea of the *'wild man'*. It is important to explore both these options for men and to learn from them.

QUESTIONS

1. Do you think the Apostle Paul's views on women have been widely misunderstood?
2. Do you think that men still have 'power' over women?
3. 'Where trust has gone and relationship is deficient, there is no point in asserting role.' Do you think men fall back on 'male authority' when they feel challenged by women?
4. This chapter makes a strong link between power and fragmentation in the lives of men. Are you aware of this in the lives of men around you?
5. It has sometimes been the case that women have been admitted into Christian leadership 'under a man'. What are the results for men of their being in leadership on their own?
6. How should men respond to stories and statistics which show the extent of the violence of men against women?

NOTES

1. Marilyn French, *Beyond Power: On Women, Men and Morals* (London: Sphere/Abacus, 1986), p. 146.
2. This quote is from a clip used by Dr Anthony Clare in his conversation with Fr Wilfreed McGreel, *In The Psychiatrist's Chair*, BBC Radio 4, 25 April 1991. Robert Bly, one of the leaders of the American men's movement says in his book *Iron John* (Shaftesbury: Element Books, 1991), 'In Christianity, it was Paul who laid the ground for the hatred of sexuality, saying in the first epistle to the Corinthians, "Let those who have wives live as though they had none." ' (p. 248.) He sees that the institutionalised drive of Christianity is 'toward the idea that sexuality inhibits spiritual growth' (p. 249).
3. ibid.
4. Although the Bible contains the word *kephale* which could be translated 'head', it does not contain the word 'headship'. Nowhere does the Bible itself suggest that an ideology should be based on this word, but that is the effect of adding the suffix '-ship' to the word 'head'. The Collins dictionary says of the suffix '-ship' . . . '1. indicating state or condition . . . 2. indicating rank, office or position.' *The Collins English Dictionary* (London: Collins, Second Ed., 1986) p. 1409. (As in 'lordship'.) By adding the suffix '-ship' to the English word 'head' we have made the Greek word *kephale* into something which indicates a state or condition which men are in which indicates 'rank, office or position'. The use of the word 'headship' is therefore a word which leaves little room for interpretation since the suffix itself indicates rank even if the word for 'head' is ambiguous.
5. Gillian Warren, *The Original Design* (Renewal, 1990).
6. The most convincing evidence of this is a perusal of *Social Trends* published by HMSO every year.
7. David Atkinson, *Pastoral Ethics in Practice* (London: Marshall Pickering, 1989), p. 118.
8. See the statement of *Christians for Biblical Equality*, section 3. (Available from 7433 Borman Ave. East, Inner Grove Heights, MN 55076, USA.)

9. See the CBE statement, section 5.
10. Phyllis Trible, 'Depatriarchalizing in Biblical Interpretation'. *Journal of the American Academy of Religion*, 41 (1973), p. 31. Quoted in Mary Evans, op. cit., p. 32.
11. John Stott, *Issues Facing Christians Today* (London: Marshall Pickering, 1990, Second ed.,), p. 258.
12. This is David Atkinson's phrase which is very vivid. His whole analysis, on pp. 89–125, is very helpful.
13. Stott, op. cit., p. 271.
14. Not only the bar-room. In her book, co-authored with Wendy Green, *Rape: My Story* (London: Pan, 1990), Jill Saward talks of the letters she received after the publicity surrounding the attack on her. Some letters included 'the chauvinist view that women are created for cooking and sex; nothing else.' (p. 64.)
15. Until recently, for instance, the law in Britain allowed rape within marriage. This gave husbands sexual rights over their wives. This has recently been changed.
16. Source: Rosalind Miles, *The Rites of Man* (London: Grafton, 1991), p. 133.
17. Jane O'Reilly, 'Wife Beating: The Silent Crime', *Time* (5 September 1983), p. 23. Quoted in James and Phyllis Alsdurf, *Battered into Submission* (Crowborough: Highland Books, 1990), p. 24.
18. In her book *Distorted Images* (London: SPCK, 1991), p. 106, Anne Borrowdale quotes research by Dobash and Dobash who found that, 'ninety-seven per cent of assaulters in the home were male, whilst ninety-four per cent of victims were female; seventy-five per cent of victims were wives, ten per cent children, and only one per cent of victims were husbands.' On this see Dobash and Dobash, *Violence Against Wives: A Case Against the Patriarch* (Somerset: Open Books, 1979).
19. Peter Rutter, *Sex in the Forbidden Zone* (London: Unwin Paperbacks, 1990).
20. Rutter, op. cit., p. 20.
21. James and Phyllis Alsdurf, *Battered into Submission: The Tragedy of Wife Abuse in the Christian Home* (Crowborough: Highland Books, 1990), pp. 13–14.

5

THE NEW MAN

Many men have been struggling to escape from the confines of an oppressive view of masculinity. As we saw in chapter two there are many different versions of contemporary masculinity, and the ideas which have become focused on the 'new man' represent an attempt by men to lay down power in some areas of their lives and co-operate with women as friends and partners. In some ways the new man represents the feelings of younger men who have been educated and brought up alongside women in the educational system and who see them as equals. Many younger men have avoided the influences of military life because there has been no conscription since the war. It is also true that, whereas the sixties rebellion against the culture of parents was a corporate sign of young people making their own way in the world, it is now the case that ideas such as the new man are a personal rather than a corporate rejection of many of the macho ideals which were at the heart of the masculinity of previous generations. In this chapter and the one which follows we evaluate these ideas as well as those of the 'wild man', recently introduced into Britain by American poet Robert Bly.

The idea of the new man has not come out of a vacuum. In many ways he is a man who is responding positively to the kind of values and questioning that has come from the women's movement over the last twenty years. Maybe the new man can afford to appear to be co-operative with other people because better education and more access to wealth means that such men do not need to be so aggressively competitive that they are constantly putting people down in order to achieve their own success. From the headlines in the newspapers about the 'caring nineties' we can also see that some of our values are changing slowly and that the aggressive individualism of the eighties is now being questioned. All kinds of people are now talking about spirituality, and the softer approach to masculinity of the new man fits well alongside this trend. Perhaps the greatest motivator has been that women who are working outside the home need new men in order to be able to survive. If men did not share the load women would face a double burden, having to prove their worth in the world of employment, but also having to take care of home and children.

The enterprise culture of the eighties gave work an exalted position among masculine values and meant that those men who did have work, and many did not, were working so hard that they had an inbuilt excuse for ignoring their domestic responsibilities. 'For the men who had never aspired to be new it was just more of the same. They had never been home of an evening in the past and, if overtime was now biting into their drinking time, at least they were getting richer.'[1]

If men did not change it would be difficult for women to have the energy and commitment required to be successful in their new careers. For this reason many of the jobs taken by women were part-time. One study found that British women work the shortest hours in Europe and that women in part-time employment lose out in terms of pay, job protection and promotion. There was already a problem with the care of children since crèche facilities at work were scant and nursery facilities in the community under-resourced. The demands of work had traditionally been felt most in the relationship between father and children. Film-maker Angela Philips, in her documentary entitled 'Bringing up Daddy' for BBC 2, says that many children practically never see their fathers and have little to say about them. British working hours have risen, the only ones to do so in Europe. She also reports that a study of two-career families found that fathers spend, on average, less than six hours a week with their children; women often get up an hour earlier than men to do housework before they leave for work. Women have considerably less leisure time than their partners.[2]

One of the key factors in the rise of the new man was his attitude to his children. Journalist Martin Plimmer saw that men could act out of their own self-interest in actually benefiting from 'the feminist advance':

The most important benefit feminism offers men is the opportunity to participate in the lives of our children. For too long we were automatically denied that. I will never forget the desolation I felt when I was sent home from the hospital immediately after the birth of my first child . . . I made sure it didn't happen with my next child. I was determined to enjoy this one to the full. And I do. It is this more than anything which marks me as new man in people's eyes. Also, the fact that my wife is the major income earner.[3]

Some men adopted a new role as nurturing and supportive partners. For many men, who had been brought up with traditional roles and who belonged to an older generation, their patterns of life were too established to make this change. The hope lay with a younger generation who were more flexible and able to adapt to the new opportunities opening up for women.

Feminist writers such as Lynne Segal acknowledged the difficulties that were experienced by men attempting to change their view of masculinity in order to support their women:

The best of both worlds is only rarely possible for women.

Although some men have embraced such opportunities as they have for entering the traditional female domain, others remain as fearful and contemptuous of it as their fathers before them. Yet, with women today permanently entrenched in the western workforce, the absurdity of the traditional gendered divide between public and private is daily more apparent. Men could continue to strive to maintain their privileges and dominance in both spheres. But it is likely they will increasingly be battling all the way. More justly and more creatively, they could join women in fighting for an end to the exploitation of women at work and at home. If they do, of course, it will spell the end of masculinity as we have known it.[4]

Such a view admits that some men have taken the needs of women on board and are trying to respond, but at cost to themselves. However, some women think that the attempt by men to find a nurturing role within the home may just be another expression of the need of men to outdo women at their own game. If this were true then it would be a tragedy since no man could be trusted, as women would suspect that at the end of the day he would claim that not only was he a success at work but better in her role at home than she had ever been herself. This view, therefore, sees the advent of the new man as fundamentally subversive to women and something which confirms rather than denies that men are intrinsically power-seekers.

Despite these suspicions the search for the new man continues and, as expressed by *Cosmopolitan* magazine, he sounds just a little familiar:

After a hard day in the business jungle what a woman executive really wants is men who will listen and be there at the end of the day. Men who will soothe, cherish, share the chores, as well as the social and sexual pleasure. They are men who recognise that what women do is as important as what men do.[5]

Perhaps those who have most interest in the idea of the new man are those who will market new products to him. Recent advertising on television and in magazines has shifted away from a hard, macho image of men, to portray men with children in a softer and more caring environment. These are the 'hunks with hearts' which *Cosmopolitan* magazine is looking for. Is the search for the new man merely the opening up of a new set of products with an image geared to men in their thirties and forties? Polly Toynbee, writing in the *Guardian* thinks so:

> I have heard tell of the new man. For many years now there have been books and articles proclaiming his advent, even his arrival. I have met women who claim that their sons will be he, or that their daughters may marry him. I have met men who claim that they are he. False prophets all, the new man is not here, and it does not seem likely that we shall see him in our lifetime.[6]

So the new father appears on the front cover of the Mothercare catalogue. He looks soft and gentle and what's more – he is not afraid to show it (at least not to a predominantly female readership). If the new man is just a new marketing ploy then many men will not be able to afford to be new men. It may then turn out to be just another middle-class fancy which is not applicable to those working men and women whose lives and lifestyle are dictated by harsher and less flexible economic realities.

The Second Stage?

Betty Friedan was one of the founders of the American women's movement with her book *The Feminine Mystique*. In the 1980s she wrote a second book, entitled *The Second Stage*, in which she evaluated the struggle of the women's movement and looked towards the future. In this book she talked of 'the quiet movement of American men'. She believed that a movement was starting which would go beyond the achievements of the women's movement. It is a quiet movement because there is no marching on the street, no anger or enemy, but a re-evaluation of old patterns of life. Men are asking whether they want to be the kind of men that they have become. They are asking questions about fulfilment and whether the ladder of promotion and success which they were brought up to believe as important is now irrelevant. Most of these men are not joining 'men's lib' groups and they may not be talking very much about their questions, nevertheless many men feel isolated, confused and different from the stereotypes that they have grown up with.

For some men the starting point was being made redundant or not being able to find a job. Other men are driven by not wanting to be like their fathers, but the questions have also been fuelled by the changes in the women around them. Many men supported the women's movement and were relieved at the questions it was asking, but when the man's partner came home from the women's group, things began to change. The first level was the arguments about his doing his share of the housework and indeed all the work, including childcare, around the home. It was no longer automatic that the woman would do all these things. The second level was that women had a right to their own interests and life, and that he had to make space for her to do that and set her free and support her in it. The third level was dealing with his own hurt. He saw himself as working very hard to support her and the children but now he was bundled with other men under labels of oppression and chauvinism:

If she didn't need him for her identity, her status, her sense of importance, if she was going to get all that for herself, if she could support herself and have a life independent of him, wouldn't she stop loving him? Why would she stay with him? Wouldn't she just leave? So he was supposed to be the big male oppressor, right? How could he admit the big secret – that maybe he needed her more than she needed him?[7]

Betty Friedan comments that such men no longer knew even what they were supposed to feel. The old, masculine stereotypes were no use in these uncharted waters. The hostility which many men showed towards women at this time was as much an admission of their insecurity and dependence on the love of women as the excesses of feminist attacks on men showed the women's dependence on men. A man could choose – either he could continue to pretend to be dominant and masculine and in control, or he could open up and enter into conversation which he could not control.

Those men who were not only struggling with feminism but with issues such as unemployment felt doubly disorientated. Unemployment left them with a struggle to separate themselves from the role of breadwinner and find themselves in other things. Some would have been willing to do things around the home to help, but in many homes their wives were now out at work and they reacted against this by becoming uncooperative, needing the solace or even the pretence of the old masculinities. Men began to ask, 'What does it mean to be a man, except not-being-a-woman?' Men had lived for too long in a world defined by the twin certainties of men in employment and women in the home. When these two things shifted the effect was startling.

In Britain we have recently seen some people in political leadership leaving high office because they wanted to spend more time with their families. Some of my friends, who have been divorced at least once and who see it as due to the demands of their work, now distinguish between their standard of living and their quality of life and are trying to improve the quality of their relationships and spend time with their children. Such men may still be in a minority, as are the men who never really cared about success at work but only about their families, but with this minority there came the new images associated with the new men and these have been given such media exposure that it feels as if a change in trend has taken place.

Others are no longer satisfied by conventional job success although they are still looking for an alternative. Those men who are unemployed and who have no prospects of employment either despair or seek some other 'life ethic' to replace the 'work ethic' which they were brought up with. Some men now see work as instrumental in that it enables them to have leisure time, including holidays, where they feel they are able to be the kind of person that they want to be. Public opinion analyst, Daniel Yankelovich, concludes from his surveys of American men that self-fulfilment has been severed from success. Men are searching for something more but find conventional life does not satisfy 'their deepest psychological needs nor nourish their self-esteem, nor fulfil their cravings for the "full rich life".' In this respect however, Britain is slightly behind America. Work is still felt to be the main area where men prove themselves as men.

Changes were also felt in the area of sexuality. Psychologist Dr Jane Loevinger, of Washington University in St Louis, found that young college women were now treating sex 'objectively' and focusing on orgasmic scores, whereas younger men were focused more on feelings. On the other hand, women who feel more confident about themselves due to their ability to earn their way in the market place are now noticing the quality of their sexual life more often and some men are finding this quite difficult. Some men feel a sense of panic that women seem to understand their sexuality better than they do themselves, yet they cannot get away from the old machismo stereotypes.

Where is all this leading? Perhaps both men and women could end up in blind alleys:

> In real life there is a danger today for men and women who may try to get out of their own binds by reversing roles. Exchanging one obsolete model of a half-life for another they may copy the worst aspects of the old feminine or masculine mystique instead of building from their own evolving, enduring strengths and liberating their buried feelings or untried potential in the new experiences now open to them until, sharing parenting and work, they create new role models of wholeness.[10]

Friedan concludes that relationships between men and women are going to be bound together in the future by a 'new emotional and economic cement' which is much more flexible than the old one-way dependency of women on men as breadwinners. Sharing the childcare and the employment is a way of enabling both men and women to discover themselves as people rather than having to capitulate to old stereotypes. The fact that they do both means that they have a choice and are not dominated by the one or the other.

This is going to be very painful for men to come to terms with, especially traditional men who view relationships with women hierarchically and their own self-identity as being tied up with employment. This transitional period for men could become a period of intense isolation and loneliness if men cannot learn to share their feelings with each other.

A Day Out with New Men

In the Britain of the early 1990s some men have responded to these issues by trying to add virtues normally considered feminine to their masculine characteristics. This has been called 'getting in touch with the feminine within'. A

small but significant network of men's groups started in
the seventies and continues to this day. The first edition
of the magazine *Achilles Heel* was in summer 1978 and
was produced by 'a working collective of socialist men'.
It was self-consciously concerned with anti-sexist themes
and took the conclusions of the women's movement as its
givens.

One of the ways secularisation has operated in Britain
and the US has been to rid analysis and discussion of
religious categories. Having done this, there was a need
to build a new context for discussions about subjects which
were formerly spiritual or religious. The way this happened
was through the broadening of the word 'political', which
seems now to be applicable to almost everything in life. The
sexual act is now political. Fatherhood is a political issue.
The relationship between men and women is dominated
by political and economic structures. From a standpoint
of the liberal nineties these things appear as a hangover
from a commitment to utopian Marxism, and the language
of Marxist socialism is prevalent, making articles and books
on masculinity difficult to read. Recently there has been
a trend to look at other sources of 'spirituality' such as
mythology and witchcraft. This disturbing trend seems to
be a secular search for the transcendent which Christians
believe can only be found within the Judaeo-Christian
tradition.

The network of anti-sexist men's groups has been greeted
ambivalently by women. Polly Toynbee, while she was
working as a journalist and features writer, went to a
conference held by these groups and had a mixed response.
The list of workshops available was quite extraordinary:
anti-patriarchal therapy; rational emotive therapy; penetration and violence; massage; Emerge – a counselling service
for men who batter; having sex with a woman; sexuality and sensuality and emotional relationships; vasectomy;
wetness in men; socialism and anti-sexism; non-verbal workshop; masturbation; men's action against porn; softness and

strength; guilt in the men's movement; men and make-up; confessions of an anti-sexist man; Jewish men, and a whole lot more:

> What sort of men were they? Many of the leading lights – yes, there were leading lights despite all attempts at non-patriarchal non-hierarchical practice – struck me as veterans of early seventies encounter groups, hooked on self-discovery, self-revelation, and a measure of self-humiliation. Others were firmly rooted in the myriad of the left or the green, veggy, anti-fascist, Crèches Against Sexism, pro-gay, CND, religious socialists as well as some hard left activists . . . remorse was the key note and many were the soul-searching revelations of past revolting sexist behaviour.[11]

The sort of subjects covered at that conference and the sort of men who attended it seem to me to be representative of the men's movement in this country. It is pro-gay, pro-feminist and pro-socialist. Other magazines and newsletters such as *Men For Change* come from the same kind of stable. A whole edition of *The New Internationalist* entitled 'Birth of A New Man: The Politics of Masculinity' came out in September 1987. It is helpful in that it gives a global perspective and some very useful statistics but it does come from the same ideological commitments as the others. There is even an article holding up non-penetrative sex as a new norm for men who feel that penetration is not necessary to sex but is only part of the male definition of what sex is.

The other magazines and newsletters are a mixture of personal biography – telling the stories of men who are struggling with their masculinity – and articles on 'big issues' such as rape, fascism, sexism and work. The content is mixed, with some of it being very helpful and moving whereas other articles seem predictable and heavy.

Most people will be aware of a very different source of

comment on men. The new 'magazines for men' such as *Gentleman's Quarterly* (*GQ*), *For Him*, and *Esquire* now jostle with each other on the newsagents' shelves. Their aim is quite different from the anti-sexist movement; for them masculinity is the key to a new market for magazines. The advertising is still 'glamorous' and the feel of the magazine is luxurious. The aim here is not *change* but *integration* of discussion of 'men's issues' into traditional models of masculinity. This approach gives the appearance of concern without the pain of change. Women can hardly complain, the market for women's magazines is one of the biggest publishing markets in the world. The debate over the new man is a debate on style: does he wear Gucci shoes and dress in Armani or sockless sandals and a pony tail? It appears that whatever is new about the new man he still comes in the same old guises.

Polly Toynbee's attitude to the conference she went to was acerbic:

I would have liked them to have had workshops on Cleaning the oven; Cooking 100 meals in a row for ten-year-olds who don't like brown rice; Hints on efficient housework to be done every day, not in bouts of patriarchalist macho spring-cleaning binges; Tolerating toddlers 24 hours a day; Remembering dinner money, new gym shoes, broken fridges, hamster food and children's dentist, while drawing up the agenda for the local Eco Party meeting, and writing an essay for an Open University course. Or maybe just on being nice to the family all day without thinking you're a saint.[12]

Women seem to divide in their support for such groups believing that even if the new man is a myth, men will have to find out for themselves what women already suspect. Some women who have been through feminism themselves feel guilty about their negative feelings about the men's networks:

. . . if women deny men the right to at least attempt to reinvent themselves, we are no better than those men who have been opposing the rights of women for the past 2,000 years. And it is those women who suffer the greatest in their own fight for equality who should be the last to deny a future generation of men the kind of fulfilment that they have only just begun to experience for themselves.[13]

Polly Toynbee concludes from her day: '. . . without the real anger and the grievance of the women's movement, without the same need for mutual support, and balm for one another's wounds, there is something a bit aimless and self-obsessed about it all.'[14]

Summing Up the New Man
One of the key problems with contemporary definitions of masculinity is that they are defined by comparison with femininity. Men are what women are not. When women change we would expect men to change the boundaries of masculinity. There have been two changes. Firstly, many men are more belligerent than they were about women; some men are grateful to have stereotypes drawn from the women's movement which can be used as a target to lash out at: this was to be expected since women were taking territory away from men. Secondly, many men view the possibility of getting rid of the stranglehold of masculinity with relief and respond to feminism through *adaptation* and *accommodation*. Such men are willing to negotiate masculinity with women. In particular they are willing to add virtues previously considered 'feminine' into the masculinity world-view. Many men quietly get on with their work but are very loving and conciliatory at home, encouraging their partners to go out to work, or to re-train, and making it possible for them to do that by doing the housework, picking up the children and cooking meals. They are willing to submerge anything they may have gained from a more aggressive and self-interested view of masculinity

under the good that is coming from serving the family as a whole.

New men are nice men, but it is only a matter of time before another change comes, trends and fashions will drift away to other interpretations of masculinity leaving new men in the cold again. Where masculinity is about style it is an expression of pluralism – after all men are free to choose what kind of man they want to be – but is this change of style the same as discovering freedom? For some men the idea of the new man is a natural expression of their mix of personal characteristics. The danger is that with the new man moving into the spotlight other men will unthinkingly react to their discontent with conventional masculinity by buying into the idea of the new man as a package deal.

The concept of human nature represented by the idea of the new man is that by adding 'feminine' qualities to those considered 'masculine', men can become more whole. This may be necessary to wholeness but it is not sufficient, for it does not deal with the issue raised by the previous chapter that men can only become whole by laying down power over women. Nor does it deal with the spiritual homelessness of men or of the problems of sin and evil which beset human nature. New men may be the ideal partner for new women but the media focus is a triumph of *style* over *content*. The new man's problem is *guilt*. He cannot get away from how he is meant to have treated women. He is hoisted on the petard of believing that 'the personal is political' and that as a man he is capable of the worst excesses which men have perpetrated. He may be changing nappies but he knows that he is not changing himself.

In summary, the idea of the new man is based on *reaction* to feminism. It accepts that men have lost contact with their 'feminine side' but adding feminine qualities will not get men out of a set of problems common to human nature and which women share. There are no answers in reaction, only in *redemption* is there any hope. The word redemption implies that a person needs to be bought out of slavery. They are in bondage. The new man may become articulate emotionally. He may learn to cry. He may even learn to listen. He is a caring man who spends time with his family. Fine. But even families can become idols. He lives in a world without God, and without transcendence.

There have always been men who have grappled with macho masculinities and have rejected them, at a cost to themselves. The focus on the new man does not necessarily mean that men are changing. In this case it is the social context which has changed, giving the appearance of change in men. The media spotlight has focused on men who have always been caring, nurturing and loving offstage. For a brief instant they have been brought on to centre stage giving the impression that men have changed *en masse*. But this is sleight of hand.

Perhaps we should distinguish between the new man who is just being himself and who is bemused by the attention his lifestyle is getting, and the 'new, new man' who is trying to emulate him because it is attractive or fashionable to do so. But when the spotlight moves on, the 'old new men' will sigh with relief and carry on with life, while the poseurs will frantically rush off to dump their cardigans and pipes and push up the price of designer-labelled animal skins, or whatever is in vogue.

The new man is one of three possible responses to the plight of men. It emphasises the *sameness* between men and women. But the claim for the 'wild man' is that if men are to discover themselves it must be in rediscovering something essentially masculine which will emphasise the *defference* between men and women.

QUESTIONS

1. How do you respond to the new man? Do you despise him or admire him?

2. 'The new man is a triumph of style over content.' Is this too harsh a judgement?

3. Do you share the view that men should be intimately involved with the care and nurture of their children?

4. Do you think those men who give up advancement at work, with its consequent status and material benefits, are correct in drawing attention to the disparity between their standard of living and their quality of life?

5. Do you think the idea of men as 'breadwinners' is helpful or harmful to a) the man concerned, or b) his family?

6. New men seem to feel guilty because of what men are meant to have done to women. How do you think they could resolve this dilemma?

NOTES

1. Angela Philips, 'Male Models', *Listener*, 18 January 1990, p. 10.
2. Philips, ibid.
3. Martin Plimmer, 'Is there a man for all seasons?', *Daily Telegraph*, 11, January 1991.
4. Lynne Segal, *Slow Motion: Changing Masculinities, Changing Men* (London: Virago, 1990), p. 319.
5. *Cosmopolitan*, March 1988.
6. Polly Toynbee, 'That Incredible Shrinking New Man,' *Guardian*, 6 April 1987.
7. Betty Friedan, *The Second Stage* (London: Sphere/Abacus, 1983), p. 127.
8. Friedan, op. cit., p. 134.
9. Friedan, op. cit., p. 142–3.
10. Friedan, op. cit., p. 145.
11. Polly Toynbee, *Guardian*, 11 June 1982, p. 12.
12. ibid.
13. Kimberley Leston, 'Love, Lust and Phoney Baloney', *Guardian*, 21 June 1990, p. 38.
14. Toynbee, (1982) op. cit., p. 12.

6

THE WILD MAN

The new man draws on the essential sameness between men and women in a shared humanity but there are also differences between men and women which are not physiological or biological. Masculinity and femininity may well describe characteristics which can be expressed by both men and women but there are some ways of seeing the world and ways of behaving which resonate more with men than with women, or with women than men. To what extent this is just a hangover from the rigid gender stereotypes which we have been brought up with is still an open question but this whole area has recently been explored by the American writer and poet Robert Bly. His contention is that there are many attributes which have been described as masculine and which are open to men and women but which have been lost by men and which men need to recover if they are to be whole.

Robert Bly is well known for his reflections on American society, especially the Vietnam war. In recent years he has drawn large audiences of men, drawing on his knowledge of mythology, to talk about masculinity. His recent book, *Iron John*,[1] has had an extraordinary impact on American men. It was on the bestseller lists for many weeks and has carved out a niche for itself in the literature on masculinity. For this reason I want to look at it in detail in this chapter.

The starting point is a comment on the effects of the idea of the new man on American men: 'The male in the past twenty years has become more thoughtful, more gentle. But by this process he has *not* become more free. He's a nice boy who now not only pleases his mother but also the young woman he is living with.'[2]

Bly finds the 'soft male' very attractive but senses that something is wrong. He feels that they are unhappy men without much energy. They are 'life-preserving but not life-giving'. He claims that it is often the women with these men who radiate energy. Such men have come to mistakenly equate their own natural male energy with being macho. Despite this Bly affirms the results of the women's movement, believing that it is essential that men discover more about those virtues which society has labelled 'feminine'. But becoming a new man is only one stage on a much longer journey and it is the attempt to chart this pilgrimage which led Bly to write *Iron John*.

Bly's response to the 'crisis in masculinity' was to dig deep into his own knowledge of mythology and poetry. He began to talk to men's groups, drawing on fairy tales which related masculinity to concepts of growth and energy. The results of these groups were quite startling:

> Often the younger males would begin to talk and within five minutes they would be weeping. The amount of grief and anguish in the younger males was astounding! . . . Part of the grief was a remoteness from their fathers, which they felt keenly, but part, too, came from trouble in their marriages or relationships. They had learned to be receptive, and it wasn't enough to carry their marriages.[3]

He concluded from this that men had lost something which was essentially 'wild'; a word he uses in opposition to the word 'tame' rather than denoting anything violent. His book, *Iron John*, brings together his views on masculinity with the exposition of a Grimms' fairy tale, a story first set down around 1820 but with a history which was much older.

The fairy story is about a boy becoming a man. An

explorer, walking with his dog in a forest, comes to a pond from which a hand emerges, and drags the dog in. The explorer gets some men, who empty the pond to find a rusty-coloured, hairy giant at the bottom. They take him to the king's castle and put him into a cage in the courtyard. The boy in the story is the king's son, who frees the hairy giant from the cage in the king's courtyard with a key found under his mother's pillow. Frightened of his parents' response to what he has done he then goes to be with 'Iron John' in the forest. Iron John sets him several tasks and he leaves the forest having failed to complete them properly, as a 'nobody'. The boy learns to be a man through facing disappointment, suffering, anonymity, servitude, courtly love and finally as a warrior. Iron John, who was his mentor in the forest, had promised that he would come to his aid if he ever needed help. The boy calls on him to provide a war-horse to enable him to fight as a warrior. The story ends with the boy saving the day by winning the battle for a king, whose servant he had become. Although he returns to the anonymity of a peasant he is found out to be the warrior hero, rewarded, marries a princess and his success frees the hairy giant from an enchantment, who returns at the end of the book as a powerful and wealthy king.

Robert Bly's interpretation of this age-old myth is complex but compelling. He is proposing that every modern man has inside him a 'wild man' who is 'hairy'. Modern men have become passive and docile, they have not made contact with the wild man within. Masculine identity can only be found by getting in touch with this wild man, by learning how to get in touch with 'forceful action, undertaken, not without compassion, but with resolve'.[4]

Bly lays men's problems at the feet of the nuclear family, which creates difficulties in two areas for boys growing up. Firstly, boys find it difficult to identify with their fathers. In our society boys sometimes feel that they can become men more quickly by rejecting their fathers than by emulating them. Secondly, our culture has made no provision for male initiation. Robert Bly seems to romanticise primitive initiation ceremonies, seeking to re-enact them within contemporary western culture.

We have already seen in an earlier chapter that although the link between masculinity and such rituals is significant, it would be difficult to introduce them into post-industrial society. Nevertheless, it is true that boys have no 'rite of passage' to becoming men. Psychologists tell us that boys have to make the break from their mothers, crossing the gender divide to identify with the male.

The Mark of the Wounded

In primitive cultures initiation is often accompanied by a wound which is given by older men, such as the deliberate knocking-out of a tooth or scarring of the skin. The scar is meant to remain for the rest of one's life and be instantly recognisable as a sign to the community that the boy so initiated has passed into manhood.

But this is not the only way of being wounded as a man. It would be inappropriate to resort to scarring men physically in some backwoods initiation. All men are wounded, and how they deal with those wounds may well affect how they face adulthood. Some have been hurt by their upbringing, by failure, by abuse, or by lack of acceptance. Within all men there is anxiety, tension, loneliness and fear. Having an absent father is an injury, or having a judgmental parent. The process of initiation, for Bly, merely recalls the other wounds in one's life and forces a man to examine them and come to terms with them. But men have been told that they become men by shrugging off their wounds and paying no attention to them.

Contemporary masculinity has never come to terms with weakness and vulnerability. There are so many grown men who have been hurt in many ways in their childhood but will not look on that hurt or admit it to other men, and yet are driven by it. Even in business life, men rub shoulders with one another but do not disclose the fact that they are wounded children.

Many men either live under their wounds or try to prove that they are somebody greater than the wounds suggest. Those who are victims can become depressed and believe what has been told to them or done to them. They actually think that they are only worthy of abuse, or are failures. Others try and beat the abuse and the wounds by proving to themselves and to others that they can rise above them. They appear to be very successful but are just as driven by the hurt and the pain. Neither the victim nor the driven person has come to terms with the reality of their situation.

It is a crucial but often overlooked insight that what Christianity can offer wounded men is the knowledge that creativity, ministry and service can arise from the wounded place. People who have been abused or who have suffered in some way can find that they have been enabled by their suffering to understand and draw closer to others who are suffering, but this can only happen if the man is willing to face his wounded nature and offer it to God.

There is another aspect to the woundedness of men. Much contemporary thinking, especially that arising out of New Age philosophy, emphasises the woundedness of humanity but neglects the sinfulness of human beings. Where do the wounds come from? Often it is from other people indulging in acts for which they are morally culpable. Some wounds are self-inflicted because we indulge in behaviour which was no part of God's intentions for our lives. It is not enough to look to God for healing of wounds, seeing life in the context of *wholeness*. If men would grow up they must also learn the old lessons of repentance; a turning away from all that is not of God, and embrace *holiness*. Bly himself points out that the search for the wild man is a search for religious life: 'Getting in touch with the wild man means religious life for a man in the broadest sense of the phrase. The fifties male was almost wholly secular, so we are not talking in any way of a movement back.'3

The Ashes Experience

Some of the ideas introduced by Robert Bly cut across what may be expected by those who suspect that the book is really an apology for the old, macho masculinity dressed up in new guise. However, Bly now turns to the idea of humility as something essential for men to rediscover. If men do not face up to the things that go wrong in their lives and learn from them then they cannot discover their full humanity or be in touch with their 'wild man'. He uses the Greek word *katabasis* to describe this descent or humbling.

The man who does not know anything about the underside of life will be weaker than the man who does. In the Bible, Joseph's ascent to power in Egypt could not have happened if he had not been put in the pit by his brothers. This humiliating episode of slavery, imprisonment and injustice was the start of a new life. Men are so achievement-orientated that a serious accident, or the loss of a job, or family breakdown, or illness cannot be seen as some kind of new path to be explored, but can only be an interruption of a normality characterised by success.

But some have found out, as the Apostle Paul said in his letter to the Romans, that nothing can divorce us from the love of God, and many have found in these experiences that the sudden wrench away from achievement has brought them back to their senses.6

Job covered himself with ashes to indicate that his former wealthy and prosperous self was dead; he was now in grief. Throughout the scriptures people respond to national repentance and private grief by heaping ashes on their head, but in our society there are meant to be no ashes. The world of advertising, marketing and media behaves as if we live in some world where nothing bad ever happens to us. We all long for a world in which our babies do not die, there are no car accidents or premature deaths, nor are we poor or driven insane. But this world is itself insane.

> Despite our Disneyland culture some men around thirty-five or forty will begin to experience ashes. . . . They begin to notice how many of their dreams have turned to ashes. A young man in high school dreams that he will be a race driver, a mountain climber, he will marry Miss America, he will be a millionaire by thirty, he will get a Nobel Prize in physics by thirty-five, he will be an architect and build the tallest building ever. He will get out of his hick town and live in Paris. He will have fabulous friends . . . and by thirty-five all these dreams are ashes.[7]

It is so important for men to let their dreams go and deal with reality. The person who has been through an ashes experience is not given to flights of fantasy. The sin that first entered our lives in the Garden of Eden was that of self-sufficiency, which draws us away from God and focuses us on our own resources. Those who suffer and those who are poor have the advantage that their lack of self-sufficiency is obvious to them every day. They are aware that they have to turn somewhere for strength and sometimes they will turn to God. People who are rich, successful or beautiful may go through life depending on their natural gifts, they do not see the necessity of depending on anybody else, especially God, but without learning dependence we cannot receive grace.[8]

It is often the case when one reads the biographies of great men and women that behind the greatness there is suffering or weakness of some description. The Apostle Paul had his 'thorn in the flesh'. The glory of Christ flows from the suffering of the cross. In the hymn that is sung in heaven, as described in the book of Revelation, the living creatures representing creation say of Christ 'worthy is the Lamb, who was slain'. Christ is worthy not just because he is God but because he willingly accepted that God's purposes could only be accomplished through his suffering. Men who wish to avoid suffering at any cost cannot be great because they cannot become like Christ.

There is a cautionary tale here for that branch of Christianity which is triumphalistic in the extreme. Those who see illness only as an opportunity for healing and do not see suffering as teaching us more about God are treading on very thin ice indeed. Because of Christ we do not have to be victims of our suffering, but pretending that it doesn't exist can lead to a pretence which deludes only ourselves. Such pretence is very wearying. We all long for the refreshment of a ministry which is rooted in the reality which faces ordinary people. Most of us want to wake up every day with something which is relevant to our human experience. We can only be led by people who have known grief and ashes as well as glory.

So to become mature a man must learn about the dark side of life. Every man's life contains the raw material of grief, failure and pain from which we can learn how to be truly human and learn how to be men. Masculinity as a cultural set of assumptions makes it difficult for us to engage in the process of grief or the time of ashes. It sees them as counter-productive, and the vulnerability and the negativity essential to them as something which is foreign to masculinity. It is this denial of what it means to be essentially human that can make masculinity such an artificial and stultifying picture for men to copy.

Heroes and Celebrities
We all need to learn from other people about what it means to be human but there seems to be a paucity of models among men whom we can admire and emulate. Our society has succumbed to the cult of the celebrity rather than the hero, but there is little to learn from celebrities since they themselves are people who are escaping from reality into fantasy. The world of the celebrity is a world of entertainment which distracts us from life's problems. The more distracted we are by media images, the less we will be able to come to terms with what is required of us as men.

In other cultures men have followed heroes whose lives contained moral and spiritual content. Within the Church there were always biographies of great men and women of God, or missionaries who did great exploits in foreign lands to inspire young men and women to emulate them and learn something from their struggles. But the best kind of mentor is found within the community: an older person who is wise and who has come to terms with his own hurt and wounds, with his own finiteness, but who has experienced something of glory as well. This kind of man can say like the Apostle Paul 'imitate me even as I imitate Christ'. All our lives we need people that we can look up to, men and women that we admire and respect and want to learn from in our own lives.

Ours is an age of cynicism and scepticism that seeks to expose and cannot sit still long enough to learn. Everything has to be instant, but the way of initiation is through apprenticeship. Jesus did not wrap up eternal life in a package deal which could be instantly experienced. He took twelve men on a pilgrimage as his apprentices, who learned from him, often making mistakes themselves. It is not enough to tell men that they must only learn from Christ. There is always a need for people who have learned from life and from their experience of God to visibly demonstrate what godliness means, and to offer to others a friendship which crosses the age divide and which is regarded by young men as something to treasure.

In my own life, I have been very fortunate in learning from a succession of older men something of their own inner spiritual life and stance on moral, economic and political issues. I have learned far more from my relationships with such men than I have from books or listening to sermons. It has been in the times of conversation and just being with them and watching them that something of their greatness has reached out to me and attracted me, because they contain something of the hero. These are those whose character shows that they have come to terms with both sin and glory. Happy is the man who has formed such a relationship and is helped to understand that the suffering we go through here is of real value when placed in the hands of God. Happy is the man who gains strength from such a relationship to be able to stand up for what he truly believes rather than merging with the crowd.

Standing Against the Crowd

Even as teenagers or children some people experience grief and ashes, but for many young people their teenage years and early adulthood are a time of great hope and optimism. The world stretches out before them and they are working hard to establish a social identity. Robert Bly calls these the 'ascenders' who are upwardly mobile, and who dare to dream dreams. At this point in their lives they are moving with the crowd and taking what the world has to offer them. Often they have a sense of career which is designed so that they plug in to it when they are young and hope that it will take them throughout their life in a straight line for promotion and seniority. But the concept of career is very different from the idea of 'calling', and if they are to learn what it means to be fully human they must grapple at some point with suffering, grief and ashes in order to fulfil what God wants for their lives.

Some boys, especially in third world cultures and those who live in poverty in the west, do not have the opportunity to be 'ascenders'. They have to accept the responsibilities of employment and provision for the family at a very early age and this turns them into mini-adults before they have really found out what it means to be young. It is often the case that the younger a person enters the labour force, the more drudgery they are expected to undertake because they have no training to make them suitable for anything more.

In the story of Iron John the boy is poised to be an ascender. Life is one big adventure and, ignoring the perils, he wants to go and discover life for himself. This activism is something which Bly draws attention to as being important to both men and women but something which has been lost by a number of men in the modern world. He says:

During the last thirty years men have been asked to learn how to go with the flow, how to follow rather than lead, how to live in a non-hierarchical way, how to be vulnerable, how to adopt consensus decision-making. Some women want a passive man if they want a man at all; the Church wants a tamed man – they are called priests; the university wants a domesticated man – they are called tenure-track[9] people; the corporation wants a team-worker, and so on.[10]

Passivity is not confined to men but it does affect men. Very few people like to stand out in the crowd or to fight their own corner. We prefer to agree and to have views which are those of the majority. But where the majority is itself lost what is needed are men and women who can turn the tide, and such people need security in themselves. They need to have a source of strength which does not come from others admiring them, agreeing with them or supporting them. They need to be people who have a source of affirmation in themselves which comes from godliness and a moral commitment rather than fame or success.

Such people are all too thin on the ground today. Following the trend has become a way of life. Both men and women need to stand up for what they believe to be right. The 'soft male' of new man fame may be extremely sensitive to other people's pain. He may be willing to be accused by women of being the source of all their oppression, but the picture which has been drawn of him is not noted for its moral discernment. He does not say 'This is right but this is wrong'. Many men that I have met in the men's movement have a kind of sincere naïvety. They wanted to be loving, gentle and nurturing but thought that the only way of doing this was by becoming a victim or a doormat.

Men do not have to lie down in the path of accusation and be trampled by it. No good will come to the world or to the future partnerships we have with women if men lose their moral insight as to what is right and wrong. There is no moral merit in feeling guilty all the time. The important thing is to act to reverse the damage that has been done. There is nothing strange about a man being open, gentle and nurturing, and about him also being a fighter for what he believes to be right. Men need to recover an activism where they have been passive for too long, they need to recover confidence in their ability to stand against the tide.

The Life of the Warrior

Fighting and violence have become synonymous with male behaviour and it is easy to romanticise the 'noble savage' by making something which is violent, honourable but also sentimental. I talked above about the passivity of the new man and that what was needed was men who also had a sense of moral outrage as well as moral courage.

Bly sees warriors as disciplined people, who have a cause to fight for which is the cause of right. They are in service to a purpose which is greater than themselves. But if man does not serve the cause of right he is not a warrior but is perpetuating violence. He is not in touch with the wild man who brings strength, 'spirituality' and wisdom, but tyrannised by savagery.

One of the hallmarks then of growing into manhood is the idea of defending and advancing a cause. One of the most startling things about recent years is that women have had a cause to fight for which they have seen as the cause of right and which has motivated them and given them life and purpose. It has united them on a campaign to defeat injustice. At the same time men had no cause. In America men were disillusioned with Vietnam; in the west there was a general replacement of moral campaigns by business strategies, which seemed at the end of the day to be empty and futile as they were fuelled by a spurious materialism. Men need a cause. They need to believe in something, to have a faith or a crusade. They are constantly asking themselves, 'What am I doing this for?' although they may not admit this to other people. They are motivated by goals and by rewards, and this need to have a purpose is so strong that men frequently delude themselves that things which are in fact worthless are of great worth.

This sense of meaninglessness which can hit men who are deeply involved in their work life is something which the Bible sees as closely related to the introduction of sin and evil into the world. We noted in an earlier chapter that one of the effects of the fall was the introduction of disappointment resulting in frustration. This was felt in the area of relationships as mutuality turned to power, but it was also one of the consequences of the fall for men that work became a source of toil which yielded little reward. After this they returned to the dust and the question is raised over the whole sorry enterprise, 'What was this for?' Men make money and status but return to the dust and this insight constantly intrudes on the ambitions of men, who are seeking to become somebody through their work but can only do this by blanking out the frustration and meaninglessness of the enterprise when it is conducted without God.

What cause will captivate the imagination of thousands of men across the world? What do we consider is worth fighting for? My belief is that it must be a spiritual cause. If we are to be released from the frustration that everything returns to the dust then we must find some way of satisfying our longing to build something out of our lives which will endure. The problem is that there are so many counterfeit spiritualities on offer at this moment. One of the keys is that Christianity is about serving the God who is the creator of all things, and who calls men and women together into a partnership in which work and family life are participated in by both partners on the basis of equality. It is this God who asks us to co-operate in the creative management of the world. Only in service to this God can we build a life which brings together our desire to build a world of peace and justice, and can make sense of the suffering of grief and sin which besets us on the way.

In this chapter I have taken some of the insights which Robert Bly shares with Christianity and commented on them, and developed them from a Christian position. His book is poetic and metaphorical, he does not present it in a strictly logical argument but works through our imagination. Nevertheless it is important to briefly summarise some of the problems which I have with the book as a Christian. The most important problem is *selfism*. Bly directs men to reach inside themselves to discover the wild man but Christianity shows us that it is the self that tyrannises us because it is fallen. Humanity needs a *saviour*.

The second problem is *relativism*. Bly is a friend to all cultures and religions. His book is a soup into which all kinds of mythology and religious stories are poured. It is not surprising to find that his work is at the centre (if the centre can be found) of the New Age movement, the defining of which is like building a brick wall round a patch of fog. Christianity cannot be included in the mix because in its biblical form it is antagonistic to pluralism. It asserts the uniqueness of Jesus Christ as the only way to God.

The third problem is *responsibility*. Bly only points out that men are wounded but he does not say that men are culpable. Christianity states that both men and women are sinful and culpable before God to whom they have to answer for what they have done to and in his world. At some point responsibility (and therefore the need for repentance) must enter the scene. Forgiveness and justice are part of relationships between the sexes just as much as becoming wild men. Bly has no real theory of change. He lets us in to great insights about ourselves but does not tell us how we are to change. Only by dealing with the problem of human sin can men have hope that they will not revert in the future to their old ways. Nevertheless although this is true the Church must face up to the fact that it has not begun to deal with the pain in men's lives in the way that Bly, and those who work with him, are currently doing.

These three points are crucial but there are others which are also important. The book does not put sexuality in any ethical framework, which means that sexuality can still be exploitative. It purports to celebrate sexuality but does not contain it. It is also the case that many men who have not grappled with the implications of the women's movement will welcome the phrase 'wild man' as a call for men to return to the old certainties of chauvinism. They will welcome the separatism of men's groups which allow them to be 'with the lads'. I have real sympathy for women who see men asserting their 'masculine' agenda and forgetting – yet again – that women exist let alone have an agenda to be addressed. Such men's groups would be a disaster for us all. They could become places for self-pity and an avoidance of the real issues. However, what I have seen in documentaries and read in articles about the men's movement in the United States and its development thus far suggests that this is not as yet a problem, and that men who have been chauvinistic and aggressive towards women have learnt to face up to this and change.

It may help to give one or two illustrations of the kind of changes that have come over men who have been on wild man weekends in the States. These are weekends when men go into the country together and build fires and are helped to get in contact with their past and their emotions through group exercises, a rediscovery of prayer in the 'sweat lodge', and even the singing of 'Amazing Grace'. BBC 2 screened a documentary entitled 'Wild Man Gatherings' in its series *Forty Minutes* in January 1992. This was accompanied by articles in the national press drawing on the experiences of those who had been filmed in the documentary. Richard Bradley and Mark Phillips interviewed some of the wives of the men who had been on the weekend, after they had returned. One wife, Gina, thought it was absurd to see this men's movement as being a threat to women and said, 'The weekend has affected everything between us . . . it is about recognising the differences between men and women – and taking down the barriers.' Her husband Greg did see a change in his life and said, 'The weekend was a super-catalyst. I can talk about what's going on without taking her head off'.

When asked what he had been like when he came back, Gina responded: 'Who came back? Well, he looked like a wild man. His hair was all over the place and his beard was in a mess. He burst through the door. We talked the whole night. He had so much energy and enthusiasm, like the stopper had blown off.'

Mary-Ann was uncertain about her husband Dan going on a wild man weekend. At least she knew the man who was going away, even if he had not really been a partner to her during their twenty-three years of marriage. On the weekend, Dan wept for the first time in thirty years, and when he returned she found she needn't have worried:

> He seems happier. He's finally become aware that he doesn't have to carry all that pain around. That he's been missing out for years . . . This weekend had nothing to do with our marriage, it was about Dan and his parents. I knew once he'd resolved all that, it could only enhance our relationship . . . This is a start. It opens the door.[11]

The wild man could become a theme which appeals to those who are overly sentimental and 'precious'. Pictures of American men in the backwoods in cowboy gear, crying their tears and doing their initiating does not seem to have rung that true with the British public, whose media gave Bly a hard time when his book was released in Britain.[12] Many writers on both sides of the Atlantic could not take it seriously. I was initially amused by the biographical sketch of American New Age author Ken Byers on his latest book on men, which states that, 'he runs week-long father and son Wilderness Relationship tours in the mountains of Arizona.'[13] At this rate being a wild man will soon become an optional extra for the complete man.

It is easy for the reserved British temperament to laugh at Americans in cowboy hats and all the cultural trappings of wild man weekends. But the laugh is on us, if these men resolve things in their lives which we refuse even to face.

Spirituality

Iron John seems at times to be drawing men towards an appreciation of spirituality. Bly's critique of men as functional people who are alienated from their true selves is very apposite. He appeals to men to 'see the big picture' and introduces ideas of transcendence, but there is nothing to stop men 'bolting on' Bly's ideas to the prevailing materialism of our age.

It seems to have been forgotten that the roots of the wild man experience was in *holy* men who had set aside the world to focus entirely on God. It shows the vacuous nature of modern culture that Bly's followers do not recognise holy ground when they find it. The writer to the Hebrews talks about wild men *and* women, who went through torture, persecution and privation for the sake of their faith: 'They went about in sheepskins and goatskins, destitute, persecuted and ill-treated – the world was not worthy of them. They wandered in deserts and mountains, and in caves and holes in the ground. These were all commended for their faith . . .'[14]

A spiritual pilgrimage of any depth has to be about risk-taking rather than the risk-avoidance of a materially obsessed world. But the wildness of God emanates from the holiness, the 'otherness' of God. There is no wildness in the human soul that does not come from the dying embers of the fire God has placed in every human being. Wildness is another way of describing the beauty of holiness. The complaint against the Church is that we have tamed the person of Jesus and made him 'gentle Jesus, meek and mild'. Secularised men, who do not know God and who only want to add new insights to their materialism or humanism, will in the end return to their old ways. The issue remains power, but Bly deals with everything but the power that enslaves, the power of sin and evil.

Wholeness cannot be found in the *reaction* to feminism of the new man nor in the *recognition* of the presence of the wild man. It can only be found in the *redemption* of the God who is man, Jesus Christ. What brings about change in men? For the new man it was a change of context that gave the appearance of men changing. This led to a triumph of *style* over content. For the wild man it was a recognition of untapped resources within each of us which would lead us into freedom: this was merely the old *self* in a new guise. But the Christian man knows that change comes from outside his seemingly helpless situation. Change comes through response to God's grace, leading to *salvation*. Which will men choose – style, self or salvation?

QUESTIONS

1. Do you think that men and women should currently be emphasising their 'sameness' or their 'differences'?
2. Is there a wild man inside every man? Would you like to be a wild man?
3. How should men deal with their wounds?
4. All of us have periods in our lives which are painful and humbling. Are we right to see these as essentially negative?
5. Do boys suffer from not having any initiation into manhood?
6. Do you have some person in your life whom you look to as a hero or mentor?
7. How important is it for men to have a cause for which to fight?
8. To what extent do the weaknesses of Robert Bly's material, when viewed from a Christian perspective, outweigh the points he is trying to make?

NOTES

1. Robert Bly, *Iron John* (Reading, Mass.: Addison-Wesley, 1990; Shaftesbury: Element Books, 1991).

2.   Keith Thompson, 'The Meaning of Being Male: A Conversation with Robert Bly', *LA Weekly*, 5–11 August 1983.
3.   ibid.
4.   ibid.
5.   ibid.
6.   Romans 8:38–9.
7.   Robert Bly, *Iron John*, op. cit. p. 81.
8.   Philip Yancey, *Where is God when it Hurts*? (London: Marshall Pickering, 1990), p. 146.
9.   An American expression for people with life-long contracts within a higher education establishment.
10. Bly, op. cit., p. 61.
11. Richard Bradley and Mark Phillips, 'Behind every wild man is a happy woman', *Independent*, 20 January 1992, p. 13.
12. For a good cross section of reviews see the following: Maureen Freely, 'Ironing out the Differences', *Independent on Sunday*, 15 September 1991, p. 34; Angela Lambert, 'Boxing Means Never Having to Say Sorry', *Independent on Sunday*, 28 July 1991, p. 23; Frederic Raphael, 'Wild at Heart?', *The Sunday Times*, 22 September 1991; Jules Cashford, 'Metaphors at High Noon', *The Financial Times*, 14/15 September 1991; John Horder, 'Huggers on the Warpath', *Guardian*, 31 August 1991; John Lichfield, 'The New All-American Man', *Independent on Sunday*, 2 June 1991, (on the American edition); Robin Skynner, 'Iron Tonic for the Soul', *Guardian*, 9/10 February 1991, and Robin Skynner, 'Bonding with the Boys', *Guardian*, 9/10 March 1991. (These are full articles based on Skynner's own experience and on the American edition. They predate the release of the book in the UK.)
13. Kenneth Byers, *Man in Transition: His Role as Father, Son, Friend and Lover* (California: Journeys Together, 1990).
14. Hebrews 11:37–9. Hebrews 11 contains heroes *and* heroines of faith, wild men and wild women.

7

MEN AND FRIENDSHIP

One of the most important lessons to be learned in this whole area is the difference between the awareness of an issue that comes through books and the awareness that comes through personal experience. In 1989 I brought together a small group of men, all of whom were Christians, who were quite enthusiastic to meet together and discuss the issues. I put it to them that I was interested in writing a book and needed to discuss the issues with a group of men. They were quite happy to meet on this basis. We met for the first time on October 2nd, 1989 in the back room of a very famous pub, The Salutation Inn, which dates back to the twelfth century. The venue was very important. They would not meet in a church or on church property nor would they meet in the home, as they felt it would cause problems for the host who might be distracted by children or by the phone and would not feel at ease. None of us were regular pub-goers, and in some senses the choice of venue was a strange one, but we were able to get this room every month on the same evening.

The first meeting set up a lot of the unwritten rules which have remained central to the group. There was to be no agenda, no chairperson, no task for the group to do. We were there to talk together and nothing else. The group was to remain small, hopefully less than six, allowing everybody to have a say on each occasion. At first we also felt that we were too similar: we were all Christians and, apart from an older man in his late fifties, we were all between thirty and forty-five. The group needed to be finely balanced between diversity and similarity and there was great talk of bringing people in who might balance us all out. Only one of the men present was single and we were all concerned about him; it was going to be very easy to start discussing issues related to our families, thereby excluding him.

Very soon we found that we were different kinds of people. Even though three of us worked in the Christian world, one was involved in the arts, another in running a business as well as counselling young people, and I was involved in communicating theology within the modern world. Of the others who met on that occasion, one was a social worker, one was a teacher and another was a senior member of the medical profession. We were all articulate, white and some could say middle-class. Nevertheless we were acutely aware of the differences of personality in the group.

Over the first few meetings of the group we began to look at issues surrounding masculinity. We talked about issues as if they were not related to us but the conversation tended to drift towards our own personal experiences. On one occasion we had a tremendous conversation about ambition and everybody in that group opened up about their sense of being driven or the amount of time they vested in some sense of career or purpose. After a few meetings the older person, who was a social worker, dropped out of the group after having missed a few sessions. The rest of us were very sad about this, as he was highly respected both inside and outside the church, and we felt the loss of his maturity.

One or two other men came and went from the group but couldn't sustain the commitment which the core group of five were now making. There was a sense of eagerness about the meetings, people would say that they had looked forward to the meeting all month. There was an openness about the group which was quite extraordinary and exhilarating.

We had already ruled some subjects out of court: those of us who were married were very concerned that our wives should feel secure about what we were saying when we were at the group. We therefore made a commitment not to speak about sexual intimacy which would draw in our wives. We also made, I think, an unspoken commitment to be loyal to them and this was important because the group decided at an early stage to be confidential. If there was to be openness between us there had to be some sense of confidentiality. Church networks are notorious for being gossipy and the group could not have existed for long or spoken about deep issues if we were unsure about what was being said.

It was this commitment to confidentiality that was to lead to a change in the direction of the group. On one occasion I happened to say to Helen that a member of the group, whom she knew, was not applying for a job that would mean promotion. I felt that this was a perfectly ordinary comment to pass on but she saw his wife later on that week and commented on it as he walked into the room. He questioned her as to how she could possibly know about it since he had only told the men's group.

Nothing much happened until the group met when he quite rightly, near the end of the meeting, accused me of betraying the very confidentiality I had been instrumental in setting up. I was hoisted on my own petard and this led to quite an emotional scene outside the pub on the pavement, which was viewed with some amazement by groups of leather-clad punks who had been meeting in another room in the pub. I acknowledged that I had done the wrong thing and was forgiven by him, but this conversation on the pavement led to the group saying that they were fed up with talking about masculinity in the third person. Basically we all wanted to talk about ourselves.

It is important to make a distinction between confidentiality and secrecy. All we were doing was extending the confidentiality which is necessary in many conversations if they are to be fruitful. But we recognised a problem with men who felt they were excluded from the group and that it was a secret group, such as the Freemasons have become.

It was never part of the aim of the group to be exclusive and the group itself may well serve a temporary purpose when looked at with hindsight.

Any group that has an identity will be exclusive to some extent and I do not think the tensions which this throws up can be resolved. Looking back I think we had learnt something from the feminist movement, which had discovered that women needed to exclude men from their groups in order to learn from one another as women. Group dynamics change when both sexes are present. For the rest of the month we were all working in teams of both men and women, and this was very important, but once a month we felt the need to come together as men. There were things we discussed together which gave us insights that could not have come even from our wives.

Those of us who were married all had very strong marriages but we were discovering that we had needs for friendship outside marriage which were very tangible. We also felt that we could talk to women friends about the *consequences* of masculinity, which were sometimes quite painful for them as women, but we needed to talk to other men about the *experience* of masculinity. None of us saw the group as being separatist in any sense from women or from other men, but we did begin to feel that the history that we had shared together had gone quite deep and that it was not fair to bring in somebody from outside the group. Several of us felt a sense of loss because there was another man whom we all admired as being extremely attractive to men and a very strong character but also extremely gentle. We were intrigued by him, and three of us were friends of his, but at the end of the day we felt the group had to stay the size it was.

A New Phase

The meetings that followed were quite remarkable. We all commented that we had been to hundreds of fellowship groups between us but had never found the commitment and openness that we were experiencing in that group.

It certainly wasn't due to the strength of the beer, most of us were driving to the meeting and found ourselves experimenting with non-alcoholic beer which was quite a dismal experience. This was no camaraderie around a heavy drinking bout, none of us were in the least interested in that.

We were all surprised by the gentleness of the group. There were times when the discussion was so fast that it was difficult to get a word in but there began to be a practice which we called 'having the floor', where somebody would come with the need to share something from his life. At those times the quality of listening was very tangible. One member of the group was particularly good at gentle, probing questions which drew people out. On some occasions people were grappling with talking about areas of their life which they had never talked about before. There were some surprises as gentle people talked of a deep anger, or those admired for their sense of control and purpose talked of being 'driven'. We often commented that we felt that this was a group where we could say the unsayable. It was possible, for instance, to be very negative about things which were sacred at other times of the year but this would be greeted with sympathy and understanding rather than a frozen, critical silence. Power was not on the agenda.

Before long each member of the group had made himself quite vulnerable; we put things from the dark side of our nature on the table among the glasses. We brought up insecurities and areas where we were very weak. On each occasion this was met by a loving acceptance and affirmation. By the end of a year we were all experiencing the same sense of exhilaration because we were discovering something more about grace. Things we feared because they were unspoken in our lives were reduced to size by the fact that we had them in common and were willing to love each other through them.

On one occasion a member of the group failed to get a job within his own institution, which would have been a promotion. This meant that he had to go back to work and learn to get on with the new person even though he felt he would have been much better at the job himself. Professionalism meant that he had to be pleasant and gracious about the whole thing and could not show his feelings. When he came to the group he asked to 'take the floor' and began to talk quite reasonably about what had happened. When we questioned him about how he felt he began to get quite irate, frequently emphasising a point by beating the table with his fist. We all looked for a word to describe his feelings and the word that stuck with us was 'petulant'. He now talks about the episode as his 'tantrum'. Although we were very concerned we were also quite amused because we did not see what was so bad about being petulant.

I spoke recently to him and asked him why this episode had been so important. His comment was that in virtually every other environment that he worked he was being judged but there was nothing to lose at the men's group. By that time people knew quite a lot about one another and the idea of having something to prove was absent. He felt that the relative light-heartedness of the group, and our delight at finding this word 'petulant' which stuck with him, made it possible for him to treat this matter lightly himself. He offered it as a contribution to the book because since then he had been able to talk about it to other colleagues and therefore it was no longer confidential. He felt he was still respected in the group and because of this he felt confident about it outside. This led to a conversation about the impact of secrecy and guilt on us. We agreed that things we harbour from other people guiltily do grow enormously in our own imagination. A small sin is like a balloon which is pumped up by guilt within our minds. What we were finding with the group was that confession was like deflating the balloon so that perspective was restored.

This does not mean that there were not times of real crisis in the group. On one occasion I was particularly insensitive to one of the members of the group, who was trying to talk about himself, and introduced my own agenda. This wounded him quite deeply and he said some things about me which came from quite deep inside him and which left me reeling. An exchange followed between us which cut out the others, who began to look out of their depth and very uncomfortable. The group closed with the issues unresolved. Typically I pretended that I was OK and did the masculine thing. I remember walking out into the car park and getting into our separate cars. One of the group shouted out to me, 'Are you sure you are all right?' 'No problem,' I replied in a suitably macho way and drove off but I was devastated by the other man's assessment of me even though I knew he was angry at the time. On getting home I was unable to stop myself talking to Helen about it. These things were very painful and led us to adopt another principle which was about 'group closure'. We decided that we would try never to leave the group with an unfinished agenda or if we did, we would try and meet soon afterwards to resolve the issue. At the next meeting we were able to resolve the issue together and I was able to see that maybe some of the things that had been said to me were true.

From time to time we talked about the fact that we had no task and no purpose; we were unused to this and mistook the lack of a stated objective for a meaning. On one occasion we began to talk about whether the group should fold, partly because we were so used to having criteria by which to judge projects that we were unused to just meeting and talking. I don't want to give the impression that all the conversation was deep, sometimes it was riotous, the humour in the group was quite wicked. We could also have sessions where we completely missed the point and could not find a way in to any kind of satisfactory discussion. One evening we spent half the time talking about cars; none of us was interested in cars and we felt we were fulfilling all the masculine stereotypes by doing it.

Later on we discussed why the group had meant so much

to us. We felt that in the rest of our lives we were to some extent 'performing' but this was a group in which we could be ourselves because we knew we could be accepted. We all felt that we had changed because of the group. We felt none of the guilt that other men's groups had reported and who were wrestling with feminist accusations of what men had done to women. We really didn't know anything about that and had no experience between us of having been in such a group before. I remember on one occasion being surprised in a communion service by the warmth of the hug I was given by one member of the group at the sharing of the peace. I was surprised because he was not given to physical gestures of affection and it meant a great deal. On another occasion I was speaking at a conference at which one of them was present. I felt very bad about the quality of my input and told the group how I felt. It was a member of the men's group who came to me afterwards and was extremely encouraging and warm. It meant so much because I knew that if he had felt it was going badly he would have told me.

Occasionally we came up against limits in the group and were uncertain of what to do. One of the group became very ill and was taken to hospital. It transpired afterwards that all of us had thought about phoning the others up and visiting him but we did not do it, neither did we visit him individually. I think he was quite hurt by this, although he expressed it in the group later as being 'interesting', really I think he felt betrayed and we felt very bad that we had let him down, especially as he was the single member of the group and the rest of us had been too concerned with busy, family life.

A Growing Friendship

We had been meeting without reminder regularly on the same day of the month but had not met outside those times, although we were friends outside the group. This brought out an interesting discussion on the limits to the group and I think it was at that point that we realised that we were becoming a circle of friends who happened to meet once a month rather than a men's group. The idea of the group had been an instrument to bring us to deepened friendships which was what we all wanted. This is interesting in the light of everything that has been said so far about masculinity. Nobody said at the outset, 'Let's all become intimate friends,' this would have been seen as completely threatening and nobody would have come. We started by discussing the issues quite cold-bloodedly then moved on to discussing ourselves, but only within the context of the monthly meeting. At present we are at the stage of enjoying our friendships together. We now meet in a different venue which is far more comfortable and quiet. We have been out for a meal together on several occasions just to enjoy one another's company and the friendships between us mean that we are now seeing each other more often between the meetings. Nevertheless the group remains the place where we come together to 'do the business'.

On some occasions the group met at a mobile home in the countryside owned by one of the group. The first time we went there one member could not make it but the change of venue made an extraordinary difference to the group. We arrived in the early evening and were completely relaxed after a long journey in the car to get there. I slumped into the corner of the caravan and began to read a John Irving novel which I found there. Two other people started playing on the swings in the playground outside. After a cup of tea we wandered over a cornfield to the local pub which did superb Yorkshire pudding with beef stew. We walked into the pub rather raucously, surprising other people who were having a quiet meal, and discovered to our delight that the pub sported a sixties juke-box which was full of golden oldies ranging from the Beatles to the Seekers. We spent the evening pumping the juke-box full of money and reminiscing about what we were doing when we first heard the records. A game of darts followed which introduced one of the few elements of competitiveness into the group.

After gloriously stodgy Yorkshire pudding we wandered back over the cornfield commenting on the resemblance to an advert for Walker's crisps, which was on the television at that time and which starred five little boys in a cornfield. I think that was about the measure of it. We felt released to have fun and later described it as the 'famous five' night. When we got back to the caravan one of the members decided to ask for 'the floor'. Immediately people became attentive and it turned out that he was really struggling with something that had come up in the previous month. The problem was quite serious and it took some time to sort it out but at the end of the day we were encouraging and he was relieved. Somehow the atmosphere was retained. It is marvellous how trust relaxes people. At no point did the atmosphere become 'heavy'. The same blend of events happened on the second visit to the caravan when we were all present. It has now become a highlight of the group's life.

One other event stands out over this period. I went out to lunch one day with the friend who had spoken out in the caravan episode. We went to a wine bar which was full of yuppies. We ended up talking about masturbation which was not a subject that either of us had discussed with anybody else very often, if at all. We had a very animated and mutually affirming discussion. I think we must have been talking quite loudly because we got some sideways glances from other diners and their conversations seemed to dry up quite frequently. At the end of the lunch we had cleared the restaurant and were the only ones there. As we went back to where my car was parked he turned, looked me in the eye and said, 'I love you.' He didn't slap me on the back, avoid eye contact, and say, 'Y' know, I really love you mate,' which I could have taken with a kind of knock-about embarrassment. At that moment all the hair on the back of my neck stood up on end and I felt like throwing up. It didn't seem to be the kind of thing that men should say to one another and yet I felt very moved by the fact that he had said it in such a direct way. In true Woody Allen style I

replied, 'Well . . . um . . . (cough) that's really nice of you
. . . I'm not quite sure I can reciprocate in like manner yet(!)'
He waved it away, got into his car and we both drove off. It
later transpired that he completely forgot about the incident,
which wasn't a big thing for him at all. I drove home sweating
profusely. Was this what we meant by intimacy? If so I was
going to have problems.

Part of my problem was that at least half of me was British
and it wasn't a very co-operative half. But I had been firmly
put on the spot and didn't know how to respond. Since then
I have thought about this a great deal and have changed a
lot. Many women who hear the story think it is crazy and
very funny, and they can't see my problem, some men from
other cultures also feel the same, but it was a turning point
for me. Since then I have been much more open about being
affectionate with other men although I am always careful to
insert words like 'really', 'mate', and a slap on the back in
order to water it down. It is extraordinary that I spend so
much time thinking and talking about the love of God and
yet feel so embarrassed about this incident.

When we discussed it at the men's group there was sympathy from some though not from all. Men find it difficult
to express themselves in a personal language. This does not
mean that men do not enjoy intimacy but that many men
sidle up to intimacy while pretending that it is not there. To
explicitly state it is seen not to be playing the game. Like hap-
piness, intimacy often surprises us. We find ourselves enjoying it because of something else that is happening in our lives,
such as honesty, trust, or mutual disclosure but intimacy
begins to tyrannise us when it becomes our objective in life
to possess it. The great thing about my friend's outburst was
that he was stating something which already existed between
us, even though it was a bit of a surprise at the time.

Recent Developments
It is interesting to see the more recent developments in the
group. At the start of the group we had decided not to

pray together or to read the Bible. I think we were all a little depressed about some of the games that Christians can sometimes play around prayer and the Bible in groups. At the end of two years we were discussing the need to talk about spirituality again. It was as if we had cleared the decks of pretence and knew that we were now ready to pray together if that was appropriate. Using the Bible was still a problem because some of us were conceptual thinkers while others were visual thinkers. Some were 'into theology', others were bored by it, and so the Bible itself could have become an area where people exerted power over one another through knowing it better and playing silly games. At the end of two years though, I think we can all say that it has been a deeply spiritual experience. I speak for myself when I say that it has been one of the most formative experiences in my Christian pilgrimage.

A second development has been a renewed willingness to confront. At the outset we were accepting and affirming and we still are, but because of that foundation we are beginning to give each other permission to be more confrontational. It is all very well to discover the fellowship of sinners but at the end of the day we are all deeply committed Christians who want to see each other grow as Christians; blanket acceptance will not do. We still believe that unconditional love is vital to discovering Christian freedom but confrontation is part of love. If I am unconditionally committed to my brother then I must 'speak the truth in love'. The problem we have in the Church is that so often we confront each other without the basis of that loving acceptance, or we go to the other extreme and refuse to confront one another because we are scared of what people might say to us. It is only when all thoughts of power and superiority have been banished by an awareness of our failure that there comes a freedom to do this.

The last development which is interesting has been a sense of ease in the presence of silence. In the early days of the group we were very uncomfortable with silence. Somebody would make a comment to try and kick off the conversation again. We talked about silence and went through a period where we thought it was a good thing to be silent but were very self-conscious about the fact that we were 'enjoying silence'. Recently we have relaxed and no longer feel the need to fill a gap. I presume many groups enjoy silence in this way but I have not been in many of them, perhaps it was me who always interrupted the silence. What it does is bring a sense of contentment into the group. It is another sign that we are not trying to perform or prove ourselves as men in front of one another and is very welcome.

Lessons to be Learned

It is important to reflect on this experience. I often mentioned the men's group when speaking in public about masculinity and, although I felt that I could not say very much about it, there was an obvious hunger among other men to be part of such a group. It is important to note that nobody in the group I attend feels that our way of doing things is normative. You cannot clone friendship. I do not think I can set up a pattern for establishing men's groups around the country which will then automatically enjoy the kind of friendship which we have enjoyed. Men are very different from one another and must find their own way but I do want to suggest that such small groups can be a help in fostering friendship. Much of the work among men that I have attended in the Church is part of the problem we are facing and not part of a solution. Many large men's groups exist up and down the country within local churches; they have meetings or breakfasts at which a sports personality or a well-known speaker addresses a gathering. It is very rare for men to talk personally together over a sustained period of time and yet this is what must happen if men are to rediscover themselves as men and not just see themselves as people. If this happens then the Church will be more whole, as men are willing to see some of their own bias and prejudice arising out of their own sense of masculinity rather than foisting it on others, including women, as being normative for all humanity. There is also competitiveness and insecurity among men in the Church as well as friendship and fellowship. We need not only to talk about grace but allow the experience of it to change our lives. Perhaps a number of pastoral problems in the Church would significantly decrease if people felt more accepted within a loving community.

Discussing Spirituality

I think that the group was important because we were all fed up with pretence. We had all been members of church fellowship groups, some of which had been extremely helpful and important to us. But we had gone to such groups with real needs only to find ourselves sharing with others at the level of 'My dog has fleas, pray for it'. At other times, even in Christian circles, we had felt under pressure to put up a false facade rather than relaxing and being the people we really were.

We had all witnessed men using spiritual things to wear still more masks. We had seen pressure put on people to believe things that were suspect, and people get excited about religious trends and 'great leaders' that came to nothing or produced splits in the church. There was an instinctive permission between us to leave the familiar landmarks behind. We wanted to find bedrock – something that we could build solidly on.

When we finally did come back to talk about spirituality as a subject on its own, after a couple of years, we found that we had developed the honesty and trust between us to be able to talk about what we really thought rather than saying what we thought would sound spiritual. In the intervening two years all of us had found strength spiritually through the love and honesty of the group. We had got rid of the need to impress one another but it had taken two years, as it went very deep in us. Some were more reticent than others about the subject of spirituality but there was a real hunger for God between us even though we expressed it differently.

At the time of writing 500 men's groups are reputed(!) to be starting each week in America and one wonders what they are looking for and what they have found. In Britain things are different, as we are much more cautious, but there is work to be done among men in this country. Church growth statistics tell us men are not being brought into the Church. I think that this is partly due to the fact that the Church has been suffering from the same delusions as the world where masculinity is concerned. It is often assumed in these meetings that we all know who men are; men are people. They are not problematic, it is women who have the problem of finding an identity for themselves, but this is a mass delusion. The reason why men can be treated as a given at such meetings is because as a gender we do not have a clue about how to develop an appreciation of what it means to be a man and what masculinity is. This should be firmly on the agenda of such groups and is a potent topic which can bring together Christians and non-Christians who will find themselves struggling with the same issues.

The experience of the group also challenged the way I thought as a Christian. I had been brought up to start with the scriptures, work out theological principles and then apply them to issues raised in the world. I still do that, but in this case I found myself experiencing things and being changed by them but also wanting to illuminate what I was going through with the scriptures. The kind of issues which I found myself thinking about in front of an open Bible were the need for confession; the nature of grace; God's acceptance of me as I am; the betrayal of Jesus by a friend; the necessity of suffering in Christian pilgrimage; and the difference between fellowship and friendship. Instead of thinking in broad, abstract terms I found myself thinking about the life of Jesus much more and comparing things that had happened in the group with stories about Jesus and his disciples. I found myself asking how he felt when

Judas betrayed him, why he wept at the grave of his friend Lazarus knowing that he was the resurrection and the life, or why he had to learn obedience through what he suffered when he was the truth about God.

Truth and Freedom

Christianity draws a direct line between truth and freedom. Jesus told his disciples that they would know the truth and the truth would set them free. (John 8:32) It is one of the characteristics of truth that it liberates people. All kinds of people who are Christians are struggling with various problems in their lives but do not share them with others because they do not think it is acceptable to do so. It is as if we think that having problems is somehow 'letting the side down' or even letting God down. So we continue to propagate an image of ourselves which does not help others because it just means that we come over as yet another person who appears to have got everything right. What a relief it is to meet somebody who is humble enough to admit their struggles.

Where people succumb to a false view of themselves or where people communicate a falsehood people are placed in bondage. This is true even when the picture conveyed is romantic or sentimental, such as in a sentimental view of the family or some illustration from the pulpit which makes people laugh. Anything which is not true places people in bondage. Only the truth liberates. If men are still powerful within society but are communicating norms which are false then the society is damaged as a result.

There are only two ways of resolving the situation. Either men lay down their power so that they do not necessarily affect others by their false picture of manhood, or they become liberated by the truth themselves. In this book I have suggested that these two things are in fact one and the same. The liberating truth which men need to put into effect is the laying down of power in order to be themselves. Men do not have more problems than women but because of their power the pervasiveness of this falsehood causes additional and unnecessary problems throughout society, not only for women but for men and children too.

In chapter four I looked at the connection between gender power and the masks which men wear leading to fragmentation. This is one of the causes of men being out of touch with themselves. The choice for men is either to allow one's true self to come out or to continue the pretence which is necessary for gender power to continue. This chapter has explored another side of the same argument. The connection made here has not been between power and wholeness but between truth and freedom. In the atmosphere of trust in the men's group we were able to bring the inside of our lives and the outside of them together. From that moment there existed people who knew as much about us as we could find to say about ourselves. This meant that the love and acceptance offered was not a love and acceptance of a projected self, which was designed to be acceptable, but of me as I am. This resulted for all of us in the same feeling that 'it is OK to be me'. But I suspect that if this were to be put into theological language it would be about the real meaning of repentance and grace.

The experience of this particular group is not one which can be cloned or repeated. Every group of men will be different and needs to be different. But I hope that small groups of men will meet together as friends and open up to one another. I also hope that the experience of this group might be helpful to them when they do that.

We now move on in the book to look directly at the person of Jesus Christ. The focus of this book is that Christ is the key to the understanding of what it means to be a man. This whole debate revolves around Jesus Christ in a way in which few other debates do. It is only as we discover the nature of friendship again and the liberation which comes through Christ that we will have something to offer those men who are still entrapped by masculinity, though they think they are free men.

QUESTIONS

1. Men can talk to women about the consequences of masculinity but need to talk to other men about the experience of masculinity. Is this true?
2. Would you like to be a member of a men's group? Why?
3. Is talking about yourself the same as 'navel-gazing'?
4. Do you think that men suffer from a gulf between the internal reality and their external image? What are the costs to such men of becoming whole?
5. Do you fear intimacy with other men?
6. What is the difference (if any) between 'fellowship' and 'friendship'?

8

THE ULTIMATE HERO?

Some men may admit that they grieve the passing of spirituality, transcendence and worship. They may acknowledge that they are stuck in a life which has become satisfied with functional and material things, and are bored with a promiscuous sexuality which they have used like a drug to distract them for too long. Why do men not seem to be able to see Jesus as a person they want to emulate? The problem is that many men feel that Christ has been taken over by institutional religion. They cannot see him as a hero because he has been hijacked by a subculture with which they do not identify. It is essential for such men to realise that the Church does not own Jesus Christ. There are some churches that will be judged by Christ for what they have done to him. Nevertheless there are still churches, and many more than some people would imagine, who follow Christ with integrity and who can be a source of new life and a new start for those who are willing to be humble enough to know that they need it.

Mentor and Hero

Jesus is both mentor and hero.[1] He is a hero because his life is a model from which we can learn. It was his claim that he did not just come to teach the truth but that he was the truth in his own person. Everything he did and said was a revelation of who God is and an expression of perfect humanity. We cannot go wrong if we focus our lives on such a person. I find myself asking, 'What would Jesus do in this situation? How would he respond to this person?' For me Jesus is the ultimate hero. He is fully human and fully divine and is therefore a bridge by which I can understand both. If I want to know about God I ask, 'What is Jesus like?' If I want to grow as a human being I ask, 'How can I be more like Jesus?'

Jesus is also mentor. He is not a dead, historic figure. The evidence for the resurrection is so compelling that it long ago led me to believe that Jesus Christ is risen from the dead and has ascended into heaven. He told his disciples that he would send the Holy Spirit to come alongside them and be with them in their pilgrimage to be Christians in the world. He promised that the Holy Spirit would be 'in them' and that there would be no difference between the character and mission of the Holy Spirit and his own presence with them. Christians are not people who read ancient books and try to copy the person described within them. Christians are people who are willing to accept the presence of the invisible Holy Spirit in their lives and have exchanged the tyranny of the sinful self for the liberating presence of Jesus Christ. This means that becoming a Christian is about entering into a relationship with Jesus. He may be invisible but he is constantly present with each of his followers. Prayer is a conversation with him through which we become more like him.

Identifying with Jesus

All kinds of people have difficulty in identifying with the person of Jesus and this difficulty is directly related to the kinds of people we identify with in our lives. In his work on masculinity, Joseph Pleck noted that when comparing themselves with various types of 'ideal men' or asked to describe the qualities most admired in a man many men are more likely to identify with minimum acceptable fulfilment rather than maximum ideal performance.[2]

So if men were given several different kinds of masculinities to choose from and were asked which they identified with the most, they may well identify with the sports-loving, competitive kind of man. It is easier to identify with this sort of man rather than some ideal person who is sensitive, nurturing and loving among other things. He may be low on the list of ideals but he is readily identifiable as a real man, according to the popular myths about what it takes to be a man. There may be more of him around walking the streets than men who have all kinds of other traits which might be 'feminine'. Nevertheless, such a man may well be seen as ideal even though fewer men could identify with him themselves. At the more 'realistic' end of the spectrum male norms are more easily recognisable as stereotypes. Pleck comments, '. . . it demands less of a man to be competitive or interested in male sports than it does to be intelligent or sensitive. Many men, therefore, spend their time competing with each other or watching sports rather than trying to be intelligent or sensitive.'[3]

Pleck notes that at the higher end of the spectrum the ideal man and women share many traits, some of which are sex-neutral and some of which are usually considered to be a characteristic of the other sex, for instance, 'intelligence, sensitivity to the needs of others, warmth and romanticism'.[4] One could imagine that at the very top of such a list would be somebody who ideally combined all the desirable characteristics of men and women. He would be capable of expressing anger but very nurturing. Strong in a crisis yet also vulnerable. We may agree that this would be an ideal person but would men own him as a 'real' man? Would anybody identify with him personally?

If we take Pleck's conclusions on board this has implications for us in the way we view the person of Jesus. All heroes contain something within their lives which is different from our experience and which we wish to emulate. It is the fact that Jesus is not in the same state as we are in that makes him a hero and a mentor. As Christians we make Jesus the norm for our lives, the person on whom we model our lives. It is this recognition of the gulf between the person of Jesus as an ideal and our own situation that makes Jesus so attractive. It is by comparison with him and his perfection that we can see our own problems. Discipleship has always been about following a person from whom one could learn and whose life could be emulated.

Yet if this was all that Christianity was about then it would make us feel very guilty because all Jesus would do for us would make us feel inadequate. The gulf between my current state as a human being and Jesus's perfect expression of humanity makes me want to emulate and follow him, but at the same time threatens me because I feel I could never be like that. If Jesus is a just a role model, and a unique role model at that, then we may worship from afar but we will feel guilty and inadequate because of the impossibility of being like him. I might even feel that he is 'cheating' since he is God and I am not.

The remarkable thing about the Christian faith is that this problem of the gulf between us and God, is recognised. At the heart of Christianity is the idea that God closes the gap between us and Christ in two ways. Firstly, in becoming a man Jesus gave up the privileges of being God. Everything that he faced in his life he faced by drawing on the same resources as are available to me. The story of the temptations is the story of this denial by Jesus of his potential for drawing on powers I do not have.

The writer to the Hebrews talks about Jesus as our high priest saying that, '. . . we do not have a high priest who is unable to sympathise with our weaknesses, but we have one who has been tempted in every way, just as we are – yet was without sin.'[5] Elsewhere Hebrews talks of Jesus being made 'perfect through suffering', and that he 'shared our humanity'. It also says that 'he had to be made like his brothers in every way'.[6] Paul writes powerfully in his letter to the church at Philippi about Christ 'making himself nothing' rather than holding on to equality with God.[7]

But if the first way the Bible closes the gulf between Christ and us is by God coming towards us, in Christ, the second way is through changing those people whose desire is to follow and emulate Christ. God does this by placing the Holy Spirit, who is Christ's invisible presence, within the lives of those who want to be Christ's disciples. This gives such people a choice where there was no choice. At every point in their lives they can choose the path of self or yield their self in favour of the Holy Spirit, creating a Christ-likeness in their lives. The very point which formerly was an indication of a gulf is now a starting point for hope and a lifelong pilgrimage. It is easy to see that if a person does not even believe in God then this view of human change seems quite ridiculous. Such a person must view Christ from a distance wondering how Christians can claim that they are becoming 'like him'. This is not a claim which is arrogant since Christians have contributed nothing of their own to it. It is due to God's initiative in Christ towards us. How different this is from guiltily worshipping an unattainable Christ from afar!

The more like Christ a person is, the more they become their true selves. The price of this is that they cannot hang on to their old self with all its sin as well as trying to emulate Christ. They must turn their back on the one in order to be filled with the other. This is what the Bible means by repentance and this is why it is expressed as new life or a new beginning.

Maleness and Masculinity Again

So who was Jesus? Certainly he was a man. He had to be either male or female. There are many conventional arguments for why Jesus was a man, which are important. For instance, if he had been a woman in the culture of first-century Israel, he could not have been a teacher and would not have been heard. According to New Testament scholar Mary Evans the position and status of women in every sphere had dramatically declined in Jesus's day even compared with the situation in the Old Testament.[7]

Jesus was born as a man and lived in a patriarchal society. He was loved and followed by his disciples. Nicodemus came to ask him about salvation. He had the power to heal, to exorcise, and even when the shadow of the crucifixion fell across his trial he was unafraid of confronting Pilate. At significant points in his ministry, such as after the feeding of the 5,000, people sought to make him king over them. Yet he constantly rejected this option, telling his disciples that they were not to lord it over each other but to become the servants of others.

What can we learn from the behaviour of Jesus? He could have been presented, against the background of a male-dominated society, as a man who had power over women.[9] He always had the option of taking power in a typically masculine sense. He could have behaved like the other men of his day, who daily thanked God in their prayers, 'Praise be to God that he has not made me a woman.' In Jesus's day, women were subordinate to men and rabbis ignored women in public, even if they were relatives.[10] For several days every month women were especially outcast during their periods, and a man committing adultery offended against his lover's husband but not his own wife.

The chronicles of ways in which women were oppressed, ignored and insulted in the time of Jesus go on and on. Although he was human Jesus was utterly distinctive in his attitude towards both men and women. He accepted the touch of a woman with a history of ten years of menstrual problems who was 'unclean'. He talked, alone, to a Samaritan prostitute at a well about the most intimate details of her life. He accepted the adoration of a woman who poured ointment over him and then wiped his feet with her hair. He constantly rejects in each of his dealings with women the possibility of acting like other men of his day. This was the difference between their masculinity and his humanity. Jesus did not just disassociate himself from the oppressive patriarchy of his day, he completely subverted it by his own behaviour, forming a kingdom which upheld completely different values.

In her book, *Is God the Only Reliable Father?*, Diane Tennis talks of the maleness of Jesus as having a positive value. Jesus calls his followers to do as he did. She states:

> Unlike women, he did not have to be a servant. He had power and access to power . . . [he] modelled in his own being a dramatic assault on male privilege. Who but a man could credibly teach and model such a revolution in relationships by giving up power? *Only a man could do that, because only men had power* [my emphasis].[11]

Here is a powerful and compelling picture of why Jesus came as a man. It is not just that he would not have been listened to if he were a woman. *It is that only as a man could he show what God was like in his willingness to give up his own life to serve others.* Women could not give up power for they had none and if they did have some power, because they had been born into a powerful family, it was an exception. But the power which Jesus laid down symbolised the power which men of his day wielded over the whole society.

The heart of the Gospel is about grace and grace is about giving up power to empower others. It is about being loved by God even though we are unworthy of that love. It is about being accepted as a child of God when a moment before we were cursing his name. There is no higher encouragement to be had or privilege bestowed than those which are rooted in an understanding of what God's grace means. The cross is a triumph because on it Jesus voluntarily gave his life away and he calls his followers to do the same.

We can now see why the life of Christ is a focus for this book. The experience of the men's group, the discussion of power, and the call to men to give up gender power in order to be whole are all brought sharply into focus when we consider what lessons we can learn from Christ and his behaviour as a man. One of the most distressing trends in the Church has been the tendency to ignore the life of Christ as a model for our behaviour. In the name of Christ wars have been waged, terrorism has been carried out and people have been exploited, yet behaviour which is unlike Christ's does not deserve the name 'Christian'.

Male But Not Masculine

It is very important to understand that there are certain things in this interpretation that we are affirming. Firstly, we are saying that Jesus is a man. Secondly, he is male in that he shares the primary sexual characteristics and other givens about maleness which enable him to share our humanity. He is of the male sex but not the masculine gender. This is of vital importance when we consider that the majority of the issues we have already discussed surround the interpretations and values associated with being masculine. Jesus does not wear the masks of masculinity as men since him have done. He does not have a division between his inner self and his outer image, nor was he trying to prove himself or be a successful man according to the criteria of his day. Jesus subverts masculinity and in doing so puts flesh on the idea of giving up power in order to be whole, or living according to the truth which makes us free to be ourselves. He did not draw on specific ways of being a man which were available in his day and age.

All too often we use our inadequate concepts of manliness and masculinity to judge others. We do it to Jesus. We ask what kind of man he was and implicitly use our culturally-bound patterns of behaviour to assess his 'performance'. On the contrary, it is his behaviour and his person that judges every inadequate stereotype of masculinity through which men interpret their own behaviour. Because he is the truth, his life provides the basis for all interpretations. He did not need to understand his own behaviour with reference to some group stereotype, for he derived his identity and his security from his relationship with the Father. He is the norm, he is the perfect expression of God's will for humanity, it is we who are the deviations from the norm. He came to demonstrate our full humanity but did so acknowledging that that humanity has to be expressed either as a man or as a woman.

Until this point we have been focusing on the masculinity of Christ by comparing his behaviour with the behaviour of men in a patriarchal society. But there is another point to be made which focuses on the maleness of Christ, something he shares with all other men. The particularity of the maleness of Jesus was sufficient for him to be able to express through it the full humanity which we seek to emulate. This is important in itself because there are many men who believe that men were not made to display those characteristics which our society considers feminine. They talk of 'the feminised male' with derision, believing that men are meant to display aggression, ambition, autonomy and control, but not tenderness, vulnerability or other emotions. If Jesus is a norm for men then he must give us hope that being a man is a sufficient basis for displaying everything that is associated with being human. There is a further point to be made. This is not only true of men since we know from the creation narrative that women were (and are) equal with men in the sight of God, then their femaleness is equally sufficient in order to express the perfection of humanity.

I have already suggested that masculinity and femininity are words which denote characteristics which are open to expression by men and women but which are usually associated with maleness and femaleness. If it were not possible for men to weep, be gentle or nurturing then the portrayal of Jesus as doing these things would be a cruel taunt. If it were not *desirable* that men should do or be these things then the person of Jesus would be a deviation from the norm for men. Similarly for women; if women are not to learn strength, courage or leadership qualities from Jesus then his life cannot be a model for them, or else they end up dissecting his life to see what is appropriate to learn from Jesus in the light of other criteria, based on traditional gender stereotypes. The fact is that Jesus is the model for men and women because all of the human characteristics he displays are available for men and women. Here is Jesus restoring God's initial vision of a shared humanity in which men and women share in a common humanity.

It is because of Jesus that Christians have hope when there is a call for men to change, for we believe that through the work of the Holy Spirit it is possible for us to become like him. Indeed we go further, claiming that as we mature as Christians we are becoming like him, through the influence of the Holy Spirit. This applies to both men and women, but it is significant that because of the incarnation this is not some ethereal transformation which has nothing to do with our bodies or our humanity. As men follow Christ they will see themselves change.

Women have argued with me that their experience is different from that of Christ. Christ is male and they are female. They are affected by their biology through having periods, becoming pregnant and going through the menopause. Christ experienced none of these things but they are events which are so important in the life of women that some women, though not all, feel that this constitutes a barrier to identifying with Christ.

The first thing to say in response is that they are right in saying that Christ did not and could not experience these things. But this is not just true of these particular things, it is also true of people who experience old age, marital break-up, illness, or of being a parent. For these are all experiences which Christ did not have. Does this mean that we can only identify with Christ when his experience accords with ours? This would, when pushed to its ultimate absurdity, mean that I could only identify with Christ if I was a thirty-year-old, Jewish, ex-carpenter. It is not in this sense that we identify with Christ.

The meaning of the incarnation is that Christ shared our humanity by living his own human life with all the detail of the incidents which happened to him. The important factor is that all his life Christ was subject to the same frailty, temptation and finiteness that we struggle with in our lives. Because God is 'one of us' we can know that when we are rejected or suffering, even if the particular incident we are going through was not paralleled in the life of Christ, he also experienced rejection and suffering and is therefore able to 'sympathise with us in our weaknesses' (Hebrews 4:15).

Despite this insight it is nevertheless true that some women feel that the maleness of Christ does constitute a problem for them because their experience of life is tied up with their bodies. It may even be true, because of the experience of women, that the fact that Christ suffered pain, betrayal and marginalisation means that women identify in some respects *more* with Christ than men. I have no intention here of submerging women's experience under the phrase 'Christ shares our common humanity', but I do not feel that the answer to this question lies in any lack in Christ's experience. Nor do I feel that women's experience gives any credence to either the divinisation of Mary or the advent of goddess worship.

There are senses in which both men and women find the behaviour of Jesus difficult to cope with. Many men have problems with Christ's rejection of masculinity because they see it as a betrayal of what men should stand for. It is important to recognise the struggle which some women have with the maleness of Christ as restricting his experience in areas they find important, and not to brush it under the carpet as an embarrassment because we cannot conveniently explain it away. If I attempted to do so, as a man, I would be using the ultimate prerogative of patriarchy by explaining that what goes on inside women's bodies is not significant theologically, and I refuse to do that.

What Kind of Man?

How does Christ relate to the models of new man and wild man which we have already discussed? Certainly Robert

Bly's analysis of the wild man falls short. You cannot plunder the person of Christ as if you can have bits of him but not others. You cannot say, 'I'll have his wisdom and love but reject his moral purity and prayer life.' Following Christ means that we decide that he is to be our hero and mentor, then it is all or nothing. We also have to be honest that it is Christ we are following. We have to name him rather than talking about a formless 'spirituality' all the time.

It is easy to see now how Jesus is the person that those who seek to be new men and those who seek to be wild men are looking for. Both strengths are found within Jesus. As an illustration take Jesus washing the feet of the disciples, recorded in John 13:1–17. John tells us that before Jesus performed this act of service, usually performed by the lowest servant in the household, 'Jesus knew that the Father had put all things under his power' (verse 3). At that point Jesus knew he was the most powerful person in the world. He didn't have to prove himself. Because he was secure in his heavenly Father he could adopt the menial task of a servant. Insecurity leads to people trying to prove themselves all the time, but true security means that they can serve others and not feel threatened.

Or take another example from John's gospel. In John 2:12–17 John portrays Jesus coming to the temple in Jerusalem for the Jewish Passover. He finds people sitting in the courtyards of the temple exchanging money and selling animals. He makes an impromptu whip and drives them out, accusing them of making his 'Father's house' into a market. This is not 'Gentle Jesus, meek and mild', this is Jesus in a fury against the desecration of the sacred. Here is a wild man. Here is a warrior fighting on behalf of transcendent purposes.

Because of this heroic act Christian men can hold their head up high. As so often happens something that a minute before looked like a disaster has now become an opportunity. The very recognition of our distorted world-view becomes a sign of the restoration work which God has begun in us.

The realisation that we, as men, do have power means that we have a task to accomplish. The motivation which Christ gives to move from power to love leads us to look for opportunities to serve others, laying down our power in order that their lives might benefit. There is, after all, another way of being a man. After the foot-washing episode Jesus makes the practice a model for his disciples to follow. 'Now that I, your Lord and Teacher, have washed your feet, you also should wash one another's feet. I have set you an example that you should do as I have done for you.' (John 13:14,15).

Matthew records Jesus as talking about authority after the mother of Zebedee's sons had come to him to ask that her sons could sit on his right and left in his kingdom. These were places of privilege. Jesus asked them whether they were willing to suffer with him ('drink from my cup') but then denies them the privilege asked for because it is in the gift of 'the Father'. He comments that they have the wrong model of authority. They had seen officials lording it over others but, 'Not so with you. Instead, whoever wants to become great among you must be your servant, and whoever wants to be first must be your slave – just as the Son of Man did not come to be served, but to serve, and to give his life as a ransom for many.' (Matthew 20:26–8)

When Jesus lays down his life for others, does he appear to be 'a wimp'? Should men, who have followed the masculinities of our age for so long, be frightened of what others will think of them if they give up all that they can retain only by power? In Jesus the answer is clear. Is Jesus meek? Meekness is the gentleness of the strong. Is Jesus a servant? Only someone secure as the Son of God can be set free to be a servant.

Following the example of Jesus, service is at its most remarkable when the one who serves could have power over the one he is serving. Meekness is at its most remarkable when the one who exhibits it is so obviously strong and powerful. All kinds of men, whether they see themselves as macho or aspire to be chief executives or generals in the army, can become more whole by openly laying down their lives, taking off the masks of acceptable masculinities, and becoming like Jesus. It is only in him that we see, in both his person and his behaviour, someone who transcends masculinities which can only exist by holding on to power.

The Two Johns[12]

Jesus had many men and women around him. Several of them seemed to be real characters: Peter, impetuous but loyal, except on one occasion when his courage failed him; Nathaniel, a person who was guileless; Mary, who sat at the feet of Jesus and listened to his teaching. But two men stand out, both called John. One was John the Beloved, the other was John the Baptist.

John the Baptist was a wild man if ever there was one. He came like an Elijah preaching in the desert of Judea. His message was 'Repent, for the kingdom of heaven is near' (Matthew 3:2). His clothes were made of camel hair, he had a leather belt round his waist and his food was locusts and wild honey. His impact was remarkable. People streamed out to him from everywhere. They confessed their sins and he baptised them as a sign of repentance and a new beginning. Like Jesus he had no time for the Pharisees and Sadducees who were the religious authorities and had tied the people up in knots with their religious rules and regulations. To them he preached judgment (Matthew 3:7–10).

John the Baptist pointed the way forward for Jesus. He announced that one was coming who would baptise with the Holy Spirit rather than water. Despite his fiery nature and uncompromising stance he was humble. 'Jesus,' he said, 'is more powerful than I am and I am not fit to carry his sandals.' (Luke 3:16) John saw Jesus as one who would come in judgement, and later from prison he sent disciples to ask Jesus whether in fact he was the one he had prophesied. Jesus told them to go back and tell John what they had seen. 'The blind receive sight, the lame walk, those who have leprosy are cured, the deaf hear, the dead are raised, and the good news is preached to the poor.' (Matthew 11:5)

John would know from this that Jesus was indeed God, come to save his people. Of John the Baptist Jesus said:

> What did you go out into the desert to see? A reed swayed by the wind? If not, what did you go out to see? A man dressed in fine clothes? No, those who wear fine clothes are in kings' palaces. Then what did you go out to see? A prophet? Yes, I tell you, and more than a prophet. . . . I tell you the truth: Among those born of women there has not risen anyone greater than John the Baptist. (Matthew 11:7–9, 11)

John was unafraid of the consequences of speaking the truth and had challenged Herod about his sexual conduct. Herodias, his unlawful wife, had John beheaded because of this. When Jesus heard the news he went in a boat to 'a solitary place'. He needed to grieve and to pray alone. John the Baptist was his cousin and a godly man. His loss was great. Jesus *admired* John and it is difficult not to feel respect for this unconventional prophet, who brought uncomfortable truths to the nation because he was passionately devoted to God. His ministry was public and his style was ascetic, yet the crowds flocked out to hear him.

We get frightened that people will dislike us if we break rank with the crowd. But we do need people who care more about what God thinks of them than the adulation of others. We have already seen that one of the characteristics of truth is that it liberates people and that is why the people flocked out to hear John. They were fed up with their sin and they were ready to repent. The same is true of our age which has had years of materialism and sexual licence. So many people feel lost and let down by it all. But where are the voices 'crying in the wilderness'?

Jesus *admired* John the Baptist but he *loved* John the Beloved as an intimate friend. John humbly refers to himself throughout his gospel as 'the disciple whom Jesus loved' (John 13:23; 19:26; 20:2; 21:7, 20). Later, writing his three letters, love was his theme. At the last supper he tells us that he was leaning on Jesus as they reclined around the table. He was the one who leant his head on Jesus's chest and asked quietly, 'Who is it, Lord?' when Jesus said that one of his disciples would betray him. On the cross Jesus places his mother in the care of John and from that moment she lived in his household. John's thoughtful and deep spirituality shines from the pages of his writings. One commentator said of his gospel that it was like a pool in which a child may wade and an elephant may swim! Here was a man who was completely immersed in his love for Jesus.

John the Beloved is a very different character to John the Baptist, yet he too lived a life whose fulcrum was Jesus. The fact that Jesus admired John the Baptist didn't stop him loving John the Beloved. They had very different pilgrimages, very different insights and callings. One of the things about following Jesus is that he doesn't coerce people to pretend to be different than they are. The Jesus who is the redeemer is also the one who created us to be the person we are. He is buying back his original vision for us. Both Johns found their fulfilment in him but they were very different men.

Some men are on a pilgrimage from the cheap masculinities which the world offers to the wholeness that can only be found in following Jesus Christ. Some will go the way of John the Beloved. In some senses he is similar to some of the aspirations of the new men in our day. He is an intimate, a friend, a man obsessed with love. Others feel the stirrings of the wild man. The character of John the Baptist resonates with their calling. Yet many of them need to discover the journey of John the Beloved before they try out their calling to be a wild man. Robert Bly quoted a beautiful Celtic proverb in his book which struck me forcefully, 'Never give a sword to a man who can't dance.'

The Apostle Paul, in his early life when he was known

as Saul, was a good example of a man who had a sword but couldn't dance. He persecuted the Church and tortured Christians because of their faith in Jesus Christ. At the end of his life he acknowledged the extent of the change that came over him when he met Christ on the road to Damascus:

. . . whatever was to my profit I now consider loss for the sake of Christ. What is more, I consider everything a loss compared to the surpassing greatness of knowing Christ Jesus my Lord, for whose sake I have lost all things. (Philippians 3:7, 8)

QUESTIONS

1. We know that Jesus identified with us but in what ways do men identify with Jesus?
2. 'Only as a man could Jesus show what God was like in his willingness to give up his own life to serve others.' How should men demonstrate that they are Christians, in practice?
3. The maleness of Jesus was a sufficient basis for him to express the whole range of human emotions. In what ways is this an encouragement for men?
4. Why do you think that the world outside the Church prefers to make other men its heroes rather than Jesus?
5. What difference would it make to the Church if every Christian emulated Jesus as the model for their own behaviour?
6. What response should men make to those women who cannot identify with Jesus because he is a man?

NOTES

1   I do not use the word 'hero' in this book in a Promethean sense of someone who exerts power and control but only

in the simple sense of a model we can admire and follow. In the Promethean sense Jesus is an anti-hero!

2. Joseph H. Pleck, *The Myth of Masculinity* (Cambridge, Massachusetts: MIT Press, 1981), p. 138.

3. Pleck, op. cit., p. 139.

4. Pleck, op. cit., p. 138.

5. Hebrews 4:15.

6. Hebrews 2:10; Hebrews 2:14; Hebrews 2:17.

7. Philippians 2:5–11.

8. Mary Evans, *Woman and the Bible* (Exeter: The Paternoster Press, 1983), p. 37.

9. For a discussion of this point and of the maleness of Jesus cf. Brian Wren, *What Language Shall I Borrow? God-Talk in Worship. A Male Response to Feminist Theology* (London: SCM, 1989), pp. 172–90.

10. Wren, op. cit., p. 175.

11. Diane Tennis, *Is God the Only Reliable Father?* (Philadelphia Penn.: Westminster Press, 1985), p. 95. Quoted in Wren, op. cit.

12. I am indebted to Father Richard Rohr for the idea behind this comparison.

9

MEN AND FATHERHOOD

Christ may have found his security in his heavenly father and he may have come to reveal to us what the father is like, but for many people the idea of the fatherhood of God does not fill them with a sense of comfort, quite the opposite. In recent years there has been an outcry about the absence of fathering in our society. Books by men and women talk of their longing for the love of their fathers. Germaine Greer's search for her father, recounted in her book *Daddy I Hardly Knew You*, is a case in point. At the same time voices are raised everywhere against the fatherhood of God. Our society had put God to death several decades ago, but now we attempt to exhume him to accuse him afresh of being a divine but distant replica of our earthly fathers. The result is confusion, not least for children.

This chapter examines whether there is any link between the pain men are expressing over their own fathers, with its concomitant confusion in their own fathering, and the rage against the parenting of a God who is meant to be irrelevant anyway. It seems God exists to be accused by us for our ills but is a delusion of those who find salvation, freedom or healing through Christ.

Times Change
In the eighteenth century men were still in the home, which was the sphere of production. The father might be a farmer

or a miller and his joys and his sorrow were part of family life. Boys growing up worked alongside their father, could be with him and learn from him. Fathers could pass on their trade to their children and by doing so feel that they were providing for their present needs, as well as training for the future. In the nineteenth century men became the distant breadwinner. Work became situated outside the home but although the father was absent his presence was still felt in the home. He was the ultimate sanction for childish misdemeanours. Mothers would promise to tell father when he got home about things that had been done wrong by the children. But the father had lost his role as the educator and the model for his children. This brought about a discontinuity for boys between father and son. Whereas girls growing up in the home had an ever-present mother from whom they could learn about motherhood and the role of the woman, boys not only had to break away from their mothers and develop their own masculine identity but had to do so when the father was not present.

In the modern period fathers continue to be absent, producing a tension between work and parenting. Some men so identify with their work that their partners plan their lives as if they are single parents. As a result women have become the chief executive of the home. It is an irony that men's work is accorded the greatest importance, yet women make decisions which have a powerful influence on the life of the next generation, shaping the minds of children as well as often making decisions about formal education, peer group, musical aptitude and much else. Over the last 300 years, then, the influence of the father has diminished. At the outset he was a powerful figure within the home. This then gave way to his absence from the home while retaining power within it. Recently he has become absent from the home without a great deal of influence within it. This means that many men now see fatherhood as providing the means to bring up the children rather than being directly involved with them to any great extent.

It is important to realise how big a shift in emphasis this is. Rosalind Miles, in her book on masculinity, comments:

> Historically fatherhood was the only parenting role of any weight or significance . . . to the child the father was god of its universe: he supervised its studies, punished its transgressions, guided it into an occupation and controlled its choice in marriage, the whole panoply of paternal power backed up by a battery of financial, legal and religious sanctions.[1]

The process of industrialisation also brought about the rise of social institutions which displaced paternal authority. Instead of education taking place within the home people began to look to institutions. The rise of the concept of social welfare meant that health and housing began to be provided by the State. Sociologist Christopher Lasch comments on the powerlessness of parents in the modern world who share their children with so many influences provided by society. The modern world is a far cry from the family of previous centuries, who were self-sufficient on their piece of land and who were largely autonomous as a family unit:

> The family economy has disappeared; children represent a financial liability rather than an asset, the school has taken over the family's educational function and the medical profession has assumed most of the responsibility for health care. These changes . . . leave parents in the position of 'executives in a large firm – responsible for the smooth co-ordination of the many people and processes that must work together to produce the final product.'[2]

For many men fatherhood has been reduced to being the breadwinner who provides the resources for the family to live on. When asked what drives them at work many men would respond in terms of providing for the family, yet in commuter households up and down the country men are mistaking a high standard of living for a high quality of relationship. In fact the opposite is true, they do not see their family and when they are at home they are tired and distracted.

The Age of Reason

From around 1750 to 1850 Europe was gripped by what historians have come to call the Age of Reason. One of the hallmarks of this period was the shrugging-off of dogmatic religion, which maintained a static society, and the elevation of reason as the means by which truth could be known. Scientific method replaced the exposition of scripture, and what was observable was seen to be the foundation of truth.

In the work of Immanuel Kant this ferment of change was applied to issues of gender. Kant distinguished between reason and intuition (or emotion) and labelled them masculine and feminine, but reason was seen as the means by which the new Enlightenment morality could be known. Reason depended on abstraction and conceptual thinking. Emotion was seen as an interruption of pure reason. Men derived a new authority from this since they alone were characterised as having the ability to discern what is morally right.

This became an impossible dilemma for women to get out of since objections to men were seen as intuitive or emotive. It is still the case in a row between a man and a woman that men often succumb to telling women that their position is not logical. Since the modern world is still convinced that logic and truth are similar, women find it difficult to break out of this corner into which they have been placed.

The cost of this was high for men as well. Men had to learn to exert control over their emotions in order to be thought of as reasonable. Fathers learned that they would fail to fulfil their obligations to their children if they got too emotionally involved with them. The absent father became the distant father. Maintaining respect within the home became synonymous with not showing their own feelings. Children who freely expressed their emotions had to learn to control themselves if they were to grow up into adulthood. This not only affected children but fathers as well, since if they were too demonstrative and 'emotional' towards their children this would affect their children's upbringing in an adverse way. Fathers learned not to be involved with their children.[3]

At the end of this process there was a double misunderstanding between the child and the father. The child does not identify with or understand what the father does outside the home, and therefore cannot admire the father or learn from him easily. But the father, who has become a problem-solver in the public sphere, treats the child as an extension of the world of problem-solving and management. Some men end up frustrated because this is seen as being insensitive and inappropriate rather than being loving and nurturing.

Modelling Masculinity for Boys

This combination of distance and distraction from fathers is devastating for all children of whatever gender. Girls may suffer in later life if they do not have strong, loving and affirming relationships with their fathers. Boys come up against particular problems. They are brought up by their mothers but have at some point to leave their mothers and identify with the world of men. The boy's mother is nurturing and loving but the boy's role model is the father whom he rarely sees. Many boys, as a result, learn about masculinity conceptually rather than copying an available person. They glean information from media images, peer group and the people to hand as to what 'being a man' is all about, but these things cannot replace a loving relationship with a mature man. As they grow up in a patriarchal society they realise that 'being a man' is meant to be a privilege. They learn that men are more important people than women. It becomes important to the boy to act more like a man and less like a woman, but he has many questions about what it does take to become a man. His insecurity is threatened, he tries harder to prove to himself and others that he really is a man. The only way he can find to do this is to cut himself off from the world of women and the way in which they express themselves. He must also deny any similar character traits in himself.

Christian psychologist Mary Stewart van Leeuwen comments on this:

> [We] can see how this masculine insecurity perpetrates itself from generation to generation. The under-fathered boy develops a fragile, ambivalent male identity; to compensate for this insecurity in adolescence and adulthood he distances himself from women and women's work, and what is most obviously women's work? Caring for young children. So he avoids nurturant contact with his own sons and unwittingly contributes to their development of insecure masculinity, dread of women, and the compensatory, woman-rejecting behaviour that can result.[4]

One of the problems which men have is that their models are derived from *not* being like a woman. However, there is another source which fathers can draw on which is invisible to a secularised society. Christian teaching claims that God is the Father from whom every family in heaven and on earth derives its name. In what ways has the loss of a vision of God's fatherhood contributed to the demise of the father in our society?

The Parenting of God

The Age of Reason displaced God and elevated rationality. Yet it is the parenting of God which is missing in all the debates on masculinity. How can we make a bridge between the practical problems of modern fathers and the ideas of Christian theology? The only bridge is the person of Jesus Christ, who was born a male human being but whose own security was derived from a relationship with his heavenly father, who was as physically invisible to him as God is to us today.

In the Old Testament God is called Father eleven times

but in the New Testament Jesus uses the word 'Father' of God 170 times and never uses another name of God when he prays. This word is not the austere distancing of Victorian fathers but is the Greek word *Abba*, which was the familiar and affectionate word which we would call 'Daddy'. It is very important to note that, whereas men are currently struggling with the distant father, the single most important characteristic of the relation of Jesus to his heavenly father is the intimacy which exists between them. *It is the intimacy between Jesus and the Father which is normative for all relationships between fathers and children today.*

Some people use their painful relationships with their fathers to reject God as Father but Jesus throws himself into the arms of the Father at the times of his greatest pain. In Mark's gospel Jesus wrestles with the will of God in the Garden of Gethsemane. He prays '*Abba*, Father, everything is possible for you. Take this cup from me. Yet not what I will, but what you will.' (Mark 14:36) This is one of the hardest moments in Jesus's ministry, he is struggling and groaning over the death which he is facing, yet at this moment – when he might be expected to curse the God who has sent him to die – he calls upon him with the most intimate affection. Jesus was not submitting to tyranny but expressing a deep trust in his father.

When he was on the cross Jesus cried out, echoing Psalm 22, 'My God, my God, why have you forsaken me?' Here Jesus calls on God without using the word 'father'. The sin of humanity had come upon him as had the darkness and suffering of the world. His last hours were marked by an intense awareness of *both* the closeness and the absence of his father. Luke shows us Jesus on the cross praying for those who tortured him, 'Father, forgive them' (Luke 23:34). His last words in Luke's account are spoken to his father: 'Father, into your hands I commit my spirit.' (Luke 23:46) Jesus dies, a victim of injustice and torture, experiencing God-forsakenness, yet even on the cross he prays two prayers: one of care for other people, one placing his life into his father's care. At the very time he had most right to doubt that God was his father he expresses his greatest trust in the father's care.

One of the problems people have is that they feel at liberty to fill the word 'father' with their own experience when the word is used of God. In John's gospel Jesus is identified as the Son of God, and God is the father of Jesus. Yet the word 'father' is not used abstractly nor is it filled with content from the behaviour of earthly fathers, as theologians Ray Anderson and Dennis Guernsey point out:

> . . . [It] is impossible from a theological perspective to equate the male role in parenting with the concept of God as father. Whatever distinctive aspects belong to the male role of parenting, they must be established on other grounds. God's fatherhood includes all the nuances of parenting represented by analogy in human parents.[5]

The idea that God is father in some general and abstract sense which it is up to us to make sense of, is foreign to the whole of scripture. The Bible does not see God as the father of all humanity, it is not the fact that we are all human beings made by God that makes God our father. The question that needs to be asked is, 'To whom is God father?' The answer which scripture gives is that God is the father of Jesus Christ.[6]

It is the relationship between the Father and the Son, Jesus, that defines all other relationships with God, for our relationships enter into the relationship between the father and the son. That is why the New Testament talks of those of us who have become Christians as being adopted into the family of God. Jesus is our elder brother and we refer to other Christians as 'brothers and sisters in Christ'. So the word 'father' either refers to God as the father of Jesus or to God the Father of believers who have entered into the Father-Son relationship by grace. Theologian Jurgen Moltmann brings out this point when he says:

Consequently in the Christian understanding of God the Father what is meant is not 'the Father of the universe', but simply and exclusively 'the father of the son Jesus Christ'. It is solely the father of Jesus Christ who we believe and acknowledge created the world. It is in the trinitarian sense that God is understood as father – or he cannot be understood as father at all.[7]

John portrays Jesus as either talking about God as 'my father' or 'your father' but never as 'the father'. Jesus is the Son of God, Christians are always the children of God. In John's gospel the male metaphor 'son' is not applied to anybody other than Jesus. This is John's way of affirming what Paul teaches when he says in Christ there is 'neither male nor female' (Galatians 3:28). To talk of God the father without adding 'of Jesus Christ' would be to succumb to patriarchy.[8]

Too many people who want to say something about human fatherhood, both radicals and conservatives, plunder the character of God to underwrite their insights on this subject. But it is God's fatherhood from which we derive our understanding of what earthly fathers should be like. Not only are earthly fathers to be fathers in the sense that God is a father but our fatherhood is accountable to God as father of Jesus Christ. God transcends the lists that we use to reduce human behaviour to male and female characteristics.

The Motherly Father

It is a painful irony that men and women who have suffered at the hands of their fathers use such hurt to alienate themselves from the fatherhood of God rather than behaving as Christ did at his moment of suffering. Nevertheless we cannot underestimate the degree of hurt and pain that women and men experience at the hands of fathers. Many men and women find it impossible to address God as Father, or think of God as loving, because of the violent images of their childhood which the word 'father' conjures up. But the fatherhood of God is a freeing fatherhood because it is already defined by the father's relationship with Jesus. We enter into the same relationship and can call God *Abba*. Matthew makes this point quite explicitly when he recalls Jesus as saying, '. . . do not call anyone on earth "father", for you have one Father, and he is in heaven.' (Matthew 23:9) Jesus acknowledges that if we look for our model of fatherhood in earthly fathers who are fallen we will miss the fathering of God.

It is easy to stereotype feminists as being the ones who cannot accept that God is a father but at least one conservative theologian falls into precisely the same trap. Werner Neuer, a respected German theologian, selectively uses human analogy and applies it to God:

> Why could Jesus not have called God 'mother' as well? This question answers itself if one considers the nature of fatherhood and motherhood. Fatherhood involves the active procreation of new life whereas motherhood is characterised by the overwhelmingly passive acts of conceiving, carrying, and bearing new life. Whoever ascribes motherhood to God introduces ideas into the concept of God that are completely foreign to his nature.[9]

Quite apart from the misconception of pregnancy as being passive, Neuer attempts to understand the fatherhood of God by considering the nature of human fatherhood and motherhood as if the fatherhood of God is a vacuum which needs content. His choice of idioms is quite partial and leaves the wrong impression, but he leaves a chink open in the door by saying later that even though God cannot be called 'mother', 'his behaviour towards mankind may be compared with the loving behaviour of a mother'.[10]

He is not alone in suggesting that although calling God 'mother' would lead to a view of God as goddess, thereby fundamentally changing our view of God, God's fatherliness includes everything possible in the way of motherly tenderness, security and love. Jurgen Moltmann has suggested a compromise between those who see fatherhood as a distortion of who God is and those who see fatherhood as a sufficient representation of who God is. We cannot give up the word 'father' for that is the word the Bible uses, but God is also a mothering God and this transcendence of gender categories is summed up in Moltmann's phrase, 'our motherly Father'.

In the 1990s the renewal of interest in the subject of men and masculinity will reveal that it is not only women who have a problem with the fatherhood of God. The opening of this chapter showed the kind of problems which boys experience with their fathers. Yet we are not at liberty to change our theology about God because of our experience of earthly fatherhood. The fact that God is the father of Jesus rather than a father like our earthly father is an important response to this pain. Feminist theologians have counselled us to replace masculine with feminine language, or at least language that is exclusive of women with language that includes everybody. It is important for us to listen to what they have to say because our current representation of God largely eradicates the way in which God expresses himself through forms which we think of as feminine.

The Psalmist portrays God as a mother-bird (Psalm 17:8), a midwife (Psalm 22:9), a mistress (Psalm 123:2), a weaning mother (Isaiah 49:15) or a mother comforting her child (Isaiah 66:13). Masculine and feminine combine in Deuteronomy 32:18: 'You deserted the Rock, who fathered you; you forgot the God who gave you birth.' Jesus uses the metaphor of himself as the mother-hen with her chicks (Matthew 23:37), and Christ is seen as embodying in himself the wisdom of God, which in the Old Testament is described as 'she' (1 Corinthians 1:30 and Proverbs 8:1).

The word used for 'compassion' (*rahamim*) is the plural of a word which means 'womb' or 'uterus' (*rehem*) and this word is not only used repeatedly to refer to God's compassion but is used of men as well. Joseph, then Prime Minister of Egypt, sees his younger brother Benjamin after a long separation, 'Deeply moved [*rahamim*] at the sight of his brother, Joseph hurried out and looked for a place to weep. He went into his private room and wept there.' (Genesis 43:30)[11]

In Psalm 103:13 a parallel is made between earthly and divine fathers using this 'womb language':

> As a father has compassion [*kerahem*]
> on his children,
> so the Lord has compassion [*riham*]
> on those who fear him.[12]

Australian theologian Charles Sherlock adds another insight by saying that we must be sensitive to:

> . . . Old Testament language, wherein God is named as 'Father' using nouns but 'Mother' using verbs. It avoids the impersonal tone elicited by the constant use of 'God'. It may help us realise more that God encompasses both 'masculine' and 'feminine' attributes. It refuses to make us choose between God as 'Mother' and 'Father'.[13]

We cannot pretend that the Bible does not use the word 'father' but, in telling us that God transcends our lists and is an intimate daddy to his only begotten Son, we are asked to turn to look to God in our hurt and pain and find in him the mothering and nurturing love that we wish our fathers on earth would give us. Elaine Storkey recognises the boundaries which the Bible gives us when she says to women, 'To reduce the deep intimacy of the fatherly (and motherly) relationship into fear of a male God is to distance oneself from the source of real self-knowledge and full womanly identity.'[14]

Why is this helpful to fathers who are trying to find their way in the modern family? It is only of help if men are willing to see that God's character and relationship with Jesus Christ is normative for their fathering. Contemporary masculinity reduces men to a stereotype which means that they cannot learn from the fatherhood of God since his fatherhood is characterised by intimacy rather than by distance. Many men will say on reading this chapter that they are intimate and loving fathers but they do not understand the source of their love. If men would be fathers like God is a father to Jesus they must self-consciously seek to honour God in their fathering. The distant father is a product of secularisation.

The Consequences for Parenting

The difference between the problems of contemporary fathers and the image of the parenting of God is striking. The distance of the one and the intimacy of the other are two ends of the spectrum. But the parallels do not stop there. All parenting should emulate the parenting of God. Avoiding this reduces parenting to problems of child management or child minding. Perhaps there are four aspects of parenting which we can learn from God.

Children are Made in the Image of God Children do not become persons, they are persons. They are not sheets of white paper that fathers can write their expectations or agenda on, nor are they clones of their parents. They are their own people with all the needs for dignity, respect and love which adults have. They are made in the image of God and are created by him to enjoy his world. The world of the abuser and the exploiter of children is a world which is under the judgement of God.

Children are Central to the Purposes of God Jesus places children at the heart of the kingdom of God. In his day children were of no importance but Jesus takes time to be with them, blesses them and commends them to our loving care and acceptance (Mark 9:36–7). Perhaps one of the greatest differences between contemporary masculinity and the fatherhood of God is the priority which children have. In a materialistic world children are a liability because they cost to keep; in an over-sexual world children are exploited by the jaded appetites of those for whom love is a four-letter word; in an ambitious world children live out their parents' dreams; in a violent world children are the victims of human malevolence. But as far as Jesus was concerned children are a sign of the presence of God and are at the heart of the kingdom of God.

Children Need Unconditional Love   One of the characteristics of Jesus's relationship with the Father was that he knew the Father and was known by him. Perfect community characterised their relationship as it had always done within the Trinity. Another aspect of their relationship is perfect love. God is love because he is both the object and subject of love within the Trinity. We learn from this that openness is necessary if love is to be given and received. Jesus and the Father were entirely open to one another. There was no mask-wearing or pretence; nothing to hide from the children or to be ashamed of, no need for dishonesty.

Perhaps the most important aspect of parenting which men and women can learn from Jesus is unconditional love. As parents we put so many conditions on our children. We tell them that if they achieve, or behave or do this or that we will love them. Such conditional love saps the human spirit. God's love brings freedom because he loves us unconditionally. He knows us yet he loves us. He is aware of every shade of darkness in our lives yet his love for us is unconditional. How liberating it would be if our children were loved like that!

Children Need Boundaries to Feel Secure   So many people are obsessed with disciplining children yet they do not seem to ask why they are behaving in the way they do. Love and admiration are powerful incentives for a child to please parents. All too often fathers see discipline as punishment but this is not the way the Bible sums it up. The word 'discipline' originally meant 'an instruction given to a disciple' and was about wisdom to live by rather than punishment. The writer of Proverbs comments, 'My son, do not despise the Lord's discipline and do not resent his rebuke, because the Lord disciplines those he loves, as a father the son he delights in.' (Proverbs 3:11–12)

How many lives would have been transformed if this connection between love and discipline had been lived out? Here the father does not reject the child but reinforces his love and delight in the child. It is often the case that children do not feel loved unless boundaries are placed around the child's behaviour. I remember one girl in her teens who was very angry. When I asked her what was wrong she said that her parents did not mind what time she got home at night. Her comment was, 'I don't think they love me.' This mixture of unconditional love and carefully laid boundaries provides children with the mix of security and freedom which they need to grow into independent children who are capable of giving and receiving love.

All these insights are based on knowledge of who God is and how he responds to us. Fatherhood is under the spotlight in the debate on gender but it is one area among many which is in confusion, since fathers who reject God's fatherhood are the blind leading the blind.

Perhaps it is in the area of sexuality that problems of parenting have their most tragic, human consequences. Our views of the 'opposite sex' are heavily influenced by the relationship between our parents, the messages we gleaned from their lives and their own relationship with us, their children. Sex promises so much joy yet it is the arena for so much pain. How, then, do men's views of masculinity affect their sexuality?

QUESTIONS

1.   Is it fair to criticise men for being 'distant' or 'absent' when they are trying to provide their families with a livelihood in a cultural context which demands a great deal from them?

2.   If your father were sitting in front of you and you had the opportunity to talk to him about his relationship with you, including your childhood memories of him, what would you say to him?

3.   What do men mean when they talk about having been 'wounded' by their experience of being parented?

4.   To what extent should Christians defend current models of parenting?

5.   If God's fatherhood is defined by the relationship between the father and the son, Jesus Christ, what can we learn from this a) about God, and b) about our own fathering?

6.   'Perhaps the most important aspect of parenting which men and women can learn from Jesus is unconditional love.' How does 'unconditional' love differ from 'conditional' love in its effects on children?

NOTES

1.   Rosalind Miles, *The Rites of Man: Love, Sex and Death in the Making of the Male* (London: Grafton, 1991), p. 135.

2.   Christopher Lasch, *The Culture of Narcissism* (London: Abacus, 1980), p. 227.

3.   Victor Seidler has written at length on the effect of the Enlightenment on masculinity. His writings are some of the best in the area of men's studies and his thesis is to be found in two books: *Rediscovering Masculinity: Reason, Language, and Sexuality* (London: Routledge, 1989), and *Recreating Sexual Politics: Men, Feminism and Politics* (London: Routledge, 1991). He has also edited and contributed to *The Achilles Heel Reader: Men, Sexual Politics and Socialism* (London: Routledge, 1991), and an essay of his entitled 'Fear and Intimacy' is included in *The Sexuality of Men*, ed. Andy Metcalf and Martin Humphries (London: Pluto Press, 1985), pp. 150–81.

4.   Mary Stewart van Leeuwen, *Gender and Grace* (Leicester: IVP, 1990), p. 137.

5.   Ray S. Anderson and Dennis Guernsey, *On Being Family:*

A Social Theology of the Family (Grand Rapids, Michigan: Eerdmans, 1985), p. 61.

6. In his book, *The Call to Personhood* (Cambridge: CUP, 1990), p. 277, note 15, Alistair McFadyen talks of the Trinity in these terms: 'It is a distinctively Christian understanding that the Fatherhood of God refers primarily to an internal relationship (i.e. trinitarian relation) within God and only subsequently and on that basis to his external relations with creation or humanity. In Christian tradition God as father is the father of Jesus Christ and does not primarily denote a relationship to humankind or to creation as a whole'.

7. Jurgen Moltmann, *The Trinity and the Kingdom of God* (London: SCM, 1981), p. 163.

8. It might be thought that in Ephesians 3:14–15 Paul is talking about God's fatherhood quite generally. He says, 'For this reason I kneel before the Father, from whom his whole family in heaven and on earth derives its name.' Some have seen in this the fatherhood of humanity but it is the family who belongs to God and owns his name. Paul has already talked of 'the God and Father of our Lord Jesus Christ' in Ephesians 1:3. This father can only be known as the Father of the Lord Jesus Christ.

9. Werner Neuer, *Man and Woman in Christian Perspective*, trans, Gordon Wenham (London: Hodder and Stoughton, 1990), p. 155.

10. ibid., p. 156.

11. See the extensive discussion on this by Phyllis Trible in Trible, op. cit., p. 33.

12. cf. Trible, op. cit., p. 34.

13. Charles Sherlock, *God on the Inside: Trinitarian Spirituality* (Acorn Press, 1991), p. 161.

14. Elaine Storkey, *What's Right With Feminism?* (London: SPCK/Third Way, 1985), p. 126.

10

MEN AND SEXUALITY

Men think about sex an average of fifteen times a day, according to a survey on masculinity carried out by *Gentleman's Quarterly*.[1] It's a wonder the 'average man' has enough time to read the magazine. At least *GQ* magazine isn't going out of its way to break up any stereotypes. Sex has the power to create an amazing joy and a celebration of our humanity as men and women, but it has also got the capacity to be wildly destructive. One of the reasons for this is that sexuality is not just about sexual intercourse. Lewis Smedes talks of sexuality as being 'the human drive towards intimate communion'.[2] When we put sex in the context of our sexuality we can see that there is a wide spectrum of responses to the sexual act. The fact that two people have high expectations of something which also involves a great deal of vulnerability means that there is a high degree of risk associated with sex. A feeling of rejection can be so debilitating that it can lead to withdrawal and violence, but openness and sensitivity can make sex into a celebration of communion between two people. This spectrum of rejection and violence to communion and intimacy shows us that our sexuality mirrors our deepest needs and drives. Sex is a good servant but a bad master.

It is central to Christian teaching on sex that it is a gift of God. It has not always been made to seem so. Sexual intercourse is hardly a refined and controlled activity. The passion of sex seems to be far removed from our view of God. Many of us view God as a serene being who is as far removed from sexual passion as it is possible to be, but God is the creator of the sexual act. Perhaps some of our pictures of God owe more to Greek thinking about the spiritual being ethereal rather than present in bodily passion. But from the outset the fact that the image of God is expressed as male and female[3] in sexual relationship means that God affirms sexuality, and the Bible is a book which is full of the exploration of sexuality.

The most well-known celebration of human sexuality in the scriptures is found in the wisdom literature of the Old Testament. A writer of the Proverbs says, 'May your fountain be blessed, and may you rejoice in the wife of your youth. A loving doe, a graceful deer – may her breasts satisfy you always, may you ever be captivated by her love.' (Proverbs 5:18–19) The Song of Songs is a quite obvious celebration of erotic love which has often been turned into a symbolic poem of our relationship with God by Victorians who could not fit the erotic into their view of God. But it does not mention God, marriage, or the procreative purposes of sexuality. It is about two people in love.[4] It opens with the words, 'Let him kiss me with the kisses of his mouth – for your love is more delightful than wine' (Song of Songs 1:2), and continues with, 'Strengthen me with raisins, and refresh me with apples, for I am faint with love. His left arm is under my head, and his right arm embraces me.' (Song of Songs 2:5–6) Phyllis Trible, the feminist theologian, comments on this:

> Male and female first became one flesh in the Garden of Eden. There a narrator reported briefly their sexual union (Genesis 2:24). Now in another garden, the lovers themselves praise at length the joys of intercourse. Possessive adjectives do not separate their lives. 'My garden' and 'his garden' blend in mutual habitation and harmony. Even person and place unite: the garden of eroticism is the woman.[5]

As in Eden, the lovers are aware of their environment and

the context of their love is the 'taste, smell, touch, sight and hearing which permeate the garden of the song'.[6] As in Eden, there is water to drink – a garden fountain, a well of flowing water (Song of Songs 4:15) – as well as animals such as gazelles, does, doves and stags. But in this garden there is no serpent to bring the temptation which has always been a threat to human sexuality.

In the garden of the song, love is harmony and intimacy. There is no power or possession in this garden but, 'My lover is mine, and I am his' (Song of Songs 2:16; 6:3). The woman also says, 'I belong to my lover, and his desire is for me.' (Song of Songs 7:10) The word desire echoes the judgment in Eden, 'Your desire will be for your husband, and he will rule over you.' (Genesis 3:16).

> In Eden, the yearning of the woman for harmony with her man continued after disobedience. Yet the man did not reciprocate: instead, he ruled over her to destroy unity and pervert sexuality. Her desire became his dominion. But in the song, male power vanishes. His desire becomes her delight. Another consequence of disobedience is thus redeemed through the recovery of mutuality in the garden of eroticism.[7]

The message of the song is about love for the sake of love, a picture of intimacy, mutuality and freedom in the erotic. It is a parallel to the starkness of Genesis 3. Yet because of Genesis 3, we cannot stay with the Song but must trace further the story of sexuality on the spectrum between tragedy and ecstasy.

Sexuality as Power

Many people do not experience sexuality in the way in which the couple of the Song did. For them sexuality is about fear, coercion and power. Within sexual relationships there is a thin line between ecstasy and violence. One of the reasons for this is the relationship between the imagination and the person. Both men and women are fed with different but equally damaging pictures of the opposite sex. Men have a tendency to objectify sex and to think of sexuality in terms of the sexual act. This tendency creates the possibility of pornography which objectifies women, making them subject to male control and disposal. But women have a tendency to subjectify sexuality, and romantic fiction can distort the expectations of women disastrously.

The biblical teaching on sex has to be seen against the background of the framework of biblical themes which we have already explored. Humanity, male and female, is made in the image of God and capable of good, but fallen and capable of evil. This means that in the area of sex, distorted expectations have great power. It also means that neither male nor female power can be construed as sacred.[8] Many women have made love to their partners and at the end have felt that their performance was being assessed by comparison with some unspoken masculine fantasy. The world of fantasy is devoid of responsibility. Women are compliant, and sex is always fantastic. But real women have ideas of their own, dignity, modesty and personal tastes. Men cannot direct sex as if it were the theatre of their imagination. Trying to do so results in coercion; women feel as if they are being exploited and used rather than loved for their own sake. They feel insecure because the man often does not disclose what it is that is in his mind. Where he does so, women are often struck by the differences between the sexual imagination of men and women. Many couples who come to the point of having sex *seem* to want the same things but in fact the different emphases of the romantic and the pornographic have created a great gulf between them.

It has become a modern proverb that 'men use intimacy to get sex but women use sex to get intimacy'. This does not mean merely that men do not spend enough time being romantic before they have sex. Sexuality is intended to be integrated with our whole personality as well as our human values. It is also meant to be an expression of commitment towards a woman in every area of life together. Sex without intimacy may be exciting but it will not further loving relationships. A man who consistently divorces the two treats both himself and his partner as sub-human. Such men seek to satisfy their sexual needs because they have little insight into their own emotional needs. They look to their partners to interpret their needs for them and feel they have been let down when they do not. As men we have been traditionally taught that our worth is found in the world of work, and this is increasingly true of women as well. We expect the sexual world to be a simple world of 'doing' rather than the adventure of 'being', which it is. Where we take responsibility for our emotional lives the first thing we learn is that we can be at fault and have to explore ourselves in order to remedy the situation.

The feminist, Alice Jardine, once commented that men still have everything to say about their sexuality. And one of the problems which men have is that they are only beginning to grasp their own view of sexuality. Looking at masculinity and sexuality is difficult because of the accusations of women that men have used sexual power to abuse them. But for men sexual activity is an area in which they feel they are able to express something of themselves. In their book *The Sexuality of Men*, Andy Metcalf and Martin Humphries comment:

> Sex for men seems less of a pure animal act, despite our fantasies, and more of a bulky portmanteau we stagger around with, desperate to unlock, but with rusted keys. Here, mingled with desire, there's the need for tenderness, the need to talk, to let skin speak to skin; there's misery that only sex seems able to right.[9]

Sex has become another world, somewhere between utopia and nostalgia, which men feel is the object of their longing but the reality of which never seems to satisfy. Men are always in search of the ultimate experience and one of the characteristics of male pornography is its addictive power. Men who read or view pornography are in search of *the ultimate without the intimate*. This search causes men to be driven by sex rather than liberated by it. Male sexuality is focused on the orgasm as a criterion of performance and achievement. But it is this constant preoccupation with performance that makes men so anxious about sex and so concerned about whether they are missing out compared to other men. Women may reassure men that 'size does not matter' and agony columns may advise that it does not matter how often you do it, but men will never be convinced. One of the ironies of the inheritance of the sixties is that 'sexual freedom' has become sexual addiction and compulsion for so many.

Yet men do not talk about sex with one another as frequently as women suppose. Of course there is the macho bravado of the man who claims great things after his first drink, but other men regard this as on a par with the fisherman's tale of the one that got away. It is a great paradox that when men read and view pornography they are supposedly interested in what people do when they have sex, but they do not have conversations about the same subject with other men, except in bravura myth-making. The challenge in explaining male sexuality is how to unlock what goes on in men's minds, for their minds are full of paradoxes. The guilt which many men feel about sex also adds the excitement to sex. The fear which comes from performance-related sexuality is tolerated because of the remote possibility that one might one day achieve one's desires. The fact that many men have an almost hydraulic or mechanistic view of sex gives them a sense of control and excitement which has to be traded off against the openness, disclosure and intimacy which many men are not willing to be vulnerable enough to admit that they want.

Another link between sexuality and masculinity is that sexuality is important to a man's sense of himself as being masculine. Sexual intercourse is very important to masculinity. If a man becomes impotent, he feels that his masculinity is threatened. The need for sexual performance figures so importantly for men that anxiety about it is a leading cause of impotence. Yet in *The Hite Report on Male Sexuality* one of the reasons most often cited by men for wanting sex was the sense of affirmation or self-validation gained through sex. In *The Hite Report* only three per cent of the answers to the question, 'Why do you like intercourse?' mentioned orgasm. Many men talked about being loved and accepted, and others said that they felt that intercourse allowed them to be more emotionally open with their partners. This is summed up by a man who said, 'Intercourse is an exquisite expression of "I love you".'[10] This kind of response shows that there is real hope for change in men, but it also shows that men disclose different responses when filling in survey forms privately to the kind of noises they make about sex when with other men, and the kind of macho stereotypes they allow to be perpetrated of them as a gender. Men may want intimacy and vulnerability but the masculinity they have created demands sex and still more sex in order for them to be 'real men'.

So men feel that the sexual act is a demonstration of love, and that being good at sex and sensitive to the physical needs of one's sexual partner is to be more loving. Yet in the next chapter on conversation we will see that such a message may not communicate itself to the woman. Men cannot stray far in a patriarchal society from the fact that it is the erect penis that symbolises masculinity.

If this is so then sexual intercourse is something which conveys many different messages, none of which can be assumed. It can be a coercive symbol of male power or it can be the time and place when men shed their masks and disclose their true selves intimately and lovingly to their partners. Nevertheless, the picture of masculinity to which modern men compare themselves views intercourse in terms of conquering or possessing. In *The Hite Report* one man expresses this very well:

I like intercourse because of the good feeling I get from it. I feel more of a man than at other times. A woman's body is always a challenge; you never know how it will respond nor to what nor when. It's like a good game of tennis; you hit a hell of a good shot, and whammo, it comes back twice as hard. A woman's body is a mountain to be scaled, a house to be inhabited.[11]

Some men do talk about women as if they are a challenge. The first edition of a documentary series on Channel 4 entitled *From Wimps to Warriors*, screened in the UK in summer 1991, focused on the lives of several men who viewed women in terms of 'the chase' and found them an embarrassment after 'the conquest', yet who couldn't work out why they could not find their ideal woman and settle down. For such men, women make their masculinity possible, like a fashion accessory which is necessary if the overall effect is to be complete. Other men gain strength from sex but one can see in the kind of strength they gain the danger signals appearing. One man commented: 'I feel stronger than I am during sex. Like I'm some macho, virile man. Like a Greek warrior. Like an Indian warrior. I feel I can do anything and everything I want to her.'[12] In this quote the warrior language and the treatment of the woman as object, which is implicit in his use of the word 'to', are danger signals for the woman.

The need for men to have sex, as in the phrase 'sex drive', may of course originate in some biological story about the procreation of the human species. If the myth about the greater reticence of women for intercourse is actually true then this may also be expressed in a biological context, which focuses on the fact that if women were like men in their desire for frequency of intercourse, they would always be pregnant. In every relationship intercourse is a matter of negotiation, and the problems that many men and women have of male resentment and female guilt about sex is that men and women may not be adept at talking together about sexual needs and preferences.

Nevertheless, not every man capitulates to masculine stereotypes in the privacy of his own home or relationships. Men can be warm, open, loving and gentle in their sexual expression. The problem is that such men have not appreciably affected the way men view sex. When together with other men it is often the loudmouth, who is insensitive and chauvinistic, who is allowed to have his say. Yet many of his male listeners are disgusted with him but would not say so to his face. Other men have to work in workshops and factories where soft porn is pinned to the wall as a sign that this is a workshop dominated by men and masculine preferences. Men often feel intimidated by this and even if they feel that such pictures exploit women and enhance male fantasies of power, they do not say so. Men must make up their minds about what they are prepared to put up with in terms of the portrayal of masculinity in our society. Are we prepared to continue to suffer stereotypes of masculinity which alienate women from men and men from themselves? Cannot men who are different in private state that they are different in public?

The Lonely Male

How can we summarise the picture of masculinity which men constantly compare themselves with? I believe there are five factors which, if men seek to fulfil them, will lead to the phenomenon of the lonely male.

Performance Masculinity is goal-oriented in its attitude to sexuality. Victor Seidler comments that for boys, sex is often an issue of 'how far' they can get with a girl. Teenage boys expect their advances to be blocked, sex is something which boys are meant to 'need' but 'good girls' are not meant to give. This conflict in the popular imagination means that 'getting it' can be seen as a conquest, and therefore sexuality can be seen as an assertion of male power over women. Over the last twenty or thirty years the discussion on women's sexuality has shifted the ground somewhat. Now the idea of sex as performance surrounds the concern to make sure that your partner has an orgasm. If she does not this still reflects back on the man. The reason this is so important is that having sex with a woman for the first time is one of the few areas of initiation that exist for men. A man can become masculine by making love to a woman.[13]

This can lead to sexuality as theatre. It is not spontaneous and joyful, for the man has a script in his head which he is trying to live out. If he succeeds to his own satisfaction this leads to the egocentric behaviour of the macho man. But for men who capitulate to this view of sexuality there is a cost involved, for the end result of performance is *anxiety*. When many men measure up to this facet of masculinity they feel inadequate and unable to perform in the way that is required of them. In *The Woman Report on Men*, instigated by *Woman* magazine and published in 1987, men expressed their most common fault as 'lack of skill'. The report observed that: 'Only one in four (twenty-six per cent) of men was completely happy with the way he made love and saw no need for change . . . among the majority of men who want to make changes in the way they make love two out of five (forty per cent) say they want to be more skilful.'[14]

One man, called Arthur, related performance to intimacy by talking of 'improving my performance so that we could introduce into our lives the warmth I so sadly miss'.[15]

Variety The modern approach to sexual intercourse focuses on variety and novelty in the sexual act. Sex manuals such as *The Joy of Sex* have become bestsellers, and it is significant that this particular book is subtitled *A Gourmet Guide to Lovemaking*. Such manuals have an ambivalence about them. Where couples are ignorant about sex or need some help to get them to discuss their sex lives, books can be very helpful as a catalyst. But there is a thin line between books that serve the imagination and books which subtly give us the message that unless our sex lives are like those in the book we are in some way inadequate.

Men seem to be particularly susceptible to the idea that sexual positions, variety, fantasy, sex toys and all the paraphernalia of sex is important to go along with. This can lead to some men never being satisfied with what they are currently doing sexually. The quest for variety is insatiable and can lead men into dark areas of the masculine imagination. In *The Woman Report on Men* one in three (thirty-three per cent) husbands who would like to change the way he makes love wants to be more experimental, and only three per cent of men ever refuse their partner's request to try a new position or technique, but ten times that many men (thirty-eight per cent) said their partner refuses their request to try something different. Half (forty-nine per cent) of the husbands wanting change wished their wife would be more experimental sexually.[16]

Variety can become a coercive source of power as men may coerce women, either subtly or overtly, to take part in sexual acts which are no part of their own preference. Variety can be wonderful when it is an expression of mutual desire, here it is entirely natural. After all, there is no one way to have sex. In a healthy relationship variety is a result of communication, where both partners feel accepted by the other and are willing to listen to the other person's needs and desires.

However, there is a great gulf between a man loving a woman as a human subject and a man treating a woman as a sexual object. Men can start to say to their partners that they would be more aroused if their partner did various things or dressed in various ways. This is the beginning of conditional love, which women can often find degrading but may go along with for the sake of their relationship. The end result of such an approach to variety is *boredom* because men have deceived themselves that variety will satisfy their desire, whereas they are in fact searching for intimacy. The difference between the two approaches is that in the first, variety is a by-product of openness and respect between people. In the other, women become the instrument which conveys variety, feeling the numbness of being thought of as an object as they do so.

Frequency It is part of the masculine myth that 'real men' have sex very frequently and this can become an unreasonable demand. Everybody gets tired or ill or depressed, and at such times the compulsion to have sex frequently can be anything but liberating. Men who find their identity through their work may be exhausted and stressed and have little interest in sex themselves. This does not prevent them from feeling that they should. But where men are more concerned with the frequency of the sexual act than with the needs of their partner, the end result can quickly be *resentment* that their expectations are not being fulfilled by their partner. Resentment can quickly turn into the feeling that men have a right to as much sex as they can take. If it is not found within marriage, the temptation is to find it elsewhere.

Potency Masculinity as we know it is obsessed with power and this finds its expression within sex with an emphasis on potency. The ability to have sex at any time, in any position, and the myth of the instantaneous mutual orgasm all reflect the quest for male potency. The potent male is self-assured in the world of men. He is a 'superstud'. But when men compare themselves to this myth of masculinity they more often feel a sense of inadequacy. Ordinary men suffer from premature ejaculation and loss of erection. They succumb to stress and depression. They may not even want sex as often as they are meant to want it and this can lead to a sense of *inadequacy*.

Self-protection It is central to masculine stereotypes that men protect themselves and do not become weak or disclose anything which could detract from their masculinity. Surveys about sexuality show that many men do not talk at all during sex and women often wonder how it is that men can expect to have sex at a time when the relationship between them is hostile and not loving. Such self-protection ultimately leads to *chauvinism*, the irrational belief in one's own superiority. But the chauvinist man is a lonely man who does not belong, does not know people, and is not truly known by them.

These five factors – performance, variety, frequency,

potency, self-protection – constitute a set of impossible demands on men. Here is the introduction of a legalism as great as any written on tablets of stone. The saddest thing about it is that many men regard such a picture as natural and normal and cannot see that the anxiety, boredom, resentment, inadequacy and chauvinistic isolation that result are too high a price to pay for something that has always been unobtainable. Sexuality is an area which needs a sense of humour, humility and self-deprecation. Both partners need to be able to laugh when something goes wrong and say 'It doesn't matter'. What is important is the closeness, friendship and intimacy that exist between them. People who are intimate with one another know that when things go wrong, the admission and acceptance leads to greater intimacy, but this masculine stereotype does not admit such self-deprecating humour and vulnerability. Macho men are 'serious' about sex. They think they are liberated but in fact they are tyrannised by masculinity.

Sex and Spirituality

The Bible makes a direct link between sexuality and spirituality in the idea of the image of God, but in the modern world this link has been broken. Relationships are at the heart of what it means to be made in the image of God. Our capacity to love and be loved reflects the love which exists between the persons of the Trinity; our community reflects their communion. The Bible has a high view of human love and sexuality, for as we have seen from the Song of Songs it is intended that it should be a celebration of humanness.

The fact that human sexuality is to do with the body is explicitly commented on in the creation stories in the fact that, 'The man and his wife were both naked, and they felt no shame.' (Genesis 2:25) Here is a picture of sexuality integrated into a relationship which characterises who God is. Lewis Smedes, in his book *Sex in the Real World*, says there are two situations in which people feel no shame. The first is in a state of wholeness, the other is in a state of illusion.[17] In the biblical view of sexuality, sex is never a subject on its own but is always a part and an expression of what it means to be human. All kinds of relationships express our sexuality including relationships between parent and child, and between men and women who are not in a sexual relationship. Single people can, within the biblical world-view, participate in all that it says about sexuality without engaging in genital sexual activity. But Lewis Smedes has chosen a good word in 'illusion' to describe the plight of contemporary sexuality. Society has lost its reference point for sexuality in God and is on a constant search for some source of meaning for sex. Instead of wholeness we have become people who trade in illusions.

Many men who are rebelling against this very hard portrayal of masculine sexuality are doing so by discovering a new tenderness and intimacy in their relationships with their partners. But some men do not feel that they can express their sexuality or their desire for intimacy with a woman, feeling that they can only find fulfilment in a sexual relationship with another man. In many respects gay culture offers men who wish to reject traditional models of masculinity an alternative set of values. In a society where masculinities are plural, gay masculinity has become increasingly an option for men. It is an option with which Christianity will always struggle ethically, and my intention in what follows is not to discuss the ethics of gay sexuality or gay relationships but to make some brief comments about gay sexuality in the light of the theme of this chapter.

Gay Sexuality

I have stated elsewhere that the upbringing of some men leads them on a search for love, acceptance and affirmation from other men. Whereas all men need love from other men but may repress it or distract themselves from it, some men are driven by their need for such love to seek it out whatever the cost. It may be that they are motivated by a lack of fathering to find what they have missed in other men. Such men live at an unfortunate time in our culture. They are under pressure in four areas.

Firstly, we live in a society where all kinds of human relationships are over-sexualised. Sexual intercourse has become an acceptable mode of human expression in situations previously considered inappropriate for genital sexuality. A man seeking intimacy and love with other men could well find that genital sexuality was considered to be an essential element of that intimacy. This is not just true of homosexual relationships but studies of homosexuality have shown that in some areas of the gay world there is a high degree of promiscuity and turnover of partners. This may be expected where masculine stereotypes about sexuality, such as those we have discussed in other sections, dominate the thinking of both homosexual partners.

Secondly, the situation is complicated by a confusion as to whether the word 'homosexual' is a description of a person's identity or of an act which they do. Is it about 'being' or 'doing'? The rise of gay culture in the west has placed great emphasis on gay identity and people who decide to 'come out' as gays find themselves in a culture which will give them a complete world-view and way of life. This idea of gay identity is developed around the assumption that gay people cannot change their orientation and need to have their own world to live in, in which they can meet other gay people and develop supportive friendships. It is important not to underrate the strength of the feelings of identification which people can have with gay identity. Nevertheless, in many cases men who commit a homosexual act may be led to think that they are automatically homosexual or bisexual in sexual orientation. However many men, who would consider themselves heterosexuals, do from time to time entertain sexual fantasies about the same kind of acts and may even do so explicitly within a homosexual context. If at some moment of vulnerability and opportunity they find themselves engaging in a homosexual act this does not mean that they are necessarily homosexual in orientation and must therefore take on a gay identity.

Thirdly, there is another problem in the absence of affectionate and demonstrative intimacy between men in our culture. Many men are looking for intimacy and are hijacked into sexual intercourse because there does not seem to be any other way of meeting it. Friendship and acceptance with other men would do a great deal to ameliorate the problem. Homophobia is rife in the world of men. In some circles any gesture or word of affection is interpreted as a sign that one is gay. Some men protect their own sexual vulnerabilities in this area with fear, and when provoked can become verbally abusive or even physically violent towards those who dare to contravene masculine conventions. Such fear can only be overcome by loving relationships of all kinds, but particularly the rediscovery of friendship between men.

Fourthly, the over-sexualisation of our society begins at an early age. Teenagers often feel under pressure to demonstrate their sexuality. When this happens at a time when a boy or girl might be going through a phase where they are experiencing homosexual affection, this is made doubly difficult when they are placed under pressure to decide whether they are 'gay' or 'straight'. Like all of us, young people can find it difficult to live with unresolved tension. If they meet a group at a club which is into gay culture, this may influence them at a time when their sexual identity is very flexible. A boy of seventeen may decide that he is gay for life when in fact he has only committed himself sexually at a point where he would otherwise pass through a homosexual period to identify himself as heterosexual.

In the UK there is pressure from some gay groups to lower the age of consent from twenty-one to sixteen, and this is seen as bringing Britain into line with Europe and the gay population into line with the laws governing heterosexual intercourse. This can only cause more problems for teenagers who need the protection of the law at a time when their sexual identity is at its most pliable. Often young people will have sexual intercourse in order to demonstrate to themselves that they are of one orientation or another. These self-imposed 'tests' can be disastrous, whatever the outcome, due to lack of experience and wise counsel.

The convergence of these four things: over-sexualisation in society, a confusion between gay identity and gay acts, an absence of intimacy with other men, and the pressure on young people to commit themselves to a particular orientation; provides a very unhelpful atmosphere for those men who may be vulnerable to such influences. This is compounded by the secrecy and guilt which surrounds men who are beginning to get involved in gay culture but do not wish to admit it to others. The effect of these two things can be to cause the issue to grow out of all proportion. The pressure of this can become intolerable and may lead to men drifting into a gay culture. They may regret this later in life but may find it difficult to escape from it.

I do not have the space to do justice to a discussion of homosexuality and ethics here, important though it is. But it would be strange in a book on masculinity to have no discussion of gay issues. It is a great sadness to me that many men who are seeking life's highest human ideal – love – become enmeshed unnecessarily in genital sexuality, when what they are looking for is intimacy and acceptance in the context of friendship.

On to Intimacy

Having seen that some men have equated intimacy with sex, and the way in which this can be destructive in their lives, it is important to examine the conditions under which intimacy can flourish. Many men do want to find ways of becoming intimate with their partners and with their friends. When discussing the more arid approaches to sexuality it is sometimes easy to see intimacy as the goal we should all pursue as a higher ideal. But should intimacy be a goal or is it a by product of other things in our lives? It certainly seems to be an elusive quality outside the pages of romantic fiction.

QUESTIONS

1. To what extent did you feel that the portrayal of masculinity and sexuality in this chapter was something you could identify with?
2. Do you think that becoming a Christian changes your attitude to sex?
3. Why do men read or view pornography?
4. Performance, variety, frequency, potency and self-protection are associated with men's attitudes to sex. Why are these so important to men?
5. Do you think that if intimacy between men was more acceptable fewer men would adopt a homosexual identity? Should the Church play a leading part in fostering such intimacy?
6. Do we live in an over-sexualised society? Is sex as important as it is made out to be?

NOTES

1. 'Are you Man Enough', *Gentleman's Quarterly*, February 1991, p. 83.
2. Lewis Smedes, *Sex in the Real World* (Tring: Lion, 1983).
3. There is no suggestion in the Genesis story that the image of God is anything to do with rationality, as is so often supposed. On this see John Goldingay, 'The Bible and Sexuality', *Scottish Journal of Theology*, 1986, 39, p. 175.
4. Goldingay, op. cit., p. 183.
5. Phyllis Trible, *God and the Rhetoric of Sexuality* (Philadelphia: Fortress Press, 1978), p. 153. Barth viewed the Song of Songs as a commentary on Genesis 2:18–25. cf. Karl Barth, *Church Dogmatics*, 3, 1, pp. 312–29.
6. Trible, op. cit., p. 154.
7. Trible, op. cit., p. 160.
8. In some feminist writings, including feminist theology, there

seems to be an assumption that male power should be overthrown, and that female power would in some sense be more congenial. Some have even seen the feminine as 'sacred'. Revolution often brings more oppression in a different guise, rather than the hoped-for social justice; tyrants can be of either gender. There is also an analysis of the development of technology, harmful to humanity – such as weaponry – which blames men alienated by their masculinity for their invention and use, suggesting that a world ruled by women would have been a world of peace. cf. Brian Easlea, *Fathering the Unthinkable: Masculinity, Scientists and the Nuclear Arms Race* (London: Pluto Press, 1983). Although I do not think we can avoid a connection between masculinity and violence, women are also implicated in what happens to our world even if its history books are written from the standpoint of men. In the Genesis account of the fall, the blame – at first sight – appears to be the woman's, but as John Goldingay remarks, 'The woman fails by her words, the man by his silence, and both by their deeds.' Goldingay, op. cit., p. 177. In our world, silence implicates.

9. *The Sexuality of Men* eds. Andy Metcalf and Martin Humphries (London: Pluto Press, 1985), pp. 4–5.

10. Shere Hite, *The Hite Report on Male Sexuality* (London: Macdonald Optima, 1990), p. 328.

11. Hite, op. cit., p. 344.

12. Hite, op. cit., p. 335.

13. Victor Seidler, *Rediscovering Masculinity: Reason, Language and Sexuality* (London: Routledge, 1989), pp. 39–40.

14. Deirdre Sanders, *The Woman Report on Men* (London: Sphere, 1987), p. 90.

15. ibid.

16. Sanders, op. cit., p. 93.

17. Smedes, op. cit.

11

MEN AND INTIMACY

Sexuality has become the currency of our society, but behind the fascination of men with sex there is a desperate quest for intimacy. The modern world is fragmented and isolated and this has created a desire in us to belong to one another. The word 'community' sums up our nostalgia for the past and our hopes for a utopian future, but in the present we are living with the break-up of the family and the mess and pain of human relationships which we cannot sustain. Our society views intimacy as the alter ego of sexuality but viewed in this way intimacy can become tyrannical, as we constantly search for something which we never find. Perhaps our longing for intimacy is another way of talking about our longing for God. If this is true our society has lost its way completely.

In the following two chapters I want to deal with different facets of our quest for intimacy as a society and our expression of intimacy within our relationships. But before we can turn to look at intimacy itself it is important to examine the social conditions that are needed for intimacy to thrive. Our relationships are not an island which is unrelated to the rest of the society we live in. We are all deeply affected by social trends. In this chapter I want to look at some of the building blocks of our culture, namely time, mobility and materialism. On the surface these three things seem to be merely a description of the way things are but probing beneath the surface we find that masculinity feeds off these three things to create an image of a man who is busy, on the move and materially successful. This image is portrayed frequently through advertising and many men aim at becoming like that. The problem is that such a view of masculinity can be quite disastrous as a basis for intimacy as we shall see.

The Value of Our Time

As social historian Michael Ignatieff has commented, we are a society separated by time zones divided into those who spend money to save time and those who spend time to save money. Some people have lots of money and no time. Others have no money but all the time in the world. A busy executive races down the motorway in his BMW talking into his mobile telephone, portable computer and fax on the seat beside him. He has all the accoutrements of wealth but he has convinced himself that he has no time. A mile away a man in a string vest stands smoking a cigarette on the twelfth-floor balcony of a high-rise block of flats. He is trying to fill his day. If he had money he could go and do things, but he has no money. There are two days before his social security cheque arrives. He has all the time in the world.

In the modern world people are not only divided by monetary wealth but by which time zone they are in. A full filofax is just as important a sign of wealth as a full stomach. This is the new materialism. Some people are so busy that one suspects that they are trying to so fill their lives that there is no time to think. Such people feel worthless when they are alone and may be at a loss to know what to do with themselves. If they do have leisure time they go at it with the same commitment as they do their work.

Such a man will not admit to something as negative as depression. He will admit to stress because it is a word of activism. Dorothy Rowe, in her work on depression, has found that many more men succumb to depression than is actually thought to be the case, but they will not call it that.

Such an attitude to life makes intimacy impossible because intimacy needs time. It is very difficult to be intimate when you have to book friends or partners into the diary in order to be intimate with them. People do not respond to being fitted in to another person's life. The highest compliment one person can pay another is that they are willing to waste time with them for hours on end, with no apparent purpose or agenda, just for the pure pleasure of being with them. Often books on marriage and relationships take the busy life as a given and make practical suggestions about how one can create time, by going away for special weekends, or taking an evening off now and then. But these things are like putting a surgical dressing on a gaping wound. If we are as desperate as we seem as a society to recover intimacy and community out of the fragmentation of our world, then at some point somebody has got to stand up and say 'enough is enough'.

Against the background of the barrenness of the busy life, those who have all the time in the world feel worthless. Nobody feels that their time is important. They are those who are made to sit waiting for hours in various waiting rooms and ante-rooms of the welfare state. Men who have been told that their value and virtue is found in work feel under threat when they are made redundant or even retire after a successful work life. In the case of redundancy a person's family life may initially improve as a man has more time to be with his partner and friends. He may go through a time of rediscovery of his sexual life but soon time will hang heavy on him and eat away at his sense of self-worth. In a society which values time so highly, such people will shrink from intimacy because they feel they have nothing to say. There is nothing to know, there is no point to intimacy because life is not going anywhere.

These two kinds of situation are interdependent. Both men are responding to their masculinity which has told them that a successful man is the busy man. Both are tyrannised by time instead of being stewards of it. If there is one thing that the ristian faith speaks out about again and again it is that everything we do is done for God and that we are to use our time wisely. Life is a gift of God, as are people, and the Christian insight which sets us free is that we are called and not driven. The man who knows what he is called to do knows his limits, he knows that God does not ask him to do everything but has so made life that there is space for worship, rest, recreation, love and friendship. Such a man may not become president of a multinational corporation but there is a contentment about his life which others may rightly envy.

Out of Sight, Out of Mind?

The modern world fosters the idea of autonomy, an idea which is hostile to intimacy. We admire 'self-made' men who are seen as strong and self-sufficient. We are brought up to try and achieve something similar in our lives. But the kind of priorities which we have to take on board to be such people are very different from the priorities of intimacy. One of these is mobility. We are a society that is always on the move in search of success. Promotion at work often means moving the home and family, a major disruption which figures high in the league of stress factors. Mobility may bring material wealth but at a very high cost. We now live at some distance from other members of our family; grandparents travel long distances to see their grandchildren, men commute sometimes hundreds of miles to work because the job is the reference point. Friendships are difficult to sustain because we are always moving on and though we promise people that we will 'keep in touch' there is nothing like mobility to distance us from people.

Mobility is not only to do with geography but is also social. We talk about 'moving up the ladder' to join those people whom we admire at the top, but we do not think about those we have left behind; whom we grew up with, who were our friends and neighbours, and whom we belonged to and who knew us. We therefore trade a higher standard of living for a lower quality of life and live on the fast track with people who are also moving so fast that we do not even know the name of their spouse. This mobility causes all kinds of problems in our society, among them a sense of anonymity in big cities, where people are just passing through. It produces a nostalgia in our society for a sense of community which we believe we have lost. It produces a lack of accountability for our environment as we pass through areas which we will not have to live in for long. But perhaps most of all, mobility destroys the framework of intimacy. In more measured communities we know people and are known by them.

Community fosters intimacy. How many of us still have one good friend from our childhood past who grew up with us and knows us in a completely different way to everybody else? Such communities have their own problems and I am not advocating that we all flee to villages and communes. In a static society it may well be that the best thing to do is to move, as I did at the age of eighteen to enjoy London life as a student. But in a society whose mobility has become demonic it may well be that the prophetic action is to put down roots. Churches cannot grow in the quality of their life together if the congregation turns over every three years. Neighbourhoods cannot become friendly, if people are constantly moving away.

Why look at mobility in a book on masculinity? One of the reasons is that men are more prone to mobility than women. They work away from the home and neighbourhood more often and do not develop as strong a network of relationships. I worked in an office in my home for many years when I worked in Lady Bay in Nottingham, and got to know the people in the community very well. I rarely saw other men during the day; they were mostly invisible in the community, appearing only at the weekends. Some seemed to treat their homes as a boarding house for bed and breakfast. Mobility is definitely part of the core identity of modern masculinity.

In this context the Christian ethic is that of contentment.

Those people who find security in speed experience contentment as boredom. In order to be able to be content such people must radically change their priorities in life from the priorities of autonomy to the priorities of intimacy.

The Material Illusion

Materialism destroys intimacy because, as Erich Fromm points out in his book *To Have Or To Be*[1], it confuses having with being. A materialistic society provides people with masks which they can wear. The advertising profession creates images for us to copy. Men are particularly susceptible to materialism when it is seen as the wearing of masks. The car is a very important symbol for men. It combines together images of power, taste, mobility and wealth to provide a potent symbol of status. The images associated with cars have long been a guide to masculine conventions and it is no surprise that car advertising in the media is pandering to the concept of the new man, believing him to be the key to a new market.

In another book I talked about the way in which wealth increases privacy.[2] Money gives us the power to control our own lives and to associate with those people who are most like us rather than having to associate with people we do not like or wish to know. Being in control, as we have already seen in an earlier discussion of masculinity in this book, is at the heart of the masculine stereotype. Materialism furnishes us with the masks and images to hide behind, but if people are comparing themselves with one another the wearing of masks will mean that not only is there no intimacy but there can be no community, only proximity. Materialism creates a sense of inadequacy which drives people to accumulate more. This comes about because we compare our inner selves, with all our problems and fears, with the masks that others are wearing to the public world. We forget that our own clothes, education, car, holidays and home can be a mask to them.

Psychologist David Smail concludes from his clinical

experience that men are no less friends to intimacy than women, but that they have been exposed to economic pressures in a different way to women:

> . . . the much-maligned characteristics of masculine insensitivity and emotional unresponsiveness are much more the consequence of spiritually mutilating economic values than of any inherently macho personality features of men themselves, or indeed any real advantage in power or status to be gained by toughness.[3]

All of us, he argues, men and women, have been driven by economic competition and by the need to 'cherish ourselves' to retreat into 'the last embattled refuge of tenderness, i.e. sex, where undefended intimacies may, if but briefly, be exchanged.'[4]

> In other times and places men seem to have been no more reticent than women in expressing their (non-sexual) love for others, and my patients (and indeed nearly all the men I have got to know intimately) experience the necessity to be stereotypically male as an imposition rather than an advantage.[5]

In the 1990s there is a reaction against materialism because of the loneliness which it engenders between people. In the public realm *ecology* is becoming a dominant world-view. In the private world there is a renewal of interest in *spirituality*, especially in New Age ideas. These two factors feature in the anti-sexist men's movement in its search for the new man, but these two paradigms are being added to conventional materialism rather than replacing it. It is only when spirituality is rooted in the Creator God that ecology can make sense as the stewardship of his creation. It is only when people see themselves as pilgrims, whose goal and destiny is a new world characterised by justice, that materialism becomes a foolish and dangerous illusion which distracts people from discovering their true identity and security in God.

There are other factors, of course, which provide a social context for the creation or destruction of intimacy, but I have chosen these three factors because they provide a bridge between the public and private worlds. Our attitude to time, mobility and material possessions serves the individualism and pluralism of our day rather than the creation of community and intimacy. The replacement of our idolatry of these three issues by stewardship, contentment and a godly spirituality is essential if we are to put them in perspective and have any chance of creating a world in which people are more important than things, but we should not underestimate how difficult some men will find this. Images of restraint are rarely used when portraying images of men to be admired.

The Limits to Intimacy
In this section I want to resolve a paradox. On the one hand conventional masculinity can find intimacy quite threatening and tends to focus on other kinds of relationship such as colleagues at work or sports or hobbies. At the same time one only has to read the lonely hearts columns in our newspapers to see what pressure there is in our society for us to be more intimate. Intimacy is not an end in itself and when it becomes the object of our desire it is not only elusive but can be disastrous if it comes to dominate our expectations of every relationship.

Am I therefore saying that men have got it right in the quest of conventional masculinity, to have all kinds of relationships in which intimacy never appears? The answer is that both sides have problems. Men find it difficult to be intimate even in those situations which should be characterised by intimacy, whereas those whose lives are dominated by intimacy may make the mistake of assuming that every relationship in their life should reflect intimacy.

To understand this we must look again at the division of

life into the public and the private. After all, intimacy is a quality which is intensely personal. There is a balance to be found between disclosure and giving ourselves away to all and sundry. The erotic freedom of the Song of Songs takes place in the context of a high-walled garden. Privacy is essential to maintain the freedom of the erotic, because being vulnerable means taking a risk and we can only be sexually intimate with one person.

In his scholarly work, *The Fall of Public Man*, Richard Sennett concludes his discussion of the way the modern world has changed our view of public life with a section entitled 'The Intimate Society'. He starts by saying that:

> The reigning belief today is that closeness between persons is a moral good. The reigning aspiration today is to develop individual personality through experiences of closeness and warmth with others. The reigning myth today is that the evils of society can all be understood as evils of impersonality, alienation and coldness. The sum of these three is an ideology of intimacy: social relationships of all kinds are real, believable, and authentic the closer they approach the inner psychological concerns of each person. This ideology transmutes political categories into psychological categories. This ideology of intimacy defines the humanitarian spirit of a society without gods: warmth is our god.[6]

Richard Sennett suggests that searching for intimacy and a high quality of personal relationships has become an obsession of our society. We have completely unrealistic expectations of what relationships with other people can do for us. One person cannot provide all the emotional resources which another person needs, and when relationships break down under the strain we conclude that there was something wrong with them, but do not think to find fault with our unrealistic expectations of the other person. This ironic state of affairs comes about because of three distortions of our world.

Driven by Longing   One of the most fundamental insights which the Christian faith has about human nature is that God has made us for a relationship with himself and when we are out of that relationship we are in disarray. One of the ways in which this comes out is through a sense of longing. Every human being has this within them, it is a longing for God and socially it is a longing for the kingdom of God. St Augustine, the great Christian leader and theologian said, 'Thou has created us for thyself and our heart is not quiet till it rests in thee.'[7]

Because our longing is a longing for God it has a tendency to make sacred those objects which we mistakenly long for instead of God. Intimacy is not a moral good which can be used as a criterion for judgment in our lives. For five years Helen and I took Bible classes for people who were enquiring about the Christian faith or who had just become Christians. I remember one girl, who had responded to Christ, coming to the group one week and saying, 'I feel so close to God when I sleep with my boyfriend.' Talking to her afterwards it was clear that she had mistaken feeling close to her boyfriend for experiencing intimacy with God. This distortion runs throughout our society. We find it very painful to accept that there may be situations in which we feel intimate but which do not receive God's blessing.

Having put God to death in our world we have displaced this longing for God. It is still present in our lives and can still only be satisfied by a relationship with God but we invest it in other things, where it becomes very dangerous. In the economic realm it can lead to an obsession with progress and growth but a confusion about why we have to grow or what we are progressing towards. In people's personal lives longing gets invested in all kinds of areas. Many people look to holidays as the time when everything will be perfect. They have been busy for so long – they have not read stories to the children, or made love, or read a good book – that the holiday becomes invested with longing. Sometimes it works but sometimes the longing creates expectations that can't be fulfilled and we are disappointed.

As Richard Sennett comments, our society is characterised by a longing for intimacy with one another; a lot of people examine their relationships with the question, 'What am I getting out of this?' We live in a fragmented world in which people often live in proximity to one another but not in community with one another. We long to belong and this has made intimacy tyrannical. It is difficult for men and women to have close friendships without feeling that the relationship would be in some sense 'deeper' if they went over some invisible line into intimacies that may be inappropriate.

The key Christian insight about intimacy is that it is a characteristic of our relationship with God. In the presence of God we are laid bare before him; he knows who we are, he knows things about us we would not even admit to ourselves, and yet he loves us. Because God is invisible people believe that this intimacy is intangible and is a delusion of those who need that kind of prop. Those who have faith in God and spend time in the presence of God know that this relationship of faith is the way in which all other relationships start to fall into place. When I am accepted by God I am not driven by longing to find intimacy in every area of life any more, I am set free from the tyranny of intimacy. Because I have come to terms with who I am as a fallen person in the presence of God, I am able to give and receive intimacy in those relationships where it is appropriate. Here again we see that in a secularised society the lack of acceptance by God leads to a need to find acceptance in others. It also leads to men and women proving themselves to others. We will not be able to accept as a society that intimacy can become idolatry, until we realise that intimacy is rooted in God.

Momentum and Meaning   Many men mistake momentum for meaning. This is another facet of our earlier discussion on mobility. Men sometimes derive satisfaction from searching for something rather than having found something. Some only feel alive when they are searching for meaning through 'working for the revolution', or in the throes of the romantic 'chase', or moving up the ladder of promotion. They work their whole lives to attain a particular position or possess a certain kind of house or car, but when they get there they feel a sense of anti-climax. Possession has not changed them, they are still the same person. Contemporary masculinity feels most fulfilled with constant change. While men are busy they feel that their lives are full and they mistake this for having clear purpose.

In churches people are being constantly challenged to do more and it is possible to feel that it is more obedient to do so. I am sure that all these things are worthy but when I talk to Christians who mistake momentum for meaning they are almost always people who do not give time to prayer. They do not have time for it and the reason for this is because the pace of their life has built up through their drive to be effective and to 'do more'. Prayer is a foolish thing; as far as people who are not Christians are concerned prayer is mere wittering into thin air. Yet it is the life of prayer that these men are being called to and real change will only occur in their lives when they cut across momentum by giving space to God in their lives. People who spend time with God and who know God are people who know that their Christian life consists of not being busy, but of being obedient to their calling, whatever that is. It is the height of irony that those who have been accepted by God displace intimacy with God by activity for God.

People as Objects It is very difficult in our culture not to be aware of the gaze of other people and of being evaluated by them. We are aware that others sometimes see us in a way that we do not see ourselves. We grow up to see ourselves as a certain kind of person and eventually derive a sort of shorthand about interpreting our own behaviour. We describe ourselves as shy or extrovert, we see ourselves as weak or strong. Instead of living with all the messiness of the constant change, dialogue and responsiveness going on inside us, we put labels on ourselves and, once we are satisfied with them, we stop listening to ourselves.

One of the hallmarks of our society is *objectivity*. We feel we can sum up people after a few moments' conversation. We meet at a party, have a conversation for twenty minutes, and by listening to what they have to say, the way they say it, the manner of their dress, the accent and their mannerisms we feel quite self-assured in summing them up and putting a label on them, something which no self-respecting psychologist would do. In doing so we close countless options. The next time we meet them we are surprised if they behave differently. They are behaving 'out of character'. Such shorthand labels pin people down. Even more dangerously we use exactly the same process on ourselves. It seems too painful to live with the open-ended *subjectivity* of the contradictions, paradoxes and ironies that pass through our head each day. So having come to the conclusion that we are this or that sort of person, we begin to behave in character, as this or that person is meant to behave.

The labels we place on ourselves we gain from other people's view of us. I used to know a woman called Mary who told people she was shy, and indeed she behaved as if she were shy, but she was also very angry. One day she answered back her husband for the first time. Being encouraged by the sound of her own voice, she ended up having a blazing row with him, telling him all the things that she had wanted to say since they had been married. He was taken aback. This was out of character. Was she ill? But it was not out of character. She was expressing the things that were really going on in her head, only she had been taught that she was a shy person and that shy people did not raise their voice.

The closer we can make our inner lives fit with the labels which we propagate, the fewer problems we cause ourselves but the greater the deception. Every human being has access in themselves to the whole range of human emotions. There is nobody in this world who does not experience anger, or irritability, or disgust. If people never show these things, why not? Intimacy is about relating to one another as human subjects rather than as human objects. It is about exploring the world behind the labels and encouraging a person to open up. The wonderful thing about intimacy is that it changes a person's own perception of himself. It opens up possibilities within them that they had long suppressed by only seeing themselves as a certain kind of person. Love sets us free to be ourselves but the person who sets us free must be free himself.

Treating people as objects is very much a part of masculine deception. Masculinity focuses on the rational and on the ability to control one's environment, but intimacy brings loose ends, messiness, pain and unanswered questions, which are the stuff of joy. Men feel more masculine if they feel that they can control, explain, predict and interpret. This is all much easier if you can sum up people, put a label on them and explain any contrary behaviour as being out of character. People are more complex than that, and it is in admitting the inconsistencies and tensions and longings in our lives that there exists a possibility of freedom.

Intimacy as an Expression of God's Love

Intimacy is therefore rooted in God's grace towards us. It is not something to be earned in our personal relationships. It is something that we mirror to other people because it is at the heart of God's love for us. We love God, says John the Apostle, because he first loved us.[8] This self-acceptance enables us to see ourselves as we really are, this frail mixture of good and evil. It enables us to accept criticism and see it as truth. It enables us to receive praise and see it in its true light. But most of all, grace enables us to be humble because we owe who we are to God and are dependent on him. Humility is opposed to autonomy. No self-made man has ever walked the Christian world. Christian men know that they owe who they are to the graciousness of God and that this spells freedom.

Without this God-framework for our lives, intimacy can become distorted and tyrannical. Men who are really looking for intimacy can mistake it for genital sexuality and its barrenness, yet the search for intimacy, and whether we have achieved it, can become the single standard of truth which stands over our society. It measures society in psychological terms. Those who have not experienced intimacy search for it everywhere, even in the most inappropriate places. It is also true that when people's lives are barren of spiritual reality, intimacy shares this barrenness between people.[9] People come with high expectations of becoming intimate, believing that they will find in this next relationship all that they have ever longed for. What they find is another person exactly like them, looking for fulfilment in them. This leads to a quiet desperation in society as the very value which everybody is searching for becomes something which nobody can find.

We have forgotten that in the story of our genesis there are two accounts of the creation of humanity. The second talked of the relationship between men and women, but the first talked of the relationship between humanity and God. We cannot find who we are in other people. We can only find who we are in God, for we are made in the image of God. When we find God we are able to put appropriate boundaries around intimacy. We do not look at all relationships with the same intensity. We do not look into every nook and cranny of life for meaning. We are quite happy to accept that there are very important aspects of life which are impersonal, political and civic, without making everything personal.

The shift in our society from the public to the private locates meaning in our emotional life. The public realm has been taken over by bureaucracies, experts and systems. Men feel swallowed up in the vast machine of public life. They wonder what it is all for. What are they building? What are they preserving? What are they fighting for? If their *raison d'être* is the next generation, what kind of world will that generation be born into? At the same time as these questions raise their head in the public realm, the private realm beckons, promising us emotional fulfilment and the perfect relationship. Yet we are all too aware that our relationships are anything but perfect, given the rate at which they are breaking down. Is it true that men find it difficult to communicate with women? There is little point in loving somebody if you cannot communicate with them.

QUESTIONS

1. In what way does the way we prioritise our time affect intimacy?
2. We are a highly mobile society. To what extent does mobility undermine friendship, intimacy and community? Is the loss of these things less important than the economic and social gains from mobility?
3. Are people more important than things? Can others looking at our lives infer that we think they are?
4. Is Richard Sennett right in concluding that 'warmth is our God'?
5. Should all relationships be characterised by intimacy? If not, why not?
6. How would you counsel a man who constantly mistakes momentum for meaning in his life?
7. What labels do you most often use of people? What labels do you think are most frequently applied to you?
8. To what extent is the longing for intimacy with others a longing for intimacy with God?

NOTES

1. Erich Fromm, *To Have Or To Be* (London: Abacus, 1976).

2. Roy K. McCloughry, *The Eye of the Needle* (Leicester: IVP, 1990).
3. David Smail, *Taking Care: An Alternative to Therapy* (London: J. M. Dent & Sons, 1987), p. 98.
4. ibid.
5. Smail, op. cit., p. 99.
6. Richard Sennett, *The Fall of Public Man* (London: Faber and Faber, 1986), p. 259.
7. St Augustine of Hippo, *Confessions: Book 1, Chapter 1* (London: Penguin, 1990).
8. 1 John 4:19.
9. Richard Sennett says about this, '. . . the experience of intimacy defeats the expectations people have of intimate encounter because "the nature of man" is in its interior so diseased or destructive that when people reveal themselves to each other, what they show are all the private little horrors which in less intense forms of experience are safely hidden.' op. cit., p. 338.

12

MEN AND COMMUNICATION

Intimacy cannot blossom if the end result of conventional masculinity is *fear* rather than freedom. In the sexual context, uncritical conformity to masculinity leads to an inner dialogue with fear in men. If men are to discover and experience intimacy they must overcome fear first. So many men are in the position which Victor Seidler describes in his essay 'Fear and Intimacy':

> I learnt not to show my fear to others as I learnt to hide it from myself. But also I discovered that in hiding my fear I hid my vulnerability. I learnt to listen to others, but not to really share myself. I had to slowly learn that in blocking my fear I was hurting my capacity for close and loving relationships.[1]

It is part of masculinity that men use language and understanding to control their personal experience and relationships. Men may experience deep emotions but seem to have dislocated the link between experiencing them and talking about them. Men are no less emotional than women but they do often seem to be less articulate. They therefore have to get in touch with these emotions, discover them again in order to be able to share them. One of the problems is that fear is unacceptable to masculinity. Throughout boyhood, courage, bravery and being a man are all mixed together in a myth which defies weakness. In the UK we are still too close to the stiff-upper-lip model of masculinity. It is difficult for men to accept that strength can be found in recognising weakness and allowing others to see it. Instead men act as they are expected to act rather than being sensitive to their own inner promptings.

Intimacy and Communication

In the previous chapter I looked in detail at the social context for intimacy and at the way in which the search for intimacy can replace our search for God and come to dominate us because of this. In this chapter the focus is on personal communication especially communication between men and women. Before I turn to the problems associated with communication between men and women I want to look at intimacy again, asking if it is anything more than 'a feeling of closeness'. If we reduce it to its lowest common denominator then it is easy to see that we can become satisfied with a feeling of warmth in our relationships. But intimacy has a moral dimension. It is possible to 'feel close' to somebody but be blackmailed emotionally by them. A man and a woman may enjoy being together but he or she may be disloyal to their partner when they are away from them. What elements does intimacy need to have in order that closeness should also convey a sense of freedom? I would like to focus on five elements.

Integrity There can be no intimacy without honesty and trust. No one will commit themselves to someone they do not trust or who is deceitful. Where men deceive themselves about their motives and about their emotions they may expect trust but they will rarely receive it. Women are not stupid. They can see dishonesty a mile off and know, as do children, whom to trust. Men who say one thing and do another, men who are dishonest at work or who are not people of integrity may wonder why people do not confide in them and why their partners do not open up to them. Over the last twenty or thirty years there has been a decline in personal moral standards in our society. Actions which our parents' generation would have called dishonest are now regarded as normal or acceptable. If men are to recover intimacy they must first recover integrity.

Faithfulness In a promiscuous world faithfulness is perceived as boring but, for those who wish to cultivate intimacy, faithfulness is essential. It has two facets. Firstly *loyalty*. No woman will be intimate with a man who is not loyal to her. I remember one middle-aged man called Douglas who was always talking about his wife to other people, and usually moaning about her. At the end of his moaning, he would always say, 'I don't know why I stay with her. There's nothing left in our relationship.' Douglas never learned that a woman will not be able to give herself to a man who may be talking about her behind her back. She needed to know that wherever he was, her best interests were being served and her reputation was intact. Disloyalty is an abuse of love in that it makes public those things that should remain private. Secondly, *commitment*. A woman will not be able to be intimate with a man who may leave her for another woman. She will always hold herself back, protecting herself against the eventuality that one day she may be on her own.

Vulnerability This is a key word for men to grapple with and often comes up in the men's group which I attend. It is characterised by two things. Firstly, *openness*; a willingness to share the good and the bad rather than hiding from other people what we think they may not like about us. It also means being willing to be hurt because we are aware of our own capacity to hurt others. Christianity is realistic because it reminds a couple that they are both sinful and capable of all kinds of evil. It is not as if we are becoming vulnerable to somebody who is all-loving. We will be hurt. But those who are intimate with one another know that love takes people through hurt and can deepen because of it.

Secondly, *disclosure*; it is one thing to be willing to share with somebody, but it is quite another to actually do it. There can be no intimacy without disclosure. Many men find talking about themselves very difficult, as if they do not like the sound of their own voice, but as we shall soon see, intimacy is dependent on conversation. Intimacy is also a two-way process. It is not enough for only one person to share while the other remains well-defended. For intimacy to exist there must be mutual disclosure. Otherwise, power can easily creep back into the relationship and it becomes one of dependency. Communion between two people is based on interdependence. The opposite of intimacy is autonomy, and disclosure is very difficult for those men who have been taught that autonomy is a sign of strength, at least in the public sphere. Modern conventions demand a split personality for men who are meant to be self-sufficient at work and intimate at home. Nevertheless vulnerability is a key to intimacy and it is one which men find particularly hard to bear in the face of masculine conventions.

Acceptance Intimacy cannot flourish where acceptance is not present. But where people cannot accept themselves they cannot offer intimacy. Acceptance mirrors the grace of God, who does not require perfection before he accepts us but loves us as we are. This has not come home to many men, who are driven to become somebody else who is more acceptable to others.

Rejection can come in many forms, both explicit and implicit. Attempts to be vulnerable can be met with incomprehension, scepticism, denial, derision or anger which instead of rewarding vulnerability with intimacy, closes the door in its face. Many people who are very well-defended emotionally are those who at some time in their lives have been vulnerable to somebody and have been scarred. It is quite often the case that when somebody has been in a close, loving relationship which turns sour and breaks up they find it very difficult to enter into another relationship. They experience the breakdown of the relationship as rejection and the deeper it had gone, the deeper the hurt. But there is no replacement for acceptance within intimacy. There is no point in marrying someone who you want to change. That will only result in conditional love, where the person is aware of the conditions but unaware of the love. Intimacy reflects the quality of our relationships and is a fragile thing.

One cannot assume that intimacy will always be there. It is not something which is static, which couples possess and others do not. But the great hope at the heart of intimacy is that anybody can foster it if they are willing to spend time with another person, give up any idea of power or possession, recognise and share their own weakness, and in a loyal and committed relationship be loving, supportive and open towards the other person. It is also dependent upon a person's willingness to listen to their partner and to put themselves in their partner's shoes and ask, how do they feel, what do they hear, what are they trying to say?[2]

Communication   While much of the feminist analysis of the behaviour of men is undoubtedly true, it is deeply flawed. It assumes that a woman's interpretation of what a man is doing or saying is also his view of it. We may expect differences in talking to people from other cultures but we expect our partners to have a similar view of the world to ourselves. If they see the world so differently that we think they must be living on another planet this shakes us. But men view the world very differently. All conversation between men and women is cross-cultural conversation. This is why it is absolutely essential that men discover in themselves a personal language with which they can express what they mean. At present men feel the victims of the accusations of women but they are victims by default, having little insight into their own world. We can only hope for partnership and mutuality if both sides can listen and understand what the other is saying *in their own terms*.

Are Men Inarticulate?

Men frequently complain that 'My wife doesn't understand me' or 'I just don't understand women'. Usually the response to this is that the man is using this as an excuse for continuing with behaviour and attitudes with which his wife disagrees.

But what if what he says is true? It may be that as far as he is concerned they talk different languages. Women complain that 'My husband doesn't talk to me' or 'My husband doesn't share himself with me'. But instead of this being the final sentence, a conclusion and a giving up on men as inarticulate, what would happen if it were the opening up of an exploration as to why this appeared to be true?

Shere Hite's study, *Women and Love*, opens with the questions: 'What is the biggest problem in your current relationship? How would you like to change the relationship if you could? Could it be better? How?' 4,500 women responded to her survey, of these ninety-eight per cent said that they would like more verbal closeness with the men they loved. 'They want the men in their lives to talk more about their own personal thoughts, feelings, plans, and questions, and to ask them about theirs.'[3] Some women said that they thought that men believed that not talking about feelings was part of being 'male'. Seventy-one per cent said that the men in their lives were afraid of emotion. Sixty-three per cent said they met with real resistance when they tried to push their husband or lover to talk about feelings. Fifty-two per cent doubted men's desire for deeper communication. Seventy-one per cent of women in long marriages, who had originally tried to draw their husbands out, finally gave up.

When asked, 'What does your partner do that makes you maddest?' seventy-seven per cent of women responding to the survey said, 'He doesn't listen', eighty-four per cent said that he does not appear to hear or want to hear, forty-one per cent of women said that men told them *not* to feel what they were feeling.[4]

These responses should alarm us. They show just how shaky the foundations of our relationships are. Women in Hite's survey obviously felt more at ease, appreciated and intimate with other women than with men. They felt invisible, overlooked and taken for granted. A third of the women felt guilty for being so self-expressive, as if it was they who were in the wrong. Many women feel that men mistake sex for communication, whereas what women want is more intimacy and that means verbal disclosure, vulnerability and openness. The end result of this behaviour is tragic; when asked when they are most lonely eighty-two per cent of women said that they are loneliest when married to someone with whom they cannot talk.[5]

Every counsellor knows that behind the lace curtains of our suburbs and the tower blocks of our inner cities, there are human tragedies being played out in great pain and misunderstanding. Many men and women seem to be caught up together in a vast irony. All their lives they believe that meeting the right partner is what they need to bring their life fulfilment, but the reality can be lonely, painful and debilitating.

You Just Don't Understand

Deborah Tannen is Professor of Linguistics at Georgetown University in the US. Her outstanding academic work, on how men and women use conversation differently, recently came to the attention of English audiences with the publication in 1991 of her book, *You Just Don't Understand: Women and Men in Conversation*.[6] Her main thesis is that misunderstanding occurs through conversation. But men and women use conversation differently. Women use conversation to seek confirmation, make connections and reinforce intimacy. Men use it primarily to protect their independence and negotiate status. Men and women live in different cultures: he in a world characterised by *independence* and she in a world characterised by *intimacy*. Because of this all conversation is cross-cultural and can cause genuine confusion.

I remember being with a couple who were obviously going through a 'dispute'. It turned out that the husband, Bill, had a habit of going out and spending money on things for the home without consulting Sue. They viewed this very differently. She expected such decisions to be made by consensus and after much discussion. She felt as if her wishes had been ignored and this made her feel unimportant.

She did not disagree that they needed whatever it was he had bought but felt she should have been consulted. He didn't want a long discussion over something he knew they wanted anyway, so went ahead and bought it. They had different views of decision-making, but they did not know that they had different views. As Tannen describes:

> If intimacy says, 'we're close and the same,' and independence says, 'we're separate and different,' it is easy to see that intimacy and independence dovetail with connection and status. The essential element of connection is symmetry: people are the same, feeling equally close to each other. The essential element of status is asymmetry: people are not the same; they are differently placed in a hierarchy.[7]

These two different strategies in conversation mirror closeness and community on the one hand, and contest and competition on the other. If people use conversation to try and be like one another they will deepen the relationship between them. But relationships of asymmetry are always adversarial in nature.

Superiority in Conversation

Consider the following scenario. Jennifer has a pain in her back and tells her husband David about it. He responds by telling her that she ought to go to the doctor, yet it is obvious to both of them that this is not the right response. She expected and wanted understanding, but he gave her advice. She wanted confirmation, but he solved her problem for her. As a result she felt belittled, but he felt hurt because he had tried to help but felt rejected. This kind of situation is mirrored up and down our country in millions of homes. Women do not want their men to approach their problems as if they are Mr Fix-It. What they want is empathy and understanding. Jennifer wanted to talk about it, to explore the pain and maybe to share some fears, but David curtailed this conversation, feeling that the rational outcome must be to go to the doctor. It is ironic that he sees his solution as an expression of his concern, but for her it is anything but. In 'troubles talk' women want the listener to reinforce the similarity between them. Other women may have responded by discussing a similar pain which they had and their fears about it. The problem is that in a conversation with a man, women so often end up in an asymmetrical conversation and feel that the giving of advice is not an expression of concern but an intimation of superiority.

However, it would not be true to suggest that men cannot create intimacy in conversation with one another, but they do it via a different means. Suppose that John has drunk too much at a party and someone at the party who knows him well suggests that he has a problem with alcohol. The next day he meets a friend called Arthur and says that people think he's an alcoholic because he drank too much at the party. John knows that by admitting this possibility he is giving Arthur the opportunity to give him advice and to confirm the diagnosis, thus showing that he is superior, and Arthur could do this but it would only make John feel worse. What Arthur could do is to deliberately ignore the opportunity for giving advice by admitting that he himself sometimes drinks too much, and by doing so he restores the symmetry of the conversation.

By admitting that they both have the same problem they create intimacy between them. They say in fact that they are the same and not different. This intimacy is not generated by assuming intimacy but by denying the opportunity for power and status to enter in to their relationship. It is not the admission by itself which creates intimacy but the convergence of three things. Firstly, Arthur also admits the problem. Secondly, he denies the opportunity to take power over John and therefore passes up the opportunity to make a judgment on him. Thirdly, he makes himself vulnerable in turn to John, who could say in riposte that he knows about Arthur's problem and it is much worse than his own. All these elements are needed if intimacy is to result.

Conversations can be divided into the message which people are talking about and the metamessage, (i.e. the message framed by the entire conversation) which asks, 'What is actually going on here?' For instance, Tannen observes that so many male drivers will not stop and ask for directions, even though they are clearly lost. They prefer to drive round and round, ever hopeful that they will stumble across the place they are trying to get to. Whereas women might be willing to ask, often men are not. She comments that the information that a stranger might offer may be a message which is helpful in finding one's way, but the fact that the stranger has the information and the driver does not sends a metamessage of superiority. Many men believe that admitting that they do not know something is humiliating. But they also believe that it is likely that, if they ask directions of somebody who does not know, that person also might find their own ignorance humiliating, leading to one of two results. Firstly, the male driver should not put himself and the other person in a mutually humiliating situation, but secondly the person may be so embarrassed that they may give false directions just to give the appearance of having the information.[8]

There is another reason why men may not ask directions, and that is that many men feel that they have to be sensitive as to who they choose to ask directions from. Many men will not wish to ask a woman, since they may startle her. For similar reasons they may not wish to ask a young person or a child, who will have been brought up not to talk to strangers. They are then left with evaluating the other men around who look as though they might know the directions and are not going to be brusque and macho about it. With such arguments men are quite able to convince themselves that their behaviour is entirely rational and appropriate.

This illustration shows us that giving and receiving information can reinforce bonds between people but it can create hierarchy as well. Many men feel rejected when their partners ask them a question which requires them to give technical information. They sit down to explain the workings of some technicality and feel hurt that the woman is suddenly not interested. He is trying to give her the very thing she requires but his offer, 'Let me explain', is seen by her as a metamessage of superiority. The same thing happens in contemporary society when men hold open the door for women or give up their seat. Men see what they are doing as polite and deferential but some women, especially younger women, see the metamessage of superiority. All these things may be invisible to the participants in the conversations. They become genuinely confused and wonder what has gone wrong. Yet to the observer, who can look at both sides of the exchange dispassionately and put the entire conversation in the context of each side's expectation (framing), it is quite clear what is going on.[9]

The Public and the Private

The examples go on and on, both of misunderstandings and of different kinds of conversation. Tannen distinguishes between rapport-talk and report-talk, asking the question, 'Who speaks more, men or women?'[10] It is often the case that men think that women talk all the time, whereas women often feel that they have to be silent while their men 'hold the floor'. Who is right?

Again it is the context which provides the key. Tannen distinguishes between public and private speaking, with men more at home with public speaking and women with private speaking; the former called report-talk and the latter rapport-talk. Women talk a lot in situations where men do not, either on the telephone or with friends. Women also have conversations that focus on the personal details of people's lives, but men have conversations which focus on events that appear important in public life. A man comes home from work and is asked by his wife, 'What happened today?' 'Nothing', he replies. Yet later in the conversation he drops the fact that two of their friends are getting a divorce. His wife feels that this is something he should have immediately disclosed, but it was obviously not at the forefront of his attention at the time.

Men and women find different things important, and women can see the lack of interest which men sometimes have in the personal details which they find important as a failure of intimacy. But men are not in the habit of verbalising their fleeting thoughts, which they do not think are worth saying. He naturally dismisses his fleeting thoughts, she naturally verbalises them. All of his training as a man leads him to suggest that he should control transient feelings that may not be important, but it does not mean that he does not think them or that he does not desire intimacy. In the public realm the situation is reversed. It is the husband who stands and speaks and the woman who is often silent. She is so aware of all the things that could go wrong if she stood to speak in public and needs time to prepare. The husband appears to be able to stand and talk spontaneously. Women are brought up not to put themselves on display or draw public attention to themselves, and if they do they have to establish their credentials for doing so, so that people will listen with respect.

Men should not dismiss what they call small talk, which in Tannen's words 'serves a big purpose'. I am constantly amazed, when attending parties, at the way in which people who are 'good at small talk' can make and keep friends effortlessly even when they appear to have nothing to say. So many men find such situations difficult socially because they want to talk about something which they view as 'important'. Yet whether it is sharing the dinner table with friends or standing drink in hand at a party, such a topic for conversation can be entirely inappropriate since it can be seen as a man looking for a group of people to whom to deliver a monologue about something which interests him. So-called 'small talk' is inclusive because it draws everybody in. It is conducted on a level of the personal, in which everybody has got something to say. Small talk cuts out the possibility of hierarchy.

Such a picture of small talk or gossip can be portrayed too positively:

For most women, getting together and telling about their

feelings and what is happening in their lives is at the heart of friendship. Having someone to tell your secrets to means you are not alone in the world. But telling secrets is not an endeavour without risks. Someone who knows your secrets has power over you: she can tell your secrets to others and create trouble for you. This is the source of the negative image of gossip.[11]

Communication and Incarnation

In seeking to understand the theological importance of this theme of communication and understanding it is important to focus on the incarnation. This shows us that Jesus was willing to leave the glory of heaven in order to become human and to share our life together.[12] God does not solve the problem of humanity from heaven but comes to earth and sees our struggle from our perspective. The writer to the Hebrews links the fact that Jesus has gone through the experiences that we have gone through, in terms of temptation and suffering, and therefore understands how we feel. It is interesting that the conclusion which is drawn from this is that we can approach Jesus with confidence, knowing that he understands us, in order to receive mercy and find grace to help us in our time of need.[13]

What can we learn from this? This chapter is calling us to try and see situations from the other person's point of view. It is not asking us to compromise what we believe to be the truth, but it is asking us to see that trying to impose our view of the world on others may lead to resentment and breakdown of communication. Furthermore, it is asking both men and women to make the effort, for although some men may be inarticulate emotionally it is by no means necessarily true that all men are inarticulate, and perpetuating the stereotype does not help. We have seen that men use different ways to achieve the same results and women must be sensitive to those ways.

Christ's own vulnerability, as demonstrated in the incarnation, means that he can only see life from our perspective if he is willing to share our sufferings and our temptations. This is what love demands of us. It is a simple matter to offer advice when what is being asked for is a sharing in suffering. Men who want to avoid opening themselves up to other pain have to pay a high cost for their self-protection, which is that they end up by avoiding intimacy itself. The writer to the Hebrews shows us that we can have confidence to approach Jesus because he sees life from our perspective and he has suffered and been tempted like us. Surely the same is true of our human relationships. If we want people to have confidence in approaching us and sharing themselves with us then they must know that we are not going to judge them or dismiss them, but are people who have been through the same experiences as them and are willing to disclose it. Here again we can see that Jesus shows us that intimacy with God is a model for our friendships and loving partnerships with one another.

We now move on from issues which focus on our relationships together to the world of work. We have already seen in this chapter that one of the reasons why relationships can break down is because men try and apply tools that they have learnt in the world of work, such as problem-solving, to the personal relationships which they have. Have men over-identified with the world of work to the detriment of other areas in their life?

QUESTIONS

1. Do men hide their vulnerability because they fear being rejected, or for some other reason?
2. Do we need integrity, faithfulness, vulnerability, acceptance and communication for intimacy to develop? Is it not possible to experience intimacy during a 'one night stand'?
3. Are men inarticulate emotionally?
4. In what ways does the difference between men and women in conversation style contribute to misunderstanding between the sexes?

5. Do you think that men are good at listening?
6. In what ways does the incarnation help us as a picture of loving commitment?

NOTES

1. Victor Seidler, 'Fear and Intimacy', *The Sexuality of Men*, eds, Andy Metcalf and Martin Humphries (London: Pluto Press, 1985), pp. 150–80.
2. See the work of Maggie Scarf and in particular her work *Intimate Partners: Patterns in Love and Marriage* (London: Century Hutchinson, 1987), which contains a great deal of material on the nature of intimacy in the context of marriage. Also, Robert L. MacDonald, *Intimacy: Overcoming the Fear of Closeness* (London: Daybreak, 1990), contains a great deal of Christian reflection on intimacy which may be helpful to work through. Victor Seidler's work has already been cited above, but he has also written about intimacy in his book, *Rediscovering Masculinity: Reason, Language and Sexuality* (London: Routledge, 1989). Shere Hite's work on male sexuality contains numerous references to intimacy. There is also a collection of essays, which can sometimes be very disturbing: *Men and Intimacy: Personal Accounts Exploring the Dilemmas of Modern Male Sexuality*, ed. Franklin Abbott (Freedom, Calif.: The Crossing Press, 1990).
3. Shere Hite, *Women and Love* (London: Viking, 1987), p. 5.
4. Hite, op. cit., pp. 11–15.
5. Hite, op. cit., p. 23.
6. Deborah Tannen, *You Just Don't Understand: Women and Men in Conversation* (London: Virago Press, 1991).
7. Tannen, op. cit., p. 28.
8. Tannen, op. cit., p. 62.
9. Tannen, op. cit., p. 33.
10. Tannen, op. cit., pp. 74–95.
11. Tannen, op. cit., p. 104.
12. Philippians 2:1–11.
13. Hebrews 4:14–16.

13

MEN AND WORK

There can be no doubt that men's attitude to work and employment is one of the defining characteristics of contemporary masculinity. The concepts of independence and autonomy which are at the heart of 'being a man' are associated with the world of work. It is no coincidence that the majority of men do not admit to vulnerability or emotional needs while at work. Work is the place where, supremely, one is proved to be a man, and that proof consists of being separate from others and achieving something for ourselves which is not owed to the efforts of others. It is in the world of work that we can see most clearly that masculinity is something which is defined externally and is 'put on' like a suit of armour.

Some of the anxieties that men feel arise out of whether they are doing a 'man's job' and there are groups of men who would view certain occupations, for instance entering the ordained ministry, as emasculating. Where men *are* dependent on each other, such as miners or those working on an oil-rig, they often develop a very macho subculture around their work so as not to be misunderstood as being weak because they are interdependent.

If our security as men is found in our work then it is a fragile security when that work depends on economic well-being. Unemployment brings a crisis to men because it destroys part of their sense of personal identity and self-worth. They have been at home in the public world of work and have come from that world to relax, albeit temporarily, at home. But many women who work in the home have made that their own domain, and when unemployment brings the man into the home setting it leads to conflict, as he has no place within the home but only in the world of work. Women tend to have a clearer sense of identity tied up with family life, child-bearing and expressing creativity within the home context. Even if they work outside the home they still have a clear idea of what they are meant to be doing when their activity is restricted to the home itself. However, many women do feel that home-based work is under threat and do not see 'staying at home' as sufficient to give them a sense of fulfilment, status and identity.[1]

Unemployment also hits at one of the most important of the stereotypes which men succumb to: that of the provider or breadwinner. The idea that men go out to work to earn money which is used by others to provide food, shelter and clothing, is embedded deep within contemporary masculinity. Many men feel a deep sense of failure if this particular role is taken away from them and, if this is compounded by their partner being able to find a job and support the family, some men can appear to visibly shrink due to the embarrassment and grief at being 'kept' by a woman. There is a great deal of pride in being a provider and not all of this pride is misplaced. The Bible has a great deal to say about men who are indolent and who refuse to provide either for themselves or for their families. Such men do exist but they are relatively few in number. The majority of men wish to work in order to provide for others and also because it is through work that they feel most fulfilled.

The demands of the women's movement fall into two categories. In the private world of relationships women are demanding that men discover more about *love*. This focuses on the need for partnership, intimacy and sharing between men and women, men and men, and men and children. But the second set of demands arises out of the public realm and is a demand for *justice*. This focuses on the need for men to make room for women in employment, at equal rates of pay and with equal access to power and preferment. These twin demands of love and justice constitute a critical confrontation with masculinity.

Men feel secure in the face of that criticism the more they have themselves become alienated from the way masculinity draws its life from the world of work. Those men who are lost and at a loss without employment and who do not wish to turn and bite the hand which gave them the job security and status which they now enjoy, feel most fear and anger at the criticisms of women, and most betrayed by the men who are attempting to find new ways of being a man in the public world.

Identity and Work

In her book, *Men: The Darker Continent*, Heather Formaini interviewed 120 men as background research. When asked, 'What is the most important thing in your life?' and, 'What is your most important achievement to date?', eighty per cent of men mentioned work.[2] One of the men she interviewed, called Michael, worked in the film industry and turned in incredibly long hours. He claimed that his work didn't give him satisfaction, he had a book to write and he would like to have been able to do that. She comments: '. . . although Michael doesn't get much satisfaction or achievement from his very high-powered job, it does give him a particular identity. He is somebody because of his work and this gives him access to the world of men where his identity as somebody is secure.'[3]

Against this background we can see why the second question we ask a stranger is about what they do. The answer to the question tells us about not what they do but who they are, and what they aspire to, or so we think. We know whether we should be deferential or superior and whether we have anything in common. It gives us a pigeonhole into which to place the person, surrounded by the pre-packaged images we have already built up about their particular employment. The idea that we talk about the weather may be true, but we talk more about work than anything else.

Women who *just* stay at home often develop the defensiveness of the downwardly mobile. As one woman said, 'If you want to know what *shunning* feels like, you go to a party and if they ask you what you do, you say, "I'm a housewife".' Employed mothers often feel poised between the culture of the housewife and the working man. On the one hand, many women feel criticised by relatives and friends who stay at home, as if under a microscope; while housewives feel threatened and militant about their declining position, especially if they become burdened and exploited with the extra tasks to help support the neighbour at work e.g. collecting delivered parcels, letting in repair men or looking after friends' children when they are sick. Their working neighbours seldom even have the time to stop or chat, let alone return favours. It seems that there are two stereotypes available to women. If you stay at home you're dull and boring, but if you work you're guilty and selfish. You can be a dull person or a bad mother.

So much of conversation revolves around work and employment that men who are unemployed often drop out of social circles, such as pubs and clubs, because they find that the conversation is work-orientated and they have little to contribute. Women who work within the home talk to one another about that world with avidity and enthusiasm, but they rarely would talk at any length about it to a roomful of men who are in employment. Women who work outside the home in the labour market find that they have more in common with male colleagues than previously.

In a world in which status is distributed with the pay-packet personal self-worth and social status are inextricably entwined with employment. The question that this raises is whether men have become over-identified with the world of work. We have already seen that the split between the private world of the home and the public world of work, which came about through industrialisation, has been a tragedy for all kinds of human relationships. Nevertheless, men often seem to be driven by their work rather than being able to put it in perspective with the rest of their life. It is as if the more they achieve in the world of work the more of a man they think they are, but the very drivenness at the heart of such a quest speaks of an inner insecurity.

I have talked to countless men over the years who have been extremely successful at their jobs yet, who in a moment of vulnerability, have told me about their inner inadequacies and insecurities. On each occasion I was surprised as I had been completely fooled by the external masks of achievement and success that they had identified with. One of the problems with building security out of achievements which are tangible is that the bigger they become the greater the loss if they disappear. Achievements borne out of economic success can be very fragile, as Luke portrays in the story of the man who built his barns bigger every year. The man was a fool because he was deluded that there was security in things which, from the perspective of eternity, are transient. The context for this obsession is the change in the world of work which came through industrialisation, but there is something more to this drivenness about masculinity and to pinpoint this we need to go back to the story of the fall in the Garden of Eden.

The Consequences of the Fall

We have already emphasised the perfect partnership between the man and the woman as a reflection of God's original intentions. Both men and women were called to subdue the world and to fill it. In Genesis 3 both the man and the woman are disobedient and through their disobedience sin and evil enter into the world. What are the consequences of this change? They are pervasive. Four kinds of relationship are distorted: between people and God, within human relationships of all kinds, between a person and their now distorted self-image, and in events happening in the public world, including the world of work and the relationship with the environment. In the latter part of Genesis 3 God explains the consequences of what they had done to the man and the woman.

This is not a judgment drawn out of thin air and pronounced by a vindictive God: Adam and Eve lived in a moral world in which immoral actions affected both them and God and had disastrous consequences. The effect of their actions is to introduce a split between them; the effects of the fall on the woman are found in the world of relationships, but the man suffers in the world of work, environment and the control of the public landscape. This is the first time such a division has been entertained. There is no hint before this that the world of work belongs to the man and the world of the home belongs to the woman. These things were included in the partnership which they enjoyed before this point.

What has happened for the man is that something which was essentially good and which was enjoyed with the woman has become distorted, provisional and frustrating. Adam is to know 'painful toil' instead of the joy of creative co-operation with God in the management of his world. The thorns and thistles (verse 18) speak not only of the hostility which now mingles with the goodness of the environment but emphasises the frustration at working at a world some of which yields weeds, which in their turn need more work to eradicate them and so on. The metaphor is applicable across the experience of human work, which can be arduous and yet constantly produces frustrating results, failure and difficulties which require us to work even harder to overcome them. Adam is reminded in verse 19 that from now on eating will be associated with sweat. It is no coincidence that it is at this point that God reminds Adam that he was taken from the dust and

he will return to the dust. It is as if God is emphasising to Adam that all his life he will work hard to
keep himself and his dependants, but without God he
moves from dust to dust. All of this could have been a
co-operative joy with God, now it is isolating, competitive
and hard.

This raises several important points for us. Christianity
has often been accused of underwriting patriarchy, but
looking at the creation narrative we find that the division of public and private is not something underwrit-
ten by Christianity, nor can it be called natural or normative. Christianity calls this division between men and
women evil, it is a result of the fall. It points to the
drivenness of working in a frustrating world as arising out
of the dislocation and disobedience which came through
the fall.

This is important as it is a starting point for many of
the divisions in our world, which theorists have sometimes
called biological and from which they have tried to create
norms. But at the heart of the Christian faith there is a
commitment to hope, that all those things that entered the
world through sin and evil can be overcome because of the
power of redemption, which frees men and women from
entrapment of the consequences of their own disobedient
actions.

The Bible places the emphasis in a different place to
the determinists and the humanists. We are responsible
for our own actions but God has stepped in, in Christ,
and has turned these things around so that good can come
of them. Yet again we see that Christian teaching is not
that this division should be continued and made normative,
but a hope that the New Testament, and in particular the
teaching and mission of Christ, will close the divide, heal
the wounds and bring a sense of vocation to heal the
idolatry of work that has arisen from this evil consequence.
Psychologist Mary Stewart van Leeuwen puts this well when
she says:

. . . [it] is precisely on the basis of creation theology that I argue for change. For if both men and women were created for sociability and accountable dominion, then any theology that defends an exaggerated separation of male and female spheres, with the 'domestic mandate' effectively limited to women and the wider 'cultural mandate' to men, is not an adequate creation theology at all. It is rather an accommodation to those social forces which have carelessly ripped apart the organic unity of homes and communities and turned us into a society of commuting wage workers (mostly men) and domestically isolated homemakers (mostly women).[4]

The Stress of Work

From this we can conclude that everything that men and women work at will be in some sense an experience which they find frustrating and hard. Even creative work, which some look to idealistically, can be work characterised by sweat. Men work in many different jobs: some have routine manual work where their problem is that nothing taps into their creativity, others communicate all day in the classroom or the lecture theatre, some make money for a living and are driven by the pace of the financial markets, others administer the manufacturing process or tend sick people. Work in some way expresses the diversity of masculinity.

Yet there is a group of ideas which many men are aware of and to which they compare themselves constantly. These ideas have produced grave distortions in the attitudes of men to work and are at the heart of what contemporary men believe it means to be masculine.

The word 'stress' is a very contemporary expression of the problem, in engineering terms a piece of metal is stressed when it is bearing a load greater than its designer intended. Any study of stress must encompass a view of what is normative or intended for us as workers and an analysis of why we are carrying loads too heavy for us. I start with the latter.

It is important to note, as Dorothy Rowe has done on depression, that men are more willing to use the word 'stress' of themselves than the word 'depression'. This is because 'stress' is a word which denotes intense activity, its companion phrase is 'burn out'. The idea is that the person involved was moving at such a high speed and carrying such great responsibilities that it was inevitable that there were consequences. Men use stress in such a way as to remain in touch with the superman image. A moment ago they were accomplishing inordinate feats but now they cannot cope, although they would not put it in this way. The word 'depression' on the other hand is a word of inactivity and is wrongly associated with failure and a sense of inadequacy. Men are unwilling to admit failure and even more unwilling to admit to other men that they cannot get out of bed in the morning to go to work, as this is a betrayal of all that they think masculinity stands for. The choice of the word 'stress' over the word 'depression' gives us a clue to the family of problems that men have introduced by attaching work to their need to prove themselves masculine.

The Barrenness of a Busy Life

All kinds of men who may have nothing in common with one another work too hard. In my experience this does provide a differential between men and women. I know women who work very hard indeed but the majority of them retain some kind of perspective on the rest of their lives. They are able to admit when they have had enough and go home. The women I know who constantly overwork are all working in a male-dominated occupation, where the men have made it a criterion of the work that exhaustion is the same as normality. They feel worn down by this and have begun to capitulate to it.

Even in Christian work many men tell me in the first few sentences how busy they are. There are several things at work here which it is important to draw out.

Substitute for Status Being busy is seen as a substitute for status. A person who is not busy is seen as somebody who is not in demand and therefore not respected. A person who is too busy is seen as somebody who is so much in demand that he cannot meet his commitments and has therefore conned himself that he is respected.

Substitute for Productivity   The second myth is that being busy is the same as being productive, but studies of men who work very long hours have shown that they are only productive for a part of the day, in most cases the mornings. In many cases this is because there is a great deal of padding in the day. They generate meetings which are unnecessary, have long lunches and even longer phone calls when a fraction of the time could have been spent making productive and fruitful decisions. Many executives, for instance, spend a lot of time massaging the culture rather than getting on with work. This is all to do with maintaining one's place in the pecking order and making sure that people know that you still have authority and are still capable. But at the heart of this overwork is a delusion. An observer could see that these men are not being productive but they themselves have chosen to avoid such a conclusion. Perhaps for some men their sense of masculinity makes them compensate for the fact that they are not in manual work but are essentially pushing papers around a desk. They cannot derive security as men from this and therefore have to create an inner momentum and drive through which they convince themselves that what they are doing proves they are a man.

Substitute for Purpose   Working too hard also replaces a loss of purpose. Men and women both need a sense of purpose and meaning in life, but men seem to see purpose in terms of a cause which motivates. Many women, on the other hand, feel that they have a sense of purpose and calling available to them in motherhood, child-bearing and family life. A crisis of meaning happens for such women when they find that they cannot have children or cannot get married. This at least is the traditional view of women, though many women today find the traditional model does not provide the meaning and fulfilment they need and look towards the world of work to provide it. Nevertheless it is certainly true that men are envious of women, who they see as having an option open to them which they cannot share. Women often do not appreciate how trapped men can feel in the world of work.

Some of the jobs that men perform do not readily provide men with meaning and purpose. Some men may respond by looking elsewhere, those whose jobs are full of boring routine may quickly develop a view of work which sees it as instrumental. It provides the money for them to go on holiday or to take up some leisure pursuit. Some men live from one holiday to the next, as if that is the only time when they come alive and are truly themselves, but other men see their work as having to provide everything they are looking for to make them a man. With no rites of initiation into manhood, starting work and leaving school is the nearest thing that we have in our culture. We invest a great deal in it. It is therefore very easy for men who are driven by their work to mistake it for a sense of purpose. This is a very dangerous view of the world because one's whole life depends on momentum; demotion or even side-ways moves within a company can cause loss of momentum and an inordinate amount of disillusionment and depression.

Substitute for Being Needed Many men enjoy the fact that their expertise at work makes them feel needed, however this 'need to be needed' is not something which they will admit to. They enjoy being asked questions, to which they alone have the answer; they enjoy the feeling of power that comes from having people working under them; and they also become addicted to the sense of momentum that they set up around them. A mid-life crisis can often be devastating because it hits a man when he feels most needed but also when he is asking questions about life itself. At this time a younger generation of workers is coming up with new ideas and a new vision, and those who looked to the middle-aged manager now focus their attention on a younger person and the momentum stops. The worst kind of blow is unemployment and some managers that I know have not even bothered to come to terms with it. I knew a man who still got up in the morning, dressed in his pinstripe suit, travelled in the same commuter carriage with his friends and then wandered around the City of London aimlessly until it was time to go home. Even immersing oneself voluntarily in this world can lead to problems.

In his book, *Working*, Studs Terkel gives an interesting example of how self-esteem can suffer. Doctor John Coleman, President of Haverford College, took a sabbatical in 1973. He worked doing menial jobs, on one occasion he was even fired as a porter and dishwasher. He commented:

I had never been fired and I had never been unemployed. For three days I walked the streets. Though I had a bank account, though my children's tuition was paid, though I had a salary and a job waiting for me back at Haverford, I was demoralised. I had an inkling of how professionals my age feel when they lose their jobs and their confidence begins to sink.

Studs Terkel comments on this: '. . . perhaps it's this fear of no longer being needed in a world of needless things that most clearly spells out the unnaturalness, the surreality of much that it is called work today.'[5]

Substitute for Identity   When men avoid facing up to their own personality, with its possibilities and limits, they can turn with relief to the ready-made identity which goes with the job. They replace who they are with what they do. Many jobs have a socialisation process associated with joining them. I remember one woman complaining to me that she had married her husband when he was a student and he was a very relaxed, fun-loving person. But when he left college he became a barrister and she watched him turn into a different person, because of the pressures of conforming to the norms and the culture of the job. It takes a great deal of security and self-assurance to stand out in the crowd, whether the crowd is a group of manual workers with a macho ethos or whether it is a group of medical consultants at a convention. Men often live in a compromise zone between the person they are and the job they do.

Some professions have an additional problem to do with professionalism itself. If a psychiatrist or social worker behaved in their work as if their clients were personal friends and that they ought to share themselves with everybody who came to them, they would be a nervous wreck within the week. Professionalism is about the wearing of masks or 'being in role'. This depends on viewing the person dispassionately and objectively. There are great strengths to that – emotional involvement with a client or patient may detract from helping them – but this means that men in professional life not only grapple with the masks and myths of masculinity but need also to be on guard against slipping into their professional persona when they want to avoid questions of personal identity.

Towards a Christian Perspective on Work

How can men restore their perspective on work? We have seen that the distortions that men are prey to arise from problems to do with status, productivity, purpose, need and identity. From a Christian perspective work may be the means by which some of these values are conveyed but the problem is that men are looking to work itself as an end rather than a means. Men and women both need purpose in life but those men who are over-identified with their work not only neglect relationships and family life but lead lives which are focused on the functional rather than the transcendent.

Many writers on masculinity have noted this loss of cause in men. Robert Bly commented on the passivity of modern men, who allow trends to wash over them like waves and hardly ever resist the consensus, even if it is evil. Men are so busy maintaining the structure of work that they no longer lift their heads up and ask what it is all for. In the Bible we are told that what we do we are to do for God, yet God is often absent from the thinking of a man who is obsessed with functional realities of work. Such a man needs to rediscover three things.

Firstly, Christ is Lord of his work. He does not start working for God when he leaves work and does religious things for the church. God is the Creator God and is present in the world of employment, however technical or obscure it may be. Too many men keep their spirituality and their work in separate compartments and it is important for men to offer their work to God. This is very difficult against the background of the sacred/secular divide, which makes us feel that repairing a car is less spiritual than singing a hymn, but everything we do is to honour God and those things that we do for God we are to do in co-operation with God.

Secondly, men must discover a sense of vocation. 'Calling' is not the prerogative of doctors. Each of us is called by God to use our talents in his service and to be stewards of the resources in our care till he calls us to account for him. Men must ask two radical questions about calling.

Is the job that I am doing reflecting my calling? Some people are not using their talents but are suppressing them. It is important that people are able to use their gifts and some people may need to consider changing what they are doing in order to do this.

What are the limits of my calling? The fact that we are finite is not a curse which we have to overcome by working even harder but is meant to be a signal that we should rest and enjoy the world around us. There are many things which people do, both in and out of the Church, which are the responsibility of other people.[6]

Thirdly, men need to rediscover prayer. I am convinced that men who overwork do not pray. They are convinced that only by working hard can they bring about results. Such a mentality is utterly destroyed by a life of prayer. Prayer is irrational, it does not link cause and effect. From the standpoint of the observer it is wasting time talking into the air, but it restores perspective. It creates quiet and calm in a world gone mad. It produces dignity and a sense of purpose. It gives both men and women a sense of acceptance, affirmation and security through being loved by God. One of the consequences of living as we do in the modern world has been the abdication of a life of prayer. If men will discover themselves again, as they really are, and be healed of the wounds which masculinity has demanded from them there is only one sure way to do it and that is to immerse oneself in God, in a commitment to a life of prayer.

QUESTIONS

1. Why do men feel such a deep sense of failure when they become unemployed?
2. To what extent do men derive their identity, status, purpose and security from employment?
3. 'Dust to dust.' Do you think men who do not know God are affected by the view of life as aimless toil?
4. 'Stress' is an over-used word today. Why do men prefer it to the word 'depression'?
5. Do men you know use work as a substitute in the sense described in this chapter?
6. Do you have a sense of calling in your life? Do you understand the relationship between 'rest' and knowing the limits of your calling?

NOTES

1. There have been several excellent studies recently on the work which women do in the home. See, for instance, the work of Anne Oakley. Also, Marilyn Waring, *If Women Counted: A New Feminist Economics* (London: Macmillan,

1989), on the consequences for the economy of the work of women not being valued in monetary terms.

2.   Heather Formaini, *Men: The Darker Continent* (London: Heinemann, 1990), p. 126.

3.   ibid., p. 127.

4.   Mary Stewart van Leeuwen, *Gender and Grace* (Leicester: IVP, 1990), p. 206.

5.   Studs Terkel, *Working* (New York: Pantheon, 1972). This story appears in John Clay, *Men at Midlife: The Facts . . . The Fantasies . . . The Future* (London: Sidgwick and Jackson, 1989), p. 25.

6.   I have talked a great deal about the need to rediscover calling in another book: Roy K. McCloughry, *The Eye of the Needle* (Leicester: IVP, 1990).

14

WOMEN'S WORK, MEN'S RESPONSE

When women talk about power being at the heart of women's issues they are talking about justice. One area where women have raised this issue has been the area of work outside the home and their access to employment. The discrimination which men denied existed for so long, but which we eventually had to legislate to attempt to end, does not only exist in exclusion from certain occupations. It is also structurally embedded in the way in which we have not bothered to provide adequate crèche facilities for working women with children, or in the way in which men expect their partners to not only work but also continue to manage the home. Women are often the ones who have to get back from work to collect children, meaning that less overtime is available to them, which is paid at preferential rates.

The educational system still does not encourage women into more highly paid professions in the same way as it encourages men. Women graduates are four times as likely to go into teaching than male graduates, a fairly low-paid, professional job. Between the ages of sixteen and twenty-four women are better qualified than men, but from the age of twenty-four men overtake them. This may be due to a combination of factors arising out of the division of roles between men and women. Men are increasingly motivated to succeed in the public arena whereas women do not have the same incentive to pursue study for further employment. In 1988 the average gross weekly salary earned by women in full-time employment was sixty-seven per cent of the average gross weekly salary earned by men.[1]

There is double discrimination against women who wish to enter the workforce. Firstly, they are not paid as much for equal work. Secondly, marriage and family life means that they are the ones who have their career interrupted, whereas men do not have that kind of interruption. Paternity leave for men is relatively unknown in the UK, where it is still the assumption that the woman's career is not as important as the man's. The level of economic activity of married women is inversely related to the presence of children. If married women are between sixteen and twenty-nine with no children they are the most likely to be in full-time employment. If the youngest child is of pre-school age economic activity falls sharply. Women are also more likely to be carers for elderly people than men.[2]

Women make up two-fifths of the labour force and their share will increase to forty-four per cent by the end of this century. In a penetrating article on women and work, Isabel Hilton states: 'Ten years ago, fifty-eight per cent of all women worked outside the home. In 1991 it was sixty-eight per cent. Ten years ago, forty-nine per cent of mothers worked. In 1991 it was fifty-nine per cent. Most significantly in 1981 only twenty-five per cent of mothers who had children under five worked. By 1991 forty-one per cent did.'[3]

Although women are entering the labour force in ever-increasing numbers they are exhausted as a result. In America seventy per cent of senior women executives cite tiredness as their main problem. In Great Britain ninety-five per cent of working women put 'feeling unusually tired' at the head of a list of their problems in a recent survey.[4]

Women are beginning to realise that they are being asked to pay a very high cost for wanting to be a part of the work place. Isabel Hilton comments:

It has come as a slow and unwelcome revelation to many women in the last few years that the price of reaching for this prize, in the present conditions, is too high. Many will still not say it out loud because they fear it will be seen as an admission of defeat. But ask a working mother if this is really what she wanted and if she is honest, she will say it is not. She will not say it publicly because she does not wish to be told, as she may still be, that it is her own fault for wanting it all, and that feminism is to blame if her children are neglected and her house untidy, if she is exhausted and her partner unhappy. So, instead of complaining, the working mother reads books on how to be superwoman and takes comfort in the myth of motherhood through 'quality time'. She scarcely admits, even to herself, that she wonders if the game is worth the candle.[5]

Hilton argues that women have won only the illusion of choice through the women's movement because they have been allowed into the world of work on terms which have been set by men. If they wish to be rewarded equally they must successfully impersonate men. Women are constantly under pressure to be the ones who do all the adjusting and if they do not like this then men will tell them that at least they have the option of returning to the home. If women do decide to impersonate men then they may suffer the risks that men currently put themselves through. Problems of stress, health, alcohol addiction and the deterioration of the quality of their relationships may quickly become the everyday background in which women go to work in a world fashioned for men.

Men are changing slowly and re-evaluating their roles as we have seen. One of the great ironies facing women is that while younger men may be calling the bluff of a male-dominated, stress-inducing work culture, women are still required to capitulate to it in order to prove themselves. In a recent survey by the Henley Centre for Forecasting men and women were asked if men should devote more time to their families. Both sexes responded strongly that they should.

However the position of the family is not just a question of private choices but also a matter for public policy. Isabel Hilton comments that the 1980s were not good years for the family. The Government privatised social care, introducing community care legislation, but at the same time reduced support for the family.

> They were the years when women were told by one Government minister that the shortage of new recruits in the labour market meant that women were needed to fill the jobs, while the same Government's social policy implied that, if women did not take care of the children, the old people and the mentally ill, then nobody would.[6]

In the 1990s the question facing families will not only be childcare but who is to care for the elderly, who are living longer and will be more likely to be living in the community. We are responding to the stresses by having fewer children. At 1.6 children per woman the British birth-rate is one of the lowest in Europe but the issue of the elderly is not so easy to respond to. There is no doubt that women are caught both ways. Moralists complain about the rate of marital breakdown and the disintegration of the family, while at the same time we are addicted to a rate of growth which can only be sustained if women join the workforce in ever-increasing numbers. When women do go out to work childcare support such as crèche facilities is among the worst in Europe. It is important, therefore, that we evaluate the changes which are happening in our society, both in terms of public policy and the consequences of private choices.

Man About the House

Women cannot retain their position in the working world if men do not co-operate with them, both at work and also at home. One of the problems which has arisen for both men and women since women started to work outside the home is who is responsible for the work that has to be done inside the home. It is not as if the man went out to work while the woman lazed around at home, waiting eagerly for his return. As women know, work within the home can be extremely strenuous and demanding. Many men have grudgingly admitted that women should work outside the home partly because they see them as bringing more money into it. Others will admit that jobs should go to women on merit. But the arguments have shifted to who is responsible within the home for the various chores and responsibilities that need to be done.

> Perfectly nice men, who would not dream of opening doors for women or calling their female colleagues a patronising 'love', turn into old-fashioned monsters, once inside the front door. The gender barriers go up, they can almost be seen calling for their carpet slippers. Some even believe they are sharing the housework. Didn't I mend the light bulb for you last week?[7]

In a rigorous, sociological study of the behaviour of two-income families, Doctor Arlie Hochschild looks at how men and women sort out this problem. The general conclusion, which may be implied from the title *The Second Shift*, is that when women come home from work they face a second shift at home.[8] Advertisers portray an image of the working mother who is fashionably dressed, calm and competent, and who holds a briefcase in one hand and a child (clean) in the other.[9] Such a woman does not exist. The superwoman of the 1970s has given way to the negotiator over domestic duties of the 1990s. In other words, the enterprise culture demands that all workers, both men and women, dedicate themselves to their jobs which can easily become all-consuming. When both return exhausted from a hard day at work there is enough work left, generated by the home, for a third person to do.

The problem intensifies AB, for life is divided into BB (Before Baby) and AB (After Baby).[10] The home which looked so clean BB, and which sparkled with a wipe of a paper towel, now looks like a downtown Mothercare store after it has been hit by a hurricane. It is when working women become working mothers that a male backlash, in terms of lack of co-operation, appears to be a problem. As Mary Brasier points out, 'In a world of dishes to be washed, children to be dressed and dustbins to be taken out, men are not pulling their weight.'[11]

Dr Hochschild's conclusion is that such dual-career families are suffering. One of the steepest increases in the divorce rate is among couples with children under five. As Angela Phillips points out, 'If Dad isn't there at all he is even less likely to learn how to be a caring, sharing partner – his sons are unlikely to learn either.'[12]

Dr Hochschild's research did not conclude that dual-career marriages were impossible but that they were dependent on the new man actually existing *and* pulling his weight. Her conclusion, and that of many other commentators, is that such men are extremely rare and that to exist they have to make fundamental changes, not only in their view of work but also in their view of themselves. Nevertheless, she ends her book a cautious optimist about the new generation of men who are willing to make the attempt:

The happiest two-job marriages I saw were between men and women who did not load the former role of the housewife-mother on to the woman, and did not devalue it as one would a bygone 'peasant' way of life. They shared that role between them. What couples called 'good communication' often meant that they were good at saying thanks for one tiny form or another of taking care of the family. Making it to the school play, helping a child read, cooking dinner in good spirit, remembering the grocery list, taking responsibility for the 'upstairs', these were the silver and gold of the marital exchange.[13]

Those who believe in traditional roles for men and women

will see this tension as pointing to the inappropriate role adopted by the woman. But it is at least as likely that such problems are generated by men, being brought up to believe in those roles and working in an environment which expects men to have no other commitments besides work. In other words, the fundamental question is still open as to whether women are wrong to change their view of themselves or whether men are wrong to retain their view of themselves. It may well be that at the end of this book we shall conclude that change is necessary for both men and women.

Successful Women, Angry Men

Many women would contend, however, that the lack of co-operation from men is not restricted to the home environment. Not only do they say that they have to work twice as hard as men in order to achieve the same recognition because of discrimination, but that the more successful they become, the more unco-operative the men around them become.

> . . . this male backlash has shocked younger women. Having avoided marrying 'traditional' men who want cosy homebound wives, they now find that the 'liberated' man they married, who promised to share their chores and encourage their professional development, reverses his ideas when his wife's career threatens his happiness.[14]

This may well be due to the fact, as journalist Joy Melville points out that, 'Men who may agree intellectually with the feminist movement emotionally fail to understand its impact in real life.'[15] Those men who feel insecure are threatened by their wives' independence and success. Joy Melville goes on to outline three stages in the breakdown of such relationships. Stage one is where husbands abdicate responsibility for household tasks then criticise their wives because of the lack of order in the home, thereby putting pressure on them to return to the home. Stage two is where subtle criticism turns into open hostility, as husbands see themselves as getting their wives' leftover time and attention. Stage three is where the partners begin to develop independent lives, sometimes turning to adultery as an outlet for hurt feelings.

Women in such a position see the backlash as unfair, since the men are having to put up with what the women tolerated with more grace for most of their married lives. Such marriages need not break down but healing is dependent on the issues being brought out into the open and seriously discussed. Where couples work from home the attitude to the home may be so different that both take responsibility for it. Where a relationship is built on friendship it is more likely to survive than any other kind of partnership.

Work in the Home

The evidence suggests that, despite a growing number of women in paid employment, the housework and childcare is almost exclusively done by women. In Dr Arlie Hochschild's book, *The Second Shift*, she cites a study done by Alex Szalai where he found that in the US working women averaged three hours a day on housework while men averaged seventeen minutes. Women spent fifty minutes a day exclusively with their children, men spent twelve minutes. On the other side, working fathers watched TV an hour longer than their working wives, and slept half an hour longer each night. This highlighted women's double day. In the 1960s Dr Hochschild came to the conclusion that women worked roughly fifteen hours longer each week than men; over a year they worked an extra month of 24-hour days.

She identified that women were experiencing one shift at the office and a second shift at home. Studies show that working mothers have higher esteem and get less depressed than housewives,[16] but compared to their working husbands they get more tired and sick and are more likely to be anxious. One of the chief reasons why women go to the doctor in the US is because of fatigue.

Strategies for Coping[17]

It seems that it is the working mother who bears the weight of contradiction between traditional ideology and modern circumstances. Women have developed strategies to deal with this overload problem.

Supermum This is a very common strategy, where women do not impose on their husbands. They put in long hours believing that the extra month is theirs to work. They develop a concept of themselves as 'on the go', organised, competent, a woman without need for rest and without personal needs. But when interviewed personally they talk of feeling numb and seem to be out of touch with their feelings.

Cutting Back at Work This involves readjusting the hours at work, detaching oneself from work-centred friends, renewing friendships with family-centred friends, or choosing a job which doesn't make emotional demands.

Cutting Back on Housework With respect to housework there are two models, traditional and egalitarian. The traditional mothers apologise for the state of the house, they feel bad when it gets messy. Egalitarian women do the opposite. They try hard not to care about the house. They feel OK about the things they're not doing around the house because they feel that they have more important things to do. Women seem to care more about how the house looks than men.

Cutting Back on Marriage Cutting back on time together is usually unintentional. Most couples feel as if they're waiting to get time together. They are always promising themselves an intimate weekend away together or looking forward to getting the front room decorated, when everything will be 'sorted out'. But the quality of their time together is deteriorating. Meals out (if taken at all) become the marriage equivalent of business meetings, discussing the mortgage or the children's education.

Cutting Back on Parenting Inadvertently in the race against time, parents cut back on children's needs as well. Corners are cut in physical care, standards are lowered when a child is sick. What is more damaging is when cuts are made in the emotional care of children, especially when a parent has received more from their own parents than they are giving to their children. They have to manage a great deal of guilt.

Seeking Help   In the UK the majority of women who work part-time depend on their husband's co-operation to provide childcare, even when this is restricted to being willing to take the children to and from school. Women who work full-time with pre-school age children depend on others: forty-four per cent depend on grandmothers, twenty-three per cent use a childminder in the family home, fourteen per cent use a crèche, playgroup or nursery. Of those with school age children forty-four per cent depend on husbands and forty per cent on an adult relative. But this is not the only kind of help. Women use babysitters to allow them to juggle their hours. Some women also have cleaners who come in to help with some of the work around the house. Where relatives are living away from family then the costs of finding help are increased, and this is reflected in the amount of money a women has to earn at work before she has money for herself.

Cutting Back on Physical and Personal Needs   Finally, some women cut back on their personal needs. They may give up reading, hobbies, TV, visiting friends, exercise, time alone, praying, reading their Bible, sex. All this has pastoral implications in our churches.

Where are women going to get support and encouragement, because if they admit to some or all of this, the guilt they may feel could be enormous?

Men's Strategies

Men also have ways of coping with the amount of work which has to be done around the home. Those who share the work seem to have a happier family life. Whether a man instinctively gets on with sharing the workload has a lot to do with the model of fatherhood which he received. In particular, how much he identified with his father and what his father was like, rather than whether his father helped around the house. In dual-career families men who earned less than their wives often refused to do anything around the house, thus retaining some kind of power for themselves. Women also balanced options by sensing whether their husband was tetchy or fragile, and warded off depression or discouragement by waiting on them at home.

In many ways men's strategies parallel those of their partners. Some are superdads, others cut back on hours at work or reduce the emotional commitment to the job. Others lower their expectations about the amount of time spent alone with their partner or seeing friends or having time for hobbies. Many men are happy to do this because they feel that it is important that their wives have an opportunity to work outside the home. But traditionally they still feel that they are judged by whether they are earning enough to provide for the family.

Some men feel that if their wives work they will lose control of them since they are no longer economically dependent. Others fear losing status in the eyes of the community or men friends. Still others feel it is a 'privilege' to have a wife willing to work at home 'being supportive'. It is a luxury they enjoy, which would be lost if she went out to work. When asked why they did not share the work at home most men responded that their career was too demanding, their job was too stressful or that they 'weren't brought up to do housework'.

Many men do try and help at home but some are actually prevented from doing so by their wives. Sometimes this is because the woman feels that this is 'her area' and that if he got involved she would lose her 'domain'. But others say things like, 'I share housework because it's fair and child-rearing because I want to.' Many men had strategies of coping which depended on resistance rather than co-operation. These fell into several patterns.

Disaffiliation   Many men alternate between periods of co-operation and resistance. When they are resistant they do tasks in a distracted way, disassociating themselves from the domestic chore they are doing. They burn the rice, forget the shopping list or don't know where the saucepans are kept. These things are meant to guarantee that they are not asked again but had got Brownie points for 'showing willing'.

Others wait to be asked hoping they won't be, forcing their partners to take on the additional task of asking itself. The woman is always the initiator in this area of life. Often she gives up because it 'feels too much like begging'. It is especially difficult if the man becomes glum or irritable when asked, which discourages the woman from asking again.

Substitute Offerings   Some men choose a different tack. They give tremendous support to their wives who are working outside the home. Their support is so complete that it has the quality of a substitute offering. They are so effusive in the fact that they are fully behind their wives going out to work that they hope that it won't be noticed that they aren't doing more about the home.

Needs Reduction   Other men reduce their needs in order to cope. When faced with shopping they say, 'I don't need anything really.' When faced with cooking they suggest a 'take-away'. If their partner is about to iron their shirt they say that they don't need an ironed shirt, they can wear it crumpled. When she is cooking he says that he doesn't need to eat; cereal or toast is fine. Such a strategy infuriates but looks helpful on the outside!

Selected Praise   Praising partners for how organised they are is another tack. Appreciating the way a wife copes with the second shift herself can be another way of keeping her doing it. Praise is so positive it can feel that the man is actually doing the job, whereas close inspection will reveal that he isn't. Countless couples describe themselves as egalitarian but when one enquires about this crucial area of work and home life, one finds that they are fooling themselves.

Many couples organise their lives as if only the man has a

calling. But every household, which has a man and woman in it, has two callings. It cannot be assumed that one is more important than another. That must be decided freely by both partners. It may be that one person's calling is important at one time and this gives way later to the other person's calling being developed. Those women who decide to exercise their gifts creatively within the home and neighbourhood are desperately needed, as value is being eroded from these traditional roles. But where women decide that they are being called to work outside the home the word 'partnership' takes on a new meaning. If men feel that the world of work is theirs by right, and withhold the co-operation that women need to sustain their position in employment, then they are using power to manipulate. The Bible gives them no right or freedom to do this. This is neither loving headship nor egalitarian partnership. It is bad, old bolshiness, and can rightly be called oppressive.

QUESTIONS

1. Do you think that women are treated equally in all respects in the area of employment?
2. Why do some women feel that they are entering employment on men's terms, or that they have to impersonate men in order to be successful at work?
3. To what extent should men co-operate with housework? Does this mean they should do less at work?
4. Which of the strategies used by the men and women in this chapter do you recognise as being used in your own home?
5. 'Every household with a man and a woman in it has two callings.' What are the consequences of believing that this statement is true?
6. If everybody goes out to work who will care for the young and the elderly in the community?
7. Do women who feel that their calling is to work within the

home now feel under pressure to go out to work? Where does this pressure come from?

NOTES

1. The actual figures were £245.80 for men and £164.20 for women. *Social Trends*, 20 (HMSO, 1990), table 5.4.
2. Twenty-four per cent of women and sixteen per cent of men are carers for an elderly or dependent relative. ibid., p. 14.
3. Isabel Hilton, 'Unfinished Business', *Independent on Sunday*, 29 December 1991, p. 15.
4. cf. Deborah Hutton, 'The Fatigue Factor', *Vogue*, October 1988, quoted in Naomi Wolf, *The Beauty Myth* (London: Vintage, 1990), p. 53.
5. Hilton, op. cit.
6. Hilton, op. cit.
7. Mary Brasier, 'Dust up in the kitchen', *Guardian*, 16 August 1989.
8. Arlie Hochschild, *The Second Shift: Working Parents and the Revolution at Home* (London: Piatkus, 1990).
9. Brasier, op. cit.
10. Bebe Moore Campbell, *Successful Women, Angry Men* (London: Arrow, 1988).
11. Brasier, op. cit.
12. Angela Phillips, 'Male Model', *Listener*, 18 January 1990, p. 10.
13. Hochschild, op. cit., p. 270.
14. Joy Melville, 'Who is first among equals?', *Guardian*, 16 February 1988.
15. Melville, op. cit.
16. On attitudes to housework see the analysis by economist, Jane Wheelock, *Husbands at Home: The Domestic Economy in a Post-industrial Society* (London: Routledge, 1990), cf. also the work done by Anne Oakley, *The Sociology of Housework* (London: Martin Robertson, 1974), and *Housewife*, (Harmondsworth: Penguin, 1976).
17. The categories and insights in the next two sections are based on Dr Hochschild's research, pp. 193–203.

15

FROM FEAR TO FREEDOM

By now I hope it will be apparent that although there is a plurality of masculinities which men use to interpret what it means to be a man, at the heart of contemporary masculinity is a collection of ideas which hold men in bondage. Men are tyrannised by modern masculinity and they need to be freed to be themselves and to enjoy life as they were meant to. There is a sinister dimension to this bondage. Men have become entrapped by it because they have been willing to sustain it. Men who stand out against the claims of contemporary masculinity can find that the cost is high. Nevertheless, it is important to point out that at the heart of the bondage to which men are subject, there is idolatry at work. Despite the problems which it causes them, men have a strange fascination with false concepts of manhood.

The central theme of this book has been that men must move from power to love, not only for the sake of justice for women but also for their own sake, in order that men might discover healing and wholeness. The idea that being a man means being superior, controlled, competitive, or any of the other typical characteristics of conventional masculinity, has held men in bondage for a long time. The problem is that nobody taught these things to men, they were not initiated into manhood but grew up breathing these ideas in through the culture. At no time were men asked to critically reflect on what it meant to be a man. But now the advent of the women's movement has forced at least some men to ask questions about their own manhood, and the stress of modern life and the persistence of family breakdown has also meant that some men have begun to question the views of masculinity they have grown up with.

It is no coincidence that the phenomenon of the wild man has been so pervasive throughout the United States. It offers men a chance to get in touch with and express emotions which they have suppressed for a long time. It invites them to confront their memories of their fathers, to recognise the wounds that they have been given by parenting, and to be willing to express that hurt in tears, in order to find healing. It introduces them to forms of prayer, transcendence, confession and a form of fellowship with other men. All these things have been missing from the secularised society which men live in, especially in the world of work. It is no wonder that so many thousands of men have found help through the ideas of the wild man.

Yet such ideas cannot ultimately lead to freedom, for men must move from power to love itself, and we need to ask what kind of love this is. All kinds of men have been named as heroes by the men's movement in the US – among them Martin Luther King, Jimmy Carter, and even Woody Allen – but there has been little consideration of Jesus Christ. I find this extraordinary, partly because Jesus is such a hero in my life, and I find it difficult to see why his life and message and call to discipleship do not immediately resonate with those men who want to move from power to love. These words describe everything about the life of Christ. Christ moved from power to love when he left heaven's glory to become a human servant; when he gave up supernatural power and advantage to be one with us in our temptations and weakness; when he denied himself the possibility of being made king by his followers; and when he went to the cross to lay down his life for us. Everything about Jesus speaks of self-denial and the love of God, and yet Jesus is not powerless, for that kind of love liberates people to be like Christ. Perhaps one of the reasons why Christ is not emulated as mentor and hero is because of the Christian Church.

The Task of the Church

The Church is called to be a counter-culture which lives in tension with what is going on in the world. This is because the Church as a visible institution is meant to be a signpost to the existence of the kingdom of God. The kind of values which Jesus placed at the heart of his ministry should be most evident within the Church if people are going to understand the difference between the Church and the world.

Where the Church merges with the world it is difficult for people to see the difference between them, and mission will be very difficult because people may wish to be saved from the human condition but they may not believe the Church is distinctive enough to give it credence when it says that it has the key to salvation.

There is another relationship which can exist: if the Church becomes so distorted in its view of its task that the world has to act in order to bring the Church back to its senses. This has recently been the case with materialistic fundamentalists operating as evangelists in America, whose behaviour was far more outrageous and exploitative than that of the vast majority of people who would not call themselves Christians.

In the area of gender the Church is in the middle of what is usually termed 'a debate'. This has centred, at least in the Church of England, on the issue of ordination of women. My own feeling is that there has not been a debate at all on the gender issue. There has been a great deal written and spoken about the changing role of women, but where has been the material on the changing role of men? There has been none. The invisibility of masculinity has yet again led those men who dominate the Church into a form of discussion which centres on men as the norm and women as the deviants from the norm. There has been much discussion about how far the Church can go in allowing women into leadership. There has been talk about theology and talk about ethics, but there has been no discussion of why men in the Church have reacted as defensively as they have done to the issue of women in leadership.

I hope that this book has shown why this is the case. In the Church masculinity is not only the norm but, as we have seen, is still a sanctified norm and this, when coupled with the conservative nature of the leadership in the Church, means that it is remarkable that there is any kind of movement at all. Certainly women are to be congratulated on having moved the Church towards greater integration in ministry.

The Church will change considerably when men humble themselves from the position which they have adopted and see themselves as men who have a particular perspective on life, which must be weighed and judged alongside the equal contributions of women. Those who believe that leadership of the Church should be male must presumably bear some responsibility for the state that the Church is in under male leadership. Although in the world of the blind the one-eyed is king, being led by a group who have very partial views of the world has been very damaging to the Church. We have seen that God gave dominion of the world to men and women together, and it is only when men and women work together to formulate the vision of the Church that we will have some chance of creative leadership. Those with traditional views often say that women in leadership should work in teams because of their weakness. But the single-person model of leadership exacerbates the mask-wearing in order to retain authority. There is power in being distant, but there is also isolation. Men also need to work in teams. In twenty or thirty years' time a future generation, which has become used to women in ministry, will look back on our debates with some incredulity.

Masculinity and Spirituality

But the application of the insights of this book to the Church does not come primarily in the area of the ordination of women. It comes in the area of spirituality and mission.

It is very interesting when reading the work of Robert Bly and asking the question, 'Why has this book been so phenomenally successful?' that it really amounts to a call for men to embrace spirituality of a sort again. Conventional masculinity is very functional. It is about getting things done, being in control, solving problems and not being vulnerable. It is not about spirituality. I find this makes me uneasy. There seems to be a paradox here, which it is important to explain.

It was the statistics of Shere Hite that made me most troubled. They pointed to the fact that men were still inarticulate about their own personal emotions. Many men were not even aware that they were needy or lonely or depressed. Ninety-eight per cent of women surveyed said that if they could improve their marriages it would be that their husbands would talk to them more. At this point a little bell began to ring, which over the months of thinking about this subject became more like a feeling of panic. If men are not talking to their wives, whom they love and can see with their eyes, can we assume that they are talking to God whom they cannot see? I began to talk about this to friends and colleagues around me, and found out that many men – I will not say the majority of men – have little or no active spiritual life of their own. Very few men that I have talked to spend regular time in prayer with God. They feel guilty about that and wish that they did. They aspire to do it but never get around to it. Yet of all the men that I talked to, including some in very large seminar groups, there was no insight at all as to why men as a group should find it so difficult to pray.

I think that when viewed against the masculine world-view the problem can be seen clearly. I spoke in a previous book, *The Eye of the Needle*, about the 'notorious unreliability' of prayer. We live in a world of cause and effect, where pressing a button causes a light to go on, but prayer is not like that. We either pray because we want to be with God or we don't pray at all. The idea at the heart of the life of prayer is relationship, or as Christian writer Sheila Cassidy put it once, 'wasting time with God'.

The fact is that if men were pouring out their hearts to God, on their knees, if they were bringing to God their loneliness and despair, or the frustrations of their fathering, or the problems in their marriages, they would change. I know of no other activity so conducive to change as regular prayer. If men were open before God and admitted their vulnerability they would find it impossible to maintain the masks of masculinity while enjoying the heady adventure of life with God. The life of prayer is multifaceted. Sometimes it is confessional and we bear our souls before God, knowing that there is no point in holding anything back from him. At other times we ask God to show us anything in our lives which may be an offence to him or to others, and declare our willingness to change, aided by the Holy Spirit. From time to time the person who prays is blessed with moments of great joy, and equally there are times of groaning and sweat and anger in prayer as we come into conflict with God.

There are two points to be made from this. The first is that those men who do have a deeply spiritual life have a great responsibility and opportunity to pass on what they know to other men. I am sure that there are many such men who in the quiet of their own lives are wrestling with God in prayer. The second point is that though Christian men are often very different from men who are not Christians, and that this difference is owed entirely to the grace of God, we are still not different enough. The Church is still gripped by the idolatry of masculinity and if we are to be a Church which has got a heart which attracts others then we must discover a true spirituality or we will die. There is so much pretence in contemporary Christianity, so many masks worn by people who believe they have to wear a false smile and be happy because they are Christians. Yet what God wants is for us to admit to the honest struggle of faith and to the fact that our lives may be very messy, but that Christ is with us in it all. So much of the pretence which we all come across in the Church, particularly the triumphalism, is put up by men. The unwillingness to cope with and admit to failure has placed us under tremendous pressure in the modern Church. We need a baptism of humility in church leadership, and to get back to a Bible and a Christ who is unashamed of the lives of ordinary people in their pilgrimage through life.

Contemporary masculinity leads to a crisis of spirituality. We are publishing hundreds of books on prayer, and holding festivals and seminars and prayer meetings, but we have not had the discernment to see that men are so gripped by the idolatry of masculinity that their mouths have been stopped by it. The masculine world-view sees prayer as foolishness because it is not efficient or functional and is dangerously near to being emotive, but it is this foolishness which men must give way to if the Church is to become full of men who are warm in their humanity and have integrity in their spirituality.

Mission to Men

Evangelists tell us that men are resistant to the Gospel. This is usually explained by resorting to a circular argument, which says that since the Church is full of women men will not join. But this merely begs the question as to how the Church came to be full of women in the first place. There seems to me to be two possibilities: either men view those in the Church as wimps, whom they do not wish to be associated with; or they are so threatened by the claims of Christianity that they will not humble themselves and become Christians.

Looking at this problem with the help of the conclusions on masculinity we have reached we can see that both are true. Contemporary masculinity portrays false images of men by comparison with which men who go to church are seen as weak. Those who lead the Church, i.e. the clergy, are often seen as having been emasculated since they wear frocks and speak in strange voices, but at the same time those men who are outside the Church are feeling the full force of a culture which is arrogant in the extreme. Christianity calls them to humble themselves and to follow Christ and it is at this point that all the values they have learnt that constitute the real man rise up and create fear in them.

If the Church is to reach men, as it can and as it must, then it must confront the issue of masculinity. For it is this that is blighting men in our culture. The problem is that the vast majority of work among men in this country may be missing the point. Over the last twenty years I have often spoken at men's breakfasts and have enjoyed the opportunities for meeting men and sharing the Gospel that this has created. They follow a similar pattern: invitations go out to men to come to a meal in a hotel or a hall, and to listen to a speaker who, it is believed, they will enjoy. The best kind of speaker is usually a famous sports person who has a Christian testimony. Usually the meetings consist of the breakfast (often cooked by women), the talk and a few questions. If the group is smaller there will be a discussion. But the men in the room are rarely, if ever, asked to talk about themselves, nor is it assumed that their view of masculinity is at all problematic. On the contrary, such meetings often use the idea of the speaker as being a 'real man' as a successful public relations tool. At other times, discussions about how we can 'reach men for Christ' utilise the stereotypes of masculinity in order to try and attract them. This is ironic, since the Church is giving the impression that it is underwriting masculinity, whereas what men need to see in the Church is the movement from power to love.

There is a desperate need for men to develop friendships

with other men, for masculinity isolates. There is also a need for men to admit that they have lost their way and to help one another to discover a Christian faith that can be integrated with the rest of their lives. When men outside the Church see men changing inside it they will come. Thousands of men are joining men's groups every week, in those groups they are confessing and sharing and grappling and weeping. How ironic it is that Christian men should still sit in their churches fully in control of their emotions and out of touch with the very world-view to which they have been subject for so long. At the end of the day the key to mission among men is not strategy, it is not getting the venue right or the speaker right or the colour of the invitations right. The issue is having something which men outside the Church are prepared to give up their masks for because it speaks to them of salvation.

The Possibilities for Change

At the outset of this book I quoted the cynicism of feminists when they said 'Men change but only to hold on to power'. I hope that the message of this book stirs men to change for their own good, not as some kind of reaction to what women are saying. For it is only as men own change that it will persist.

There are all kinds of change. Sometimes the context in which we live changes and this can be mistaken for people changing. The new man is a good example of this. The media decided that there was a need for a new man and that his advent would make a good theme for articles, documentaries and the advertising of products. No one person or body decided this but it became clear that this was a shift in perception in public life. All of a sudden we find ourselves reading about the lifestyles of new men and being told that men are changing, but these men have been there all the time. They are the ones who have always rejected contemporary masculinity and have tried to live lives which are open, loving and nurturing. These are they who ten months before were being called wimps, now they can all work for the advertising profession for they are in great demand. It is important then that we do not mistake the spotlight of public opinion for a fundamental change in people.

The second kind of change is a change in aspiration. We can continue with the new man paradigm to illustrate this. The fact that there is so much talk about the new man leads men to reflect on the gulf between their own lives and the lives of such men. A desire is born within them to become like that and they begin to try and emulate that lifestyle. They may change their fashion, they may even change their job, they may wake up from the delusions of contemporary masculinity. The growth of the men's movement owes a great deal to such men who have a yearning to be different. The human heart has not changed, even if they find themselves dressed in the clothes of the new man and wearing his after-shave they will still find that they have an unresolved longing in their life. In this case it is not that one wants to prevent this movement for, as Robert Bly comments, these men are good to know and we need more of them. The problem is that the answer to the question which contemporary masculinity is asking is not to change masculinity into another form, which is more pleasant to live with. The fact is that contemporary forms of masculinity are all problematic and the only way of resolving the issue is through men turning back to God.

At the heart of men's world-view is the idea of autonomy and the fact that we are meant to be self-made men and self-reliant. *The issue is not style, it is self.* Until the self is yielded to God and we discover our place in his world as creatures and not creators we will not find rest as men. Nor will tacking on any New Age version of spirituality help us, even if it is the age of Aquarius. The issue at stake is between a man and his creator, God. Only Christianity can resolve the paradox of human nature: human culture constantly struggles between optimism and pessimism as to who we are. Richard Holloway, Bishop of Edinburgh, put this dilemma eloquently:

This is my dilemma . . . I am dust and ashes, frail and wayward, a set of pre-determined behavioural responses, . . . riddled with fears, beset with needs . . ., the quintessence of dust and unto dust I shall return. . . . But there is something else in me. . . . Dust I may be, but troubled dust, dust that dreams, dust that has strange premonitions of transfiguration, of a glory in store, a destiny prepared, an inheritance that will one day be my own. . . . So my life is stretched out in a painful dialectic between ashes and glory, between weakness and transfiguration. I am a riddle to myself, an exasperating enigma . . ., this strange duality of dust and glory. . . .[1]

There is a third kind of change which comes from seeing the world in a new light: seeing the light as coming from God. This is not change for the sake of change nor is it mistaking momentum for meaning or pace for purpose, this dawning of realisation sees life as a pilgrimage towards God, it sees character development as being transformed into the person of Jesus Christ. It sees the motivation of life as reflecting the love of God sacrificially to those around us. This kind of change is all-embracing because it admits our struggles and our pain as well as our strengths and our joy. It tells us that everything we are we owe to God and everything we do we do for God. It is as if the sun has come up and we have awakened in a different world.

This book has been critical of contemporary masculinity, but in rejecting many of the ideas which are at its core we cannot get rid of it. There will always be ideas and values associated with being a man. What I am calling for is the transformation of masculinity, to change the values and the ideas, so that men will be liberated to be themselves. This book is not a book about rejection, it is a book about celebration, for men need to celebrate their masculinity rather than suppress it.

It is also important to realise that there are many men who have been on such a pilgrimage and who are deeply spiritual, wise men. Not everybody has been deluded by the claims of masculinity, but those of us who have been on the fast track for a long time may not have seen such men as having anything to offer us, as we busy ourselves being 'real men'. In our communities and in our churches there are men who have been learning how to celebrate and feed on God for many years. Those men who, at the end of this book, find a growing hunger in them to start such a pilgrimage would do well to seek out such men. They may not be found easily, they may not be on platforms as speakers or on book covers as writers, they may not be sports people or personalities. Such men may be in wheelchairs, or be unemployed or retired. They may not be articulate or have a successful career behind them, but they will be men who find their security in God and who remind us of Jesus Christ.

When we ask, 'What will change men?' it is important to be accurate about the response. If we say the Church will change men then people may lift an eyebrow. Is not the Church one of the greatest bastions of patriarchy in our society? We have to admit that in this area there is a need for transformation within the Church as well as outside it. But if we respond, Christ changes men, that is quite different. It is possible for men to become Christians but then to revert back to a life of playing games with one another, but the man who has a passion for being like Jesus Christ, in laying down power to express self-giving love, can never be the same. His life is lived in the security of God's love alone. He does not care what others think of him but only of what God thinks of him. He does not need to prove himself continually before other men because he has been accepted by God. At the heart of this great issue of men and masculinity, the offer open to every man is quite simple. God's grace reaches out to men and fills them with his love, desiring that they mirror that love to the rest of the world. It is God who equips men to move from power to love.

QUESTIONS

1. If men are not talking to their wives about what is going on in their lives are they talking to God? Do men pray?
2. Should people behave as if they are living happy and fulfilled lives if they are not, simply because they are Christians and do not want to let the side down?
3. Why do you think men do not respond to the Christian faith as readily as women?
4. The Church is often stereotyped as being dominated by men but full of women. Is this stereotype true?
5. How do you think the Church could be more effective in putting over its message to men?
6. What stops Christian men from sharing their lives with men who are not Christians, through friendship?

NOTES

1. Quoted in John Stott, 'The Glory and the Shame', *Third Way*, 13, no. 12 (December/January 1991), pp. 20–2.

BIBLIOGRAPHY

The following represents a selection of the books used in research for the compilation of this book. Inclusion in this list does not constitute a recommendation of the book listed. Additional bibliographical references can be found in the notes at the end of the chapters.

Abbott (ed.), Franklin. *Men and Intimacy*: *Personal Accounts Exploring the Dilemmas of Modern Male Sexuality*. Freedom, California: The Crossing Press, 1990.

Abbott (ed.), Franklin. *New Men, New Minds*: *Breaking Male Tradition. How Today's Men Are Changing The Traditional Rules of Masculinity*. Freedom, California: The Crossing Press, 1987.

Abulafia, John. *Men and Divorce*: *Coping, Learning, Starting Afresh*. London: Fontana, 1990.

Adams, Carol and Rae Laurikietis. *The Gender Trap*: *A Closer Look at Sex Roles*. London: Virago/Quartet, 1976.

Allan, Graham. *Friendship*: *Developing a Sociological Perspective*. London: Harvester Wheatsheaf, 1989.

Anderson, Ray S. and Dennis B. Guernsey. *On Being Family*: *A Social Theology of the Family*. Grand Rapids, Michigan: Eerdmans, 1985.

Anderson, Ray S. *On Being Human*: *Essays in Theological Anthropology*. Grand Rapids, Michigan: Eerdmans, 1982.

Archer, John and Barbara Lloyd. *Sex and Gender*. Cambridge: Cambridge University Press, 1985.

Argyle, Michael and Monika Henderson. *The Anatomy of Relationships*. Harmondsworth: Penguin, 1990.

Aries, Philippe and Andre Bejin. *Western Sexuality*: *Practice and*

Precept in Past and Present Times. Oxford: Blackwell, 1985.

Badinter, Elisabeth. *Man/Woman: The One is the Other*. London: Collins Harvill, 1989.

Barth, Karl. *The Doctrine of Creation: Vol III, Part 4*. Edinburgh: T. and T. Clark, 1961.

Bauckham, Richard. *Moltmann: Messianic Theology in the Making*. Basingstoke: Marshall Pickering, 1987.

Berger, Brigitte and Peter. *The War Over the Family: Capturing the Middle Ground*. Harmondsworth: Penguin, 1983.

Berry (ed.), Patricia. *Fathers and Mothers*. Dallas, Texas: Spring Publications, 1990, 2nd ed.

Black (ed.), Clementina. *Married Women's Work: Being the Report of an Enquiry undertaken by the Women's Industrial Council*. London: Virago, 1983.

Bly, Robert. *Iron John*. Reading, Massachusetts: Addison-Wesley, 1990: Shaftesbury: Element Books, 1991.

Borrowdale, Anne. *A Woman's Work: Changing Christian Attitudes*. London: SPCK, 1989.

Borrowdale, Anne. *Distorted Images: Christian Attitudes to Women, Men and Sex*. London: SPCK, 1991.

Brain, Robert. *Friends and Lovers*. St Albans: Paladin/Granada, 1977.

Brannen, Julia and Peter Moss. *Managing Mothers: Dual Earner Households After Maternity Leave*. London: Unwin Hyman, 1991.

Breen, Dana. *Talking with Mothers: About Pregnancy, Childbirth and Early Motherhood*. London: Jill Norman, 1981.

Brittan, Arthur. *Masculinity and Power*. Oxford: Blackwell, 1989.

Brod (ed.), Harry. *The Making of Masculinities – the New Men's Studies*. London: Allen and Unwin, 1987.

Brothers, Dr Joyce. *What Every Woman Should Know About Men*. London: Grafton, 1987.

Broughton Knox, D. *The Everlasting God: A Character Study of God in the Old and New Testaments*. Homebush West, Australia: Lancer, 1988.

Chapman, Rowena and Jonathan Rutherford (eds.). *Male Order: Unwrapping Masculinity*. London: Lawrence and Wishart, 1988.

Chesler, Phyllis. *About Men*. London: Harvest/Harcourt Brace Jovanovich, 1989.

'Christianity and Feminism', *Christian Scholars Review*, 17, no. 3 (1988).

Clark, Keith. *Being Sexual . . . and Celibate*. Notre Dame, Indiana: Ave Maria Press, 1986.

Clark, Stephen B. *Man and Woman in Christ*. Servant, 1980.

Clay, John. *Men at Midlife*: *The Facts . . . The Fantasies . . . The Future*. London: Sidgwick & Jackson, 1989.

Cockburn, Cynthia. *Brothers*: *Male Dominance and Technological Change*. London: Pluto Press, 1983.

Cohen, David. *Being a Man*. London: Routledge, 1990.

Coleman, Peter. *Christian Attitudes to Homosexuality*. London: SPCK, 1980.

Cook, David. *The Moral Maze*: *A Way of Exploring Christian Ethics*. London: SPCK, 1983.

Coote, Anna and Beatrix Campbell. *Sweet Freedom*: *The Struggle for Women's Liberation*. Oxford: Blackwell, 1987.

Corneau, Guy. *Absent Fathers*, *Lost Sons* – *The Search for Masculine Identity*, trans. Larry Shouldice. London: Shambhala, 1991.

Court, John H. *Pornography*: *A Christian Critique*. Exeter: Paternoster Press, 1980.

Crabb, Lawrence J. *Men and Women*: *The Giving of Self*. London: Marshall Pickering, 1991.

Craston, Colin. *Biblical Headship and the Ordination of Women*. Nottingham: Grove Pastoral Series, 27, 1988.

Daly, Mary. *Beyond God the Father*. London: The Women's Press, 1986.

Dominian, Jack. *Sexual Integrity*: *The Answer to AIDS*. London: Darton, Longman and Todd, 1987.

Dowell, Susan and Linda Hurcombe. *Dispossessed Daughters of Eve*: *Faith and Feminism*. London: SPCK, 1987.

Easlea, Brian. *Fathering the Unthinkable*: *Masculinity, Scientists and the Nuclear Arms Race*. London: Pluto Press, 1983.

Easthope, Anthony. *What A Man's Gotta Do*: *The Masculine Myth in Popular Culture*. London: Paladin/Grafton, 1986.

Eden, Martyn and Ernest Lucas. *Being Transformed*: *Applying the Bible to Modern Life*. Basingstoke: Marshall Pickering, 1988.

Ehrenreich, Barbara. *The Hearts of Men*: *American Dreams and the Flight from Commitment*. London: Pluto Press, 1983.

Ehrenreich, Barbara Elizabeth Hess and Gloria Jacobs. *Remaking Love*: *The Feminization of Sex*. London: Fontana/Collins, 1987.

Etherington, Jan. *Men! A Collector's Guide*. Wellingborough: Grapevine, 1989.

Evans, Mary. *Woman and the Bible*. Exeter: Paternoster Press, 1983.

Farrell MD, Warren. *Why Men Are the Way They Are: The Definitive Guide to Love, Sex and Intimacy*. London: Bantam, 1990.

Fast, Julius. *Body Language*. London: Pan, 1981.

Feirstein, Bruce. *Real Men Don't Eat Quiche*. Sevenoaks: New English Library, 1982.

Fernando, Ajith. *Reclaiming Friendship: Relating to Each Other in a Fallen World*. Leicester: IVP, 1991.

Figes, Eva. *Patriarchal Attitudes*. Basingstoke: Macmillan Education Ltd, 1986.

Fogel, Gerald I., Frederick M. Lane, and Robert S. Liebert (eds.). *The Psychology of Men: New Psychoanalytic Perspectives*. New York: Basic Books, 1986.

Ford, David and Jeff Hearn. *Studying Men and Masculinity: A Sourcebook of Literature and Materials*. Bradford: University of Bradford, 1988.

Formaini, Heather. *Men: The Darker Continent*. London: Heinemann, 1990.

French, Marilyn. *Beyond Power: On Women, Men and Morals*. London: Sphere/Abacus, 1986.

Friedan, Betty. *The Second Stage*. London: Sphere/Abacus, 1983.

Gaebelein Hull, Gretchen. *Equal to Serve: Women and Men in the Church and Home*. London: Scripture Union, 1987.

Gill (ed.), Robin. *Theology and Sociology: A Reader*. London: Geoffrey Chapman, 1987.

Goldingay, Rev. Dr. John. 'The Bible and Sexuality', *Scottish Journal of Theology*, 39, 175–88, 1986.

Haddon, Celia. *The Powers of Love*. London: Michael Joseph, 1985.

Hayes, Trudy. *The Politics of Seduction*, Dublin: Attic Press, 1990.

Hearn, Jeff. *The Gender of Oppression: Men, Masculinity, and the Critique of Marxism*. Brighton: Wheatsheaf, 1987.

Hearn, Jeff and David Morgan (eds.). *Men, Masculinities and Social Theory*. London: Unwin Hyman, 1990.

Hearn, Jeff and Wendy Parkin. *'Sex' at 'Work': The Power and Paradox of Organisation Sexuality*. Brighton: Wheatsheaf, 1987.

Heine, Susanne. *Women and Early Christianity: Are the Feminist Scholars Right?*. London: SCM, 1987.

Hite, Shere and Kate Colleran. *Good Guys, Bad Guys and Other*

Lovers. London: Pandora Press, 1989.

Hite, Shere. *The Hite Report on Female Sexuality*. London: Pandora Press, 1976.

Hite, Shere. *The Hite Report on Male Sexuality*. London: Macdonald Optima, 1990.

Hite, Shere. *Women and Love: A Cultural Revolution in Progress*. London: Viking, 1987.

Hochschild, Arlie with Anne Machung. *The Second Shift: Working Parents and the Revolution at Home*. London: Piatkus, 1990.

Hodgkinson, Liz. *Sex is not Compulsory*. London: Sphere, 1988.

Houston, James. *The Transforming Friendship: A Guide to Prayer*. Oxford: Lion, 1989.

Hudson, Liam and Bernadine Jacot. *The Way Men Think: Intellect, Intimacy and the Erotic Imagination*. London: Yale University Press, 1991.

Hurley, James B. *Man and Woman in Biblical Perspective: A Study in Role Relationships and Authority*. Leicester: IVP, 1981.

Illich, Ivan. *Gender*. London: Marion Boyars, 1983.

Jackson, David. *Unmasking Masculinity: A Critical Autobiography*. London: Unwin Hyman, 1990.

Jewett, Paul K. *Man as Male and Female*. Grand Rapids, Michigan: Eerdmans, 1975.

Jozef Perelberg, Rosine and Ann C. Miller (eds.). *Gender and Power in Families*. London: Routledge, 1990.

Kimmel (ed.), Michael S. *Changing Men: New Directions in Research on Men and Masculinity*. London: Sage, 1987.

Laffey, Alice L. *Wives, Harlots and Concubines: The Old Testament in Feminist Perspective*. London: SPCK, 1990.

LaHaye, Tim and Beverly. *The Act of Marriage: The Beauty of Sexual Love*. Grand Rapids, Michigan: Zondervan, 1976.

Lasch, Christopher. *The Culture of Narcissism*. London: Abacus, 1980.

Lee, Carol. *The Blind Side of Eden: The Sexes in Perspective*. London: Bloomsbury, 1989.

Leech, Kenneth. *True God: An Exploration in Spiritual Theology*. London: Sheldon Press, 1985.

Lewis, Charlie and Margaret O'Brien (eds.). *Reassessing Fatherhood*. London: Sage, 1987.

Littler (ed.), Craig. *The Experience of Work*. Aldershot: Gower, with Open University, 1985.

Lloyd, Genevieve. *The Man of Reason: 'Male' and 'Female' in Western Philosophy*. London: Methuen, 1984.

Loades, Ann. *Searching for Lost Coins: Explorations in Christianity and Feminism*. London: SPCK, 1987.

Lyon, David. *Sociology and the Human Image*. Leicester: IVP, 1983.

Lyon, David. *The Steeple's Shadow*. London: SPCK, 1985.

MacDonald, Gordon. *The Effective Father*. Wheaton, Illinois: Tyndale House, 1977.

MacDonald, Robert L. *Intimacy: Overcoming the Fear of Closeness*. London: Daybreak, 1990.

McClung, Floyd. *The Father Heart of God*. Eastbourne: Kingsway, 1985.

Mangan, J. A. and James Walvin (eds.). *Manliness and Morality: Middle-class Masculinity in Britain and America, 1800–1940*. Manchester: Manchester University Press, 1987.

Mead, Margaret. *Male and Female: A Study of the Sexes in a Changing World*. Harmondsworth: Pelican/Penguin, 1962.

Metcalf, Andy and Martin Humphries (eds.). *The Sexuality of Men*. London: Pluto Press, 1985.

Miles, Rosalind. *The Rites of Man: Love, Sex and Death in the Making of the Male*. London: Grafton, 1991.

Miller, Stuart. *Men and Friendship*. London: Gateway, 1983.

Millett, Kate. *Sexual Politics*. London: Virago, 1977.

Mitchell, Juliet and Ann Oakley (eds.). *What is Feminism?* Oxford: Blackwell, 1986.

Moltmann, Jurgen. *The Trinity and the Kingdom of God: The Doctrine of God*. London: SCM, 1981.

Moore, John H. *But What About Men? After Women's Lib*. Bath: Ashgrove Press, 1989.

Morley, Janet. *All Desires Known*. London: MOW, 1988.

Morris, Desmond. *Intimate Behaviour*. London: Triad/Grafton, 1979.

Mount, Ferdinand. *The Subversive Family: An Alternative History of Love and Marriage*. London: Jonathan Cape, 1982.

Neuberger, Julia. *Whatever's Happening to Women? – Promises, Practices and Pay Offs*. London: Kyle Cathie Ltd, 1991.

Neuer, Werner. *Man and Woman in Christian Perspective*, (trans.) Gordon Wenham. London: Hodder and Stoughton, 1990.

Neuhaus (ed.), Richard John. *Virtue – Public and Private*. Grand

Rapids, Michigan: Eerdmans, 1986.

Nicholson, John. *Men and Women: How Different Are They?* Oxford: Oxford University Press, 1984.

Norwood, Robin. *Women Who Love Too Much*. London: Arrow, 1986.

Nouwen, Henri. *In the Name of Jesus: Reflections on Christian Leadership*. London: Darton, Longman and Todd, 1989.

Osiek, Carolyn. *Beyond Anger: On Being a Feminist in the Church*. Dublin: Gill and Macmillan, 1986.

Parke, Ross D. *Fathering*. London: Fontana, 1981.

Pawson, J. David. *Leadership is Male: A Challenge to Christian Feminism*. Crowborough: Highland Books, 1988.

Payne, Leanne. *Crisis in Masculinity*. Eastbourne: Kingsway, 1988.

Pirani, Alix. *The Absent Father: Crisis and Creativity*. London: Arkana, 1989.

Radcliffe Richards, Janet. *The Sceptical Feminist: A Philosophical Enquiry*. London: Penguin, 1980.

Radford Ruether, Rosemary. *Sexism and God-Talk: Towards a Feminist Theology*. London: SCM, 1983.

Ramey Mollenkott, Virginia. *Women, Men and the Bible*. Nashville, Tennessee: Abingdon, 1977.

Robertson, James. *Future Work: Jobs, Self-employment and Leisure after the Industrial Age*. Aldershot: Gower, 1985.

Rogers, Barbara. *Men Only: An Investigation into Men's Organisations*. London: Pandora Press, 1988.

Roper, Michael and John Tosh. *Manful Assertions: Masculinities in Britain since 1800*. London: Routledge, 1991.

Ross, Michael W. *The Married Homosexual Man*. London: Routledge & Kegan Paul, 1983.

Ruse, Michael. *Homosexuality: A Philosophical Inquiry*. Oxford: Blackwell, 1990.

Rutter, Peter. *Sex in the Forbidden Zone*. London: Unwin Paperbacks, 1990.

Sanders, Deirdre. *The Woman Report on Men*. London: Sphere, 1987.

Saward, Jill with Wendy Green. *Rape: My Story*. London: Pan, 1990.

Scanzoni, Letha and Nancy Hardesty. *All We're Meant To Be: A Biblical Approach to Women's Liberation*. Waco, Texas: Word Books, 1975.

Scarf, Maggie. *Intimate Partners: Patterns in Love and Marriage*. London: Century Hutchinson, 1987.

Segal, Lynne. *Slow Motion: Changing Masculinities, Changing Men*. London: Virago, 1990.

Seidler (ed.), Victor J. *The Achilles Heel Reader*. London: Routledge, 1991.

Seidler, Victor J. *Recreating Sexual Politics: Men, Feminism and Politics*. London: Routledge, 1991.

Seidler, Victor J. *Rediscovering Masculinity: Reason, Language and Sexuality*. London: Routledge, 1989.

Sennett, Richard. *Authority*. London: Secker and Warburg, 1980.

Sennett, Richard. *The Fall of Public Man*. London: Faber and Faber, 1986.

Showalter, Elaine. *Sexual Anarchy: Gender and Culture at the Fin de Siecle*. London: Bloomsbury, 1991.

Skynner Robin, and John Cleese. *Families and How to Survive Them*. London: Methuen, 1985.

Smail, David. *Illusion and Reality: The Meaning of Anxiety*. London: J. M. Dent, 1984.

Smail, David. *Taking Care: An Alternative to Therapy*. London: J. M. Dent, 1987.

Smedes, Lewis. *Sex in the Real World*. Tring: Lion, 1983, 2nd ed.

Soelle, Dorothee. *The Strength of the Weak: Toward a Christian Feminist Identity*. Philadelphia, Pennsylvania: Westminster Press, 1984.

Stearns, Peter N. *Be A Man! Males in Modern Society*. New York: Holmes and Meier, 1990.

Stewart van Leeuwen, Mary. *Gender and Grace: Women and Men in a Changing World*. Leicester: IVP, 1990.

Storkey, Elaine. 'What Will Happen to God', by William Oddie *Scottish Journal of Theology*, 41, 117–24.

Storkey, Elaine. *What's Right With Feminism?* London: SPCK/ Third Way, 1985.

Stott, John. *Issues Facing Christians Today: New Perspectives on Social and Moral Dilemmas*. London: Marshall Pickering, 1990, 2nd ed.

Swartley, Willard M. *Slavery, Sabbath, War and Women*. Pennsylvania: Herald Press, 1983.

Tamez, Elsa. *Against Machismo*. Oak Park, Illinois: Meyer Stone, 1987.

Tannen, Deborah. *You Just Don't Understand: Women and Men in Conversation*. London: Virago, 1991.

Thielicke, Helmut. *Theological Ethics Vol 3: Sex*. Grand Rapids, Michigan: Eerdmans, 1964.

Thistlethwaite, Susan. *Sex, Race, and God: Christian Feminism in Black and White*. London: Geoffrey Chapman, 1990.

Tolson, Andrew. *The Limits of Masculinity*. London: Routledge, 1988.

Trachtenberg, Peter. *The Casanova Complex: Compulsive Lovers and Their Women*. London: Angus & Robertson, 1988.

Trible, Phyllis. *God and the Rhetoric of Sexuality*. Philadelphia, Pennsylvania: Fortress Press, 1978.

Tuttle, Lisa. *Heroines: Women Inspired by Women*. London: Harrap, 1988.

Tweedie, Jill. *In the Name of Love*. London: Pavanne/Pan, 1979.

Vanier, Jean. *Man and Woman He Made Them*. London: Darton, Longman and Todd, 1985.

Wakefield, Gavin. *Where Are the Men? A Study of an Endangered Species*. Nottingham: Grove Pastoral Series, 34, 1988.

Walczak, Yvette. *He and She: Men in the Eighties*. London: Routledge, 1988.

Walker, Andrew. *Restoring the Kingdom: The Radical Christianity of the House Church Movement*. London: Hodder and Stoughton, 1985.

Waring, Marilyn. *If Women Counted: A New Feminist Economics*. London: Macmillan, 1989.

Westermann, Claus. *Creation*. London: SPCK, 1971.

Westermann, Claus. *Genesis*. Edinburgh: T. and T. Clark, 1988.

Wheelock, Jane. *Husbands at Home*. London: Routledge, 1990.

White, Alistair. *Poles Apart? The Experience of Gender*. London: J. M. Dent & Sons, 1989.

White, John. *Eros Defiled: The Christian and Sexual Guilt*. Leicester: IVP, 1978.

Wogaman, J. Philip. *A Christian Method of Moral Judgment*. London: SCM, 1976.

Wren, Brian. *What Language Shall I Borrow? God-Talk in Worship: A Male Response to Feminist Theology*. London: SCM, 1989.

Wright, David F. '"Incidentalism" in theology – or a theology for thirty-year-olds?', *Themelios*, 11, no. 3 (April 1986), 88–90.

INDEX